Ardeth

LAND LOTTERY: 1901

The Diary of Miss Minnie Johnson

by

Ardeth Elling Denney

Blue Beaver Publishing
P. O. Box 6188
Lawton, Oklahoma 73506
or e-mail
blubeavpub@aol.com

COVER DESIGN: aabgraphics

Denney, Ardeth Elling
     Land lottery: 1901 the diary of Miss Minnie Johnson/by
     Ardeth Elling Denney. -- 1st ed.
     p. cm.
     Includes bibliographical references
     Preassigned LCCN: 98-93736
     ISBN: 0-9667576-0-2
     1. Johnson, Mina Randina --Diaries. 2. Pioneers--Oklahoma--
Biography. 3. Frontier and pioneer life--Oklahoma--Indian
Territory. 4. Indian Territory (Okla.)--Biography. 5. Land
grants--Oklahoma--Indian Territory. 6. Land settlement--
Oklahoma Indian Territory. 6. Land settlement--Oklahoma--
Indian Territory. I. Johnson, Mina Randina. II. Title

     F697 J64D46 1999   976.65'04'092 {B}

Printed in the U.S.A.
by
Morris Publishing
3212 E. Hwy 30
Kearney, NB 68847
800-650-7888

Dedicated to

Carl E. and Florence Hawthorne Elling
1909-1994 and *1909-1998*

Preface

This book was inspired by a very real and interesting person. Mina Randina Johnson "Minnie" kept a diary during the time her father was on a quest for land during the opening of Indian Territory by the United States in 1901.

I met great Aunt Minnie a couple of times. The time I remember best was in 1958. She and her daughter Mina, drove to Oklahoma to visit relatives and relive old memories. I remember that Minnie's eyes danced as she listened to a person. She was warm, open and laughed easily. She made me, a uncertain fourteen year-old, feel as if I was as interesting and worth listening to as people closer to her own age. At seventy-seven she still had a youthful spirit and a spring in her step. I liked her.

The diary first came to my attention in 1971. My father's cousin, Tod Pool, of Edmonton, Alberta, Canada, had discovered the diary in his mother's belongings after her death in 1968. Making a trip to Oklahoma in 1971, Tod and his wife, Florence, brought with them a typewritten copy. Carl E. Elling—my father/Minnie's nephew—was greatly interested in the journal. His father, Otto H. Elling, Sr. had also been a 1901 homesteader. Otto lived and raised his family a mile south of where the Johnson family homestead had been located. Tod gave my father a copy of the diary.

The opening days of Lawton became more and more interesting to me over the years as a result of the opportunity I'd had to glimpse into those days through Minnie's diary. (Who could forget the image of her climbing Mount Scott in her long dress, accompanying petticoats and carrying a parasol?) I became intrigued as my grandmother, father, uncles, and aunts told and retold stories their parents told them.

Eventually I obtained my own copy of the diary. As I studied it I began to think there might be more to the story. More she might have wanted to say. Or—more likely—more I wanted her to say. For twenty-eight years I nurtured a dream of sharing Aunt Minnie and her diary with others. I believed I could use it as a framework from which to build a story set against the background of the land lottery, the opening of Lawton, Oklahoma and surrounding areas. I hoped that it would be interesting, enjoyable and perhaps contain at least a sliver of historical significance.

Lawton will soon be celebrating the centennial anniversary.of the opening. At the same time it will be 100 years since Minnie kept her diary. Having retired a couple years ago from being an elementary school principal, I now had the needed time to research and write. The perfect time had arrived for me to follow through on my dream.

I began to dig through endless books, periodicals, newspaper accounts, official records and photographs of Minnie's era and the Land Opening of 1901. We made a trip to Canada to talk with Minnie's daughter, Mina and meet other relatives there.

Finally, my book is ready for publishing.

But first, a caution. It is historical fiction. There are many scenes in this book, all set within the context of carefully authenticated events. But the actions and conversations of the characters are of course the inventions of the author.

I must acknowledge some of the people who helped me get through this first effort at writing. My husband, Jerry, for encouraging me in this project and giving me lots of rope, interest and assistance;

Cousin Mina Pool, for giving enormous assistance in helping me understand the personalities of her mother, father, grandmother and grandfather;

Florence Lee Pool for taking the time to type up the diary all those years ago and sharing copies with so many of us;

Brad, for his efforts in keeping the cousins of Canada, Iowa and Oklahoma in touch-and his wife Jennie, who welcomed us on a trip to Canada when we were tracking down facts;

Hank, for proof-reading and offering valuable suggestions,

Uncle Laddie, Mr. Folsom, Emma, Chris, Lenson & Gina, for showing an interest in my project, never hinting that perhaps, I couldn't do it;

Jan Roberts and Ralph Brown, an especially big "Thank You" for reading, editing, and offering suggestions.

And, of course, to the wonderfully spirited, indefatigable great Aunt Minnie for having kept the diary and leaving it behind for the rest of us.

Enjoy the story!

Introduction

Typically diaries kept by women of wagon trains were records of tedious detail. They recorded the time they started each morning, the time they stopped for the noon meal, when they did the washing and baking, packing and unpacking, the number of miles traveled, the presence or absence of grass and a fit source of water. They reflect a focus on action. Although most of those diaries predate Minnie's by several decades, we found that in the same way, Minnie does a fair amount of recording of the same details.

After a great deal of consideration it was decided that Minnie's diary entries should be left as she wrote them; in the belief that each thing she wrote might have merit someday to someone. It is faithfully transcribed here in its entirety–*exactly as she wrote it*–with one notable exception. The names of the older couple who made the trip with the Johnsons were changed, since the personalities created for them are caricatured. However; names of places the Johnsons visited, individuals they met, Minnie's sentence structure, abbreviations, and spelling are just as she wrote them. You will notice that at times Minnie changes or corrects her own writing as she learns the correct name or spelling for a creek, mountain, or person. For example: she refers to Lookout Mountain first as Observatory Mountain then Signal Mountain. And when she first meets Rev. and Mrs. E. C. Deyo, she incorrectly spells their name "Dayo". Perhaps that was the way it sounded when they introduced themselves. She later changes the spelling.

As you read keep in mind that Minnie wrote these words a century ago. Some words at that time were commonly spelled differently than they are today. In the same way Minnie always refers to the noon meal as "dinner", and the evening meal as "supper." She will say that they "camped for dinner", and mean that it was a temporary stop in the middle of the day.

And finally, to differentiate Minnie's writings from mine, her diary entries are set in a different font (like this).

Oliver and Mary Johnson
circa 1890

Chapter 1
Leaving Home

Minnie turned up the collar of her coat. Gathering it more tightly around her, she pulled her head down deep into its recesses and hugged her thin body against the morning chill. She and her father, Oliver, rode the wagon seat as it heaved and swayed high above the waves of prairie grass.

Staring sleepily at the sunrise, she watched the last remnants of orange and pink surrender the dawn to the day.

"Need my coat, girl?"

"Nah, I'll be okay, Papa."

"Soon be warmer. Sun's gettin' higher."

Minnie nodded.

"You can tough it out," Papa told her.

"Yeah," she answered, finally feeling the warmth of the sun on her face.

"I'm taking Minnie with me," Papa had announced out of the blue one morning back in April.

"The fresh air'll do her good," he added, speaking to the family of nine seated around breakfast table. He'd used his I've-got-this-all-figured-out-don't-question-me voice. So, no one did. Their mother, Mary, rankled silently at the announcement. They already knew Arnold would be going, but Minnie?

Minnie was as surprised as anyone. Her heart skipped a couple of beats while the idea sank in. She was too young to qualify for a homestead–by just nine months. They'd already discussed that issue–Papa hinting that maybe Minnie could pass for twenty-one; Momma putting her foot down about the dishonesty of it.

It sounded to Minnie that her father had decided she would probably come in real handy. Seeing as how he couldn't read, he'd need her along–just in case. She would be able to read things for him, explain them to him and write down any important information. She could also cook and mend and wash dishes. And besides, Minnie was quite sure her Papa truly did believe the fresh air and change of climate would do her good.

"How long will it be before you send for the rest of us? Momma asked."

"Don't know. Soon as we know somethin' for sure."

***

Papa tugged and slapped the reins, keeping the matched set of black ponies headed in a southeasterly direction.

Fifteen-year-old Arnold, Minnie's blond-haired, blue-eyed brother, rode proudly beside the wagons on their feisty new sorrel, Red. She watched how gracefully he moved with the rolling motion of the horse, and couldn't help but envy him. She grinned remembering how his head had swelled two sizes when he heard he would have the responsibility of being "scout" for their small party. Though they would be traveling some pretty well-worn trails, his job would be to ride up ahead now and again, over the next rise, to check for the best places to cross streams, creeks, and gullies.

Cradled in her lap inside her wrap, Minnie clasped the

brown essay book she'd gotten in which to keep notes of their adventure. She loved writing and looked forward to keeping a daily log of their experiences. Minnie already had taught school for two years, but had spent the last year at home trying to shake the lingering effects of a severe bout with typhoid.

Their little wagon train consisted of two wagons. Five people–the three Johnsons–Arnold, Minnie and their Papa Oliver. Then there were Mr. and Mrs. Hawp, a childless couple in their mid-fifties, who followed them in a light wagon. More people, wagons. a buggy and a surrey were set to join them at Cambridge, Nebraska.

Papa's optimism about the land opening in Indian Territory had been contagious. He had a confident way about him that caused folks to believe in things he did and projects he undertook–till they got to know him.

"DAD GUMMIT EARNIE, don't lag so far behind!"

"Huh?" Earnie's mind wasn't always *here* with Myrtle.

"I said, move these lazy mules. Your lettin' em poke along here. First thing you know we won't be able to see 'em up there and we'll get lost out here behind one of these sand hills."

Arnold heard Myrtle Hawp's screechy voice and turned to see what was going on. Myrtle spoke like she made salad or cleaned house in a staccato of chops. A skinny woman; folks said she was worn to the bone from doing her house chores over and over again. Everything had to be flawless, above and beyond clean and tidy. She fidgeted and fretted endlessly. It got so people tried not to sit beside her in church, her fidgeting worried a person so.

Earnie's lacadasical attitude toward just about every-thing disturbed her so much that sometimes it looked like she might bust a blood vessel or some such thing. Earnie tried to ignore her most of the time–much as a body could. He gave the reins a good slap, pushing the team into an awkward trot that shook and jolted the wagon.

"Ea-r-r-r-nie," Myrtle's voice bounced along with the wagon. He kept them going till their noses were almost inside the rear of the Johnson's rig.

"Not that close, you idiot," she said through gritted

teeth as she slapped him.

Earnie raised his arm to fend off her blows, and leaned away from her, his belly dancing in silent laughter. Experience had long ago taught Earnie Hawp that the best way to handle Myrtle's "high-strung" personality was to let her yammer on, while he wordlessly took her instructions to the brink of stupidity. She'd get so mad it looked like she'd spit nails.

This strategy seemed to gain him the most points in their particular version of "matrimonial misery." It never failed.

For this small victory, Earnie licked his finger and chalked up three bonus points for himself on the imaginary chalkboard he kept hanging in air.

***

"This is just an excuse for Oliver to scratch that wanderlust itch of his," Mary Johnson had seethed in confidence to her friend Abigail, three days ago.

"You know what he told me ?"

"I couldn't begin to guess what that man of your's might have said, Mary," Abigail said in true sympathy.

"He said, 'Aw, for Gawd's sake Mary, it's been eight or ten years since the Indians killed anybody down there." She mimicked the way he'd said it. It was when she'd dared to bring up the question of the safety of her children after they'd gone to bed.

"Well, I don't care what he says, there are dangers in that land. He thinks I'm a fool."

"I've seen it called 'Outlaw Territory' in the news-papers. It says right there on the map 'Indian Territory.'"

"I tell you this–thieves, rustlers, gangs, and Indians was all you ever heard out of Oklahoma till this land thing came along. And, this lunatic I'm married to will have us living there." Mary needed to bring a halt to this complaining session, it wasn't doing her any good, and she was developing a headache.

"Comanche–Kiowa–Apache ceded lands..." Abigail read the words from a newspaper clipping.

"Abigail, those three words make the hair on the back of my neck stand up just as if you'd said 'war parties, raiding, and scalping." Mary shuddered.

There was something else bothering Mary–something deeper. The fact that Minnie was of marrying age now, caused a deep sense of foreboding. She worried that her oldest daughter might be swept of her feet by some sweet talking, no-good, son-of-an-immigrant down in Indian Territory before Papa ever sent for her and the rest of the family. She would have no way of influencing Minnie's choices way off up here in Nebraska. Then, where would her dreams for her beloved daughter be?

"In these same worn out shoes I'm wearing–that's where." Mary stewed, feeling that old regret come rising to the surface.

***

"YOU'LL BE SMART to hold off marrying for awhile." her mother commented brightly; as if saying it for the first time. Minnie turned her head. Looked like she would be hearing her mother's confidential "just between you and me" talk again.

Minnie and her mother knelt beside the families' hand-carved wooden trunk, packing it with items needed for the trip. The trunk was a family heirloom with the year 1771 carved into its front. It'd been in her mother's family for many years before it came to America with Mary, her parents and five siblings in 1867. Sunlight shining through the lace window curtains made dancing shapes across it.

"The fellahs down in the new territory aren't going to be looking for just land," Mother seemed compelled to warn her again. "Most of them will be looking for a wife for free labor–some vulnerable young thing, about marrying age. You mark my words, Minnie..."

Standing now, one hand on her hip while the other punctuated the speech with a wooden coat hanger–keying unseen cymbals and drum rolls.

"...they're going to be wantin' a woman to cook for 'em–to clean, wash and sew, feed the chickens, keep a garden, milk the cow and have babies. AND, make those babies BOYS--if you please Ma'am, while you're at it!"

She'd added that last part on the spur of the moment for effect. But her purpose was lost when she ran out of breath enough to say it with any verve at all.

"I want more for y–*you deserve more* than that. More than being a milk maid or a harvest hand for some two-bit farmer."

She took her Minnie's hands in her own. "You have talent that should be appreciated," she said unaware of the yoke she placed upon her daughter. The yoke of her own unspoken, unrealized dreams.

"Now, Momma, don't you worry about me." Minnie said trying to break the seriousness, "I am pretty sure those men are *NOT* going to be lining up at our door...uhm...tent flaps," she added with a good-natured hoot. You don't need..."

Looking into Minnie's eyes, Mary silenced her and put her arms around her in a bear hug. For a long moment, she stared out the window at a point years away. She *knew* Minnie didn't think it would happen. Girls her age never did. Most were pretty sure they'd been left out of life's social circle, doomed to old maid martyrdom by virtue of the fact that they were too plain, too pragmatic or too intelligent. That was just the point. This thing was like a predator, preying upon a girl's self-doubt and innocence. This unreasonable, totally unpredictable thing that romantics these days rhapsodized as "love" was really just lust and nothing more. It passed soon enough into "motherhood" and other unappreciated labors. Never made a lick of sense after a couple of years.

Mary placed her roughened hands on either side of her daughter's sweetly expressive face. Her voice changed; now it was sincere and gentle. A twitch beginning below her left eye,she said, "Minnie, honey, your life is *your* life. It should be a wonderful adventure, for *you*." She paused for a second, thinking that actually–that was all she needed to say. But she just couldn't help adding, "Just don't be too hasty and close off your options too soon. Now, that'll be my last word on that."

Momma turned on her heel, made her way immediately to the kitchen where she began intently peeling potatoes for supper. Minnie glanced over at the grandfather clock, then back at her mother. She shook her head in sympathy. Poor Momma. What a state she must be in. It was only 2:00 p.m.

***

A person would sure have a lot of time to think up here on this wagon seat for five hundred miles, Minnie mused watching the prairie grass disappearing endlessly beneath the wagon. Her thoughts kept returning to her mother. She squirmed remembering their leaving this morning.

Mary Johnson never cried. She was much too staid for that. But this morning she'd more than just "teared up." Minnie hadn't anticipated this and was in no way prepared for it. It'd made the parting unbearable.

She'd done just fine while saying "good-bye" to her husband and then when she'd hugged and kissed them each one. No tears. But when she'd reached out to hold Arnold and Minnie one more time, her strength wavered. She'd drawn in a long, shuddering sob–her face contorted–mouth open in a silent cry. Minnie could still hear the sob and taste the saltiness of her own unexpected tears.

She knew it wasn't so much that her mother was going to miss Oliver. It was that she would so dearly miss her oldest son and daughter. Though there would still be five children left at home–the youngest only a year old–these two were her eldest and somehow symbolized something different. Minnie knew her mother was wrenched with fear that this might be the last time she rested her eyes lovingly upon them.

<u>May 27, 1901</u>
Mr. and Mrs. Hawp and O. H. Johnson, Minnie and Arnold Johnson left Gordon, Nebraska, May 27, 1901 at 8:45 a.m. in two light wagons loaded with food and clothing enough to last all summer. Camped for dinner at 11:20 at Alva Marp near a bridge crossing the Niobara River. The men went fishing. Cooked coffee on a campfire and ate a lunch. Started at 2:45, arrived at camp at 6:00 p.m. Camped for the night.

There now. Minnie finished the first entry in her new diary with a flourish. From her pallet inside the wagon–it's endgate opened–Minnie stared at the last traces of sunset. Head propped on her hands, her eyes locked on the horizon where the sun had slipped from view; many thoughts clamored for attention in her mind.

Would the land be all it was promised–all Papa hoped? Would the Indians be hostile toward them? Would Papa get a farm? What if he didn't? *Oh, brother.*

And the big question; what if she accidentally happened to meet THE man? What if the perfect man for her just stumbled right into her life? Poor Momma.

Minnie smiled and shook her head. She took a deep breath and released a dramatic sigh, "Well, like it or not, a new chapter in my life is beginning. May the good Lord help me--*and Momma*--be ready for it."

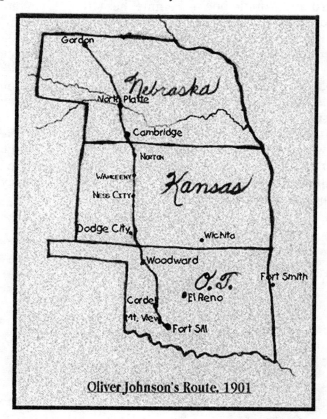

Oliver Johnson's Route, 1901

Chapter 2
Mr. Hawp's Incident

Around Gordon, Nebraska, Minnie Johnson was mostly thought of as *nice*. If her name came up at a quilting bee, the ladies of Gordon, seated around a quilt making thousands of tiny stitches, would say things like:

"Minnie Johnson? Oh, yah, now she's a pretty one–a little thin since the typhoid–but so *nice*."

"She's smart, too."

"Sure, but not in a highfalutin' way. She smiles at you, and she's always friendly."

The Ladies Aid of the First Methodist Episcopal Church would have said:

"Oh, sure, our Miss Minnie is a truly good person, so very thoughtful and kind. Her mother has every right to be proud of that daughter."

"Oh, and on the piano, now. That girl does something heavenly with a prelude. I'll tell you that right now."

Truth was, Minnie hadn't had the opportunity–nor the

inclination–to be anything but nice. This trait had evolved over time as she observed that life went along a lot easier for a person that way. Her "niceness" had never come up against a real challenge.

She'd inherited her father's brains and her mother's good sense–and there was a difference. She played the piano as did her mother. No, let's get that right–Minnie was a gifted pianist–her mother played the piano well. It was one of those gifts that ran in the family. Mary's grandfather, John Brotan, had composed and conducted music for the festival held in Endsvold in 1814 in celebration of the union of Norway and Sweden.

It had been Mary's father, Ludvig Brotan, and her mother, Anna Rustad, who immigrated to America with their six children in 1867. So, how did Mary get the maiden name, "Johnson"? (Yes, she was a Johnson, and married a Johnson) Well, it is said that captains of some ships in those days didn't particularly care for the paperwork and would lazily indicate the same surname for the entire manifest of persons on board.

Having finished her own schooling Minnie took and passed the Nebraska State Rural Teachers Exam. At age seventeen she was hired to teach. The school board members of Gordon figured she, being bright and level-headed, she'd make a right nice teacher. And, of course, she did.

***

IN 1892, ELDERS of the Kiowa, Comanche, and Kiowa-Apache tribes met in a series of talks with federal land commissioners headed by David Jerome near Fort Sill. After days of talks, the tribal representatives finally signed the commissioners paper agreeing to sell most of their land for ninety-two cents an acre. Every man, woman and child would be allotted 160 acres of their own.

Later, these same men whose names/marks were on the aggreement would make an impressive case that they had been misled either by the commissioners or the interpreters–they couldn't know which–as to the actual contents of the agreement.

You see, to give the Indian men a picture of the amount of money their tribes stood to gain by signing with them, they told them it was *like* ten wagon loads of silver dollars. It wasn't made clear that this money would be kept in the U.S. Treasury forever, with the interest being distributed to tribal members at intervals over the years.

"Trickery, nothing but trickery and deceit!" the Indians said, kicking themselves for ever once believing a white man. Together the tribes fought congressional ratification of the Jerome Agreement. They went right up to Washington, D.C.

During the decade of the 1890's these men learned to fight in a new way. Every year they sent a delegation of the most powerful men from each tribe: Quanah Parker, Lone Wolf, Big Tree, Apiatan, Gotebo, Eschiti and others. These tribal representatives were viewed with great interest and curiosity on Capitol Hill.[1]   Walking through the halls and office buildings in their native garments and braids, speaking in their dramatic way, they endeared themselves to the congressmen. Consequently, doors opened to them and they became quite proficient at lobbying–the white man's way of solving disputes without shooting or scalping anyone–usually.

Oliver Johnson had been observing the progress of legislation that would open the Kiowa-Comanche-Apache lands in southwest Indian Territory. He'd missed out on the Land Run of '89 and a couple since then. So, for seven or eight years now, he'd been paying close attention. He took notice as the Jerome Agreement continued to be brought before Congress each year. And, as each year it failed to be ratified. Though he didn't read, he was able to keep up with the news by having different ones of his children practice their reading skill by reading the newspaper to him.

The general store which Oliver owned in partnership with another man in Gordon was the center of many conversations with customers and drifters about the status of the Indian land.

"There's the Kiowas, the Comanches, the Kiowa-Apaches (*a very small tribe*) and the Texas ranchers standin' on one side of it and then there's the folks who just want a piece of land and the Oklahoma and Kansas Congressional representatives on the other. Long as they keep on goin' toe-to-toe like that the agreement's gonna be stuck up there in Washington. They bring it up fer a vote ever year. And ever year its voted down."

In June of 1900, the Jerome Agreement was finally ratified. It had happened at a time when congress had been distracted by unrest in Cuba and the Philippines along with election-year politics. Then, this previous March, in a move to hasten the opening, Dennis Flynn, a representative from Oklahoma Territory was able to slide a bill through congress the day before President McKinley's second inauguration, directing the president to make the arrangements for the opening of the ceded lands. The bill gave him a deadline for doing so.

He currently had his Department of the Interior working out the process.

"...Congressman Charles Curtis, who just returned from Washing-ton D. C. says that by the terms of the act of Congress opening the Kiowa, Comanche and Apache reservations the manner of the opening is left with the president, and he adds that; therefore, there will be no grand rush or horse race, and all sooners will be shut out. Two plans are proposed, says Mr. Curtis. One is to allot the land to the persons first sending letters after a specific date. The other is to heap all the letters containing cards with the number of quarter sections of land marked on them, together with a sufficient number of blanks to make the required number equal to the letters, and draw them after the lottery plan. The opening will be about August 1" [2]

Now, Oliver Johnson, et al, were on their way to the opening of the Kiowa-Comanche-Apache ceded lands. It wasn't clear to him exactly how the opening would proceed but Oliver meant to get his 160 acres of land. And he'd make good things happen for his family there or die trying–he swore by the Almighty.

***

Two men sat on stools at the counter in the Sunshine

Diner in Corning, Iowa. Friends from college days, Clarence Pool and George Corvah were drinking coffee, rehashing yesterday's talk and bringing up any new business for discussion. It was a daily routine. The conversation went along pretty predictably most of the time.

"LOOKS LIKE THAT land down in Indian Territory is going to be opening up this summer after all."

"Say, it sure does, doesn't it? Has McKinley made any announcements yet?"

"Nah, looks to me like they're having a heck of a time coming up with a better method than a land run."

"They'd better get on it, if they're going to have it done this summer."

"That's for sure."

"Clarence, why don't you go down there and try for a piece of that land?" George said introducing a surprising new twist. "They say its beautiful land."

"You mean *me* go down to Indian Territory for the land opening?" Clarence asked. Here was another person telling him what he ought to do.

"Well, why not? I mean, you're perfect for it. Not married or tied down with kids. Still trying to recuperate from that "bug" you picked up in the Philippines. The change of climate might do you good. Didn't the Doc say something about trying a more arid climate?"

Clarence Pool just three years ago had been a tall, nice-looking, healthy, bright young man with good–if not great–possibilities for a future in law when he'd joined the army for the Spanish-American war. Now, just a scant three years later, he was still losing weight, unable to work–other than teaching school–because of this amoebic dysentery. He lived at home with his parents and school teacher sister, Hellen. Younger brother, Garfield, was away from home, working.

"Oh, I don't know, George. I really hadn't thought to be a farmer. What I want–what I studied for–is the law."

"Clarence, you're gonna have to face reality sometime." he spoke with all the kindness he could muster, knowing his friend did not want to hear this. "Just exactly how're you gonna practice law, feeling so weak half the time?

How can a person argue a case in a court of law with exuberance and power never knowing when he's gotta make a run for the privy? Besides, you know as well as I do, most of the people getting ready to go down to the territory aren't looking to be farmers either. They're looking to win a prize–a one-hundred-and-sixty-acre prize."

Clarence felt the anger well up inside. His best friend had now turned on him. George, of all people.

"You sound just like Dad." Clarence responded, trying to keep from yelling. "If I'da wanted to be harassed about going down to that infernal land opening, I could've stayed home. I don't need every Tom, Dick and Harry tellin me what to do. My brain, contrary to popular belief, has not been affected by the dysentery."

Clarence stood up, tossed a nickel onto the counter for their coffee and walked out. George watched him leave and shook his head. He sure hadn't wanted to be so hard on him, but–dang it...

> <u>May 28</u>
> *Started 4:45 a.m. After travelling a few miles, Papa and Mr. Hawp got out of the wagons to hunt as they walked along. As we neared a barn and windmill, Mr. Hawp's shotgun went off accidentally and shot a hole in the watering tank about 2 inches in diameter. We passed Hewett and Morey's ranch, also Comstock and Richard's, Henry Garrow's and stopped at 10 a.m. and let the horses feed--also ate a lunch. Started in about an hour and reached Stephenson Lake at 3 p.m. Camped for the night. Cooked 4 o'clock dinner and then we went fishing (at Heart Lake). Mr. and Mrs. Hawp and myself in one boat and Papa and Arnold in another. We caught 123 all told (bass and croppies) and went to camp and fried fish for supper.*

UP BEFORE DAWN the second morning, Oliver started a pot of coffee, sliced some bread, and put some salt pork in the skillet in preparation for making corn meal gravy for breakfast. It wasn't long before the others smelling the enticing aroma rolled out of the sack as well.

Before long they were on the road again.

About mid-morning the men got out to walk beside the wagons--hopefully to shoot game for supper. Short, plump, bald-headed Mr. Hawp nearly strutted alongside Papa. His face took on a furrowed look of intensity as he watched for the opportunity to show he could bag game.

As he approached a small, faded-wood barn close to a windmill, a covey of quail erupted from a clump of grass near his foot, scaring him silly. Reacting in panic to the noise, he managed to get his feet tangled up in a dead tree branch mostly hidden by the tall grass. Trying to save face he attempted a sideways leap over it. A graceful leap it was not. He landed on the ground with an indignant expression on his swiftly reddening face.

Oliver chuckled and walked over to Mr. Hawp who was kicking angrily at the branch. Extending his hand, he said, "Here, Earnie, let me help you."

Just as Oliver began to pull he saw little red crawling things all over Mr. Hawp--then on himself!

Forgetting his helpful hold on Earnie's arm, Papa reflexively jumped back, hollering. "What the...!" He started swatting at his legs with his hands and his hat then stomping his boots in the dust.

Mr. Hawp, it appeared, had jumped from the frying pan into the fire--so to speak. His ungainly lurch landed him smack in the middle of a red ant den. But, that wasn't all of it--unfortunately. While both men were hollering, dancing and slapping, the trigger on Mr. Hawp's shotgun got pulled.

The buckshot made a hole in the watering tank that stood beside the windmill. The gun's discharge spooked the Johnson team which Minnie was currently in charge of. She pulled on the reins, worked the team, steadying them. Arnold dismounted and hurried over, grabbed Cole's bridle, and spoke to him in a calming voice.

"Whoa, whoa--ho there, Cole!"

After the team simmered down, Minnie heart still pounding, glanced over at Arnold who was biting his lipand looking at Myrtle Hawp.

Her initial look of annoyance at her husband's clumsiness had turned into shock when the gun went off. She'd let out a yelp, scrambled down off the wagon seat, and hustled toward him.

"Ba-by, are you all right, hon-ey?" Myrtle squawked in that voice of hers, tramping through the tall prairie grass and arriving close to her husband, out of breath. Just as she got there, Mr. Hawp spied the water wasting out onto the ground from the hole he'd shot in the water tank. Bolting over to it he plunged head-long into its blessed coolness. There he lay allowing it to wash the ants off and soothe the stings they'd inflicted.

"Oh, for goodness sake!" Mrs. Hawp huffed, folding her arms in disapproval. Minnie covered her mouth, changing what was almost a laugh to a cough. Arnold had to clear his throat a few times. Then–thank goodness–Mrs. Hawp started to laugh. Though they felt sorry about Mr. Hawp's ant stings, they were so glad when Myrtle's laughter allowed them to indulge in wonderfully intoxicating laughter. Mr. Hawp finally grinned a little after his stings began to feel some relief in the water.

May 29
Stayed in camp to-day. Myrtle Hawp and I cleaned fish nearly all fore-noon while the men fished carp and bull-heads of whom they caught 5 carp and one bull-head. This afternoon we all went out in the boats and caught 95 more. Arnold caught four fishes only and Mr. and Mrs. Hawp and I caught the rest. This evening while eating fish, of course, Jim and Connie Saults drove up and we had a real nice chat.

May 30
Started at 5:15 a.m. Passed Gregory P.O. where Mrs. Piester is Post-mistress, also a lovely ranch near Pull-man and passed a sod house where Rote Abbotts live which is on this side of Gregory. Are camped at Pull-man this noon which is on one side of a lovely valley 3 or 4 miles long. Cloudy this noon and looks like rain because it is thundering. This is the head of Middle Loup River. This afternoon we started at one and for night camp, we stopped at a bachelors ranch. Their cat came over and made friends and stayed all night.

Courtesy Buffalo Bill Museum

aahgraphics

Courtesy Hellen Pool Elling Album

American Heroes

Chapter 3
Movin' Along

The laughter following Earnie Hawp's accident didn't completely stop for a long time after the fact. If Minnie and Arnold so much as looked at each other that afternoon, they had to smother a laugh. Sometimes it erupted into their ears and noses, carrying them off into another fit that racked their bellies. It was a silent, happy torment; seriously trying to wipe the grin off one's face while the belly insists on keeping the laughter bubbling up and spilling over the top.

Every trip needed its running joke. Oliver was sure this one would serve as fodder for a few laughs during the rest of this trip.

Both the ladies cleaned the fish for supper. Mrs. Hawp put out the fixings: bread, pickles, plates, and silverware. Minnie fried the fish.

"Be careful now, Minnie. Don't let that grease get so hot it pops out on you."

"And watch how you turn that fish over, now. You don't want that hot grease slopping out on you. It can make a real bad burn and takes a while to heal."

"I know, Mrs. Hawp, I'll be caref--."

"But, don'tchu worry, if you do burn yourself, I have some gentian violet to put on it. I wondered if I ought to put it in or not. Then I decided, you just never can tell."

Minnie decided to wait and see if there was anything else Mrs. Hawp wanted to say. It was blissfully silent for a little bit. Only the sound of the grease bubbling around the fish.

"I- -" Minnie tried.

"Turn that one over--there on the left, Minnie."

"Okay..."

About that time, Minnie had an idea.

"Say, why don't you and Mr. Hawp go ahead and start eating. Don't want your fish gettin' cold."

"Well, okay. Are you sure? That's awful nice of you, Minnie-girl. Be careful now."

Minnie started to say, "Yes, Mrs. Hawp, but decided she'd just be silent and hope that Myrtle would act on the suggestion.

The Hawps sat down in their ladderback chairs using the endgate of their wagon for a table. They bowed their heads and closed their eyes for Earnie to return thanks. He'd just gotten the words, "Dear Lord," out of his mouth when an cruel assault on his reverence began. For it was just at this moment that Myrtle remembered she'd not called Arnold for supper.

"Arrr--nooold, supper's ready!" she screeched in her loudest, most piercing voice, scaring the living daylights out of Earnie.

When things had settled down again Papa, plate-in-hand, stood near Minnie about to serve himself from the platter of fish. He nudged Minnie, still tending the last of the fish in the cast iron skillet, with his elbow.

"Listen to this," he whispered in a conspiratorial tone.

Changing to Norwegian, the language spoken enough at home so that the Minnie and Arnold understood, he said in a contemplative voice:

"Noen ganger må enmann putte en sokk i sin kones

munn før han kan få fred." which translated into English means, "Sometimes a husband must first put a sock in his wife's mouth before he can get any rest."

Oliver allowed not the faintest hint of a smile to cross his face as he seriously regarded the platter of fish. He peered over his shoulder at Minnie doubled over in a giggling fit and hiding behind the wagon. Arnold, on his way in from tending the horses did an abrupt turnabout on the path before his laughter started again.

The Hawps happily eating their fish never missed a bite.

<u>May 31</u>
This fore-noon we passed no ranches--but windmills and spoke with a cowboy regarding the road. Noon: camped in Lone Calf Valley. Started 1:05, passed some lovely farms in dry valleys and camped for the night on the Loup River. A lovely stream and timber dotting the banks and hills--cedars, elms, cottonwoods and fruits.

<u>June 1</u>
5:07 a.m. drove two miles and reached Mullen at 6:00. a little town located in a valley between the Sand Hills, a new town but small, all alive. Lumbering and wagon shops, two livery barns, stores and hotels. Started at 7:35 and reached the U.B.I. ranch at 11:00, where we camped for dinner. When we got water at the wind-mill an old hound tried to bite papa and the gent that came out to call her off happened to be Joe Robinson, the foreman, who used to be the U/foreman. At noon he came out and visited with us, also invited us to take dinner with them. 12,000 head of cattle. This afternoon we crossed the Dismal River, a horrible road. Camped for supper at Thompson's at 6:00 (Came into Hooker Co. north of Mullin, County seat and came out 20 miles north of Tryon County seat.)

Changing localities was nothing new to Minnie. The family had moved four times in her life. This would be the fifth relocation but not the last.

Papa was a chronic pioneer.

Minnie had been born in Barron County, Wisconsin, in 1882. In 1884, Papa moved her, her mother and sister Helen to Buffalo County, South Dakota, into a dug-out. From there they moved on to White River in Jackson County, South Dakota. Again, in 1897, they moved 75 miles south to Gordon, Nebraska, where Oliver and a partner owned and operated a general store, trading mostly with the Sioux. It was here in Gordon, Nebraska that the older children were able to complete their schooling.

June 2, Sunday

Started at 5:20 and intended to camp at the courthouse at Tryon but missed it and camped at 12:20 for dinner. Very hard to get water. On account of travelling 30 miles this for-noon, we drove only about 6 miles this afternoon and are camped close to a ranch where a great many trees grow around the house. Met a fellow this morning that was an old friend of Mr. Wallace. His name was Mr. Sparks. We have had no rain so far, but looks a great deal like rain. Arnold has ridden horseback ever since we left home. I have ridden a little. Time for camp, 4:45 to-night.

There was a lot more to Minnie than just this "niceness" observed by others. In her short life, she'd developed a strength of character that might be described as quiet determination. She would do only what she chose to do. Anyone--*with the exception of her father*-- would be 'hard put' to convince her otherwise.

June 3

Started at 5:15. We have 26 miles to drive to make North Platte City. Noon. 12:00. We came over sand hills for a ways, then came to White Horse Creek. Many dams placed in it a mile apart and fish above each dam. Lovely trees grow on the dams. We passed three school houses to-day, the only ones except the one at Mullin since we left home. We followed the White Horse River to the Platte Valley. The valley is about

> three miles to the river. The river about half a mile wide.
> We came across on a wagon bridge. Saw many small
> islands and some there were farmers living on. The town
> lies south of the river, as also does Buffalo Bill's ranch.
> The town is large, and has a lovely Courthouse (brick).
> We are going to stay here till morning. Mrs. Hawp and
> I are going up town as soon as the men come back. After
> coming back I will tell you more. We went and visited
> Buffalo Bill's house, also went through Courthouse park.
> Passed the jail--a 2 storey and the school house--a three
> storey brick, a very large beautiful piece of architecture.

Buffalo Bill Cody was famous. They'd heard and read much about him. Arnold was particularly interested in seeing his ranch. His eyes sparkled with interest as they toured the home and grounds. Arnold would turn sixteen on July 6, while on the trail. Just the right age to enjoy the reputation; the "show"of Buffalo Bill.

"Did you hear what they said about him?" Arnold asked Minnie as they walked back through town.

"About what?" Minnie asked.

"That he killed 4,280 buffalo in eight months, back in 1967-68."

"That'd make a lot of buffalo robes."

"And besides all that they say he rode the Pony Express for a season, and he was an Army Scout for the Fifth Cavalry and then got elected to the Nebraska Legislature."

"You sure remembered a lot."

"Yeah," Arnold smiled

Touring the United States, Buffalo Bill took the wild and woolly west to the doorsteps of eastern dudes with his Wild West show. His latest venture was a partnership with James A. Bailey of Barnum and Bailey fame, to take the show to Europe. In 1886, Cody instructed his brother-in-law/ranch manager to build the house they toured today. He left the design to his sister. His one stipulation was that it contain a parlor and a bedroom with a bathroom. A contractor was engaged and built the house for $3,900. No expense was spared.

<u>June 4</u>

Eastern Time 6:15. We crossed the South Platte a little ways south of town. It is also bridged but scarcely any water in it and about the width of the North Platte. We are through the sand hills. Came over rolling country, passed many farm houses surrounded by trees. Are camped for dinner in a draw 1/2 mile from a farm house where we watered, and filled our kegs. N.P.(North Platte) is a division town employing about two hundred men in this place. Eva Coker lives 10 mi. from N.P. at Sutherland. Started 1:00 p.m. Camped on head of Medicine Creek for the night.

<u>June 5</u>

Started 6:10 a.m. It sprinkled a little last night and this morning. We drove about 2 hours and arrived at Maywood. Then we followed the creek down 7 miles and came to Curtiss for dinner. Camped near the Mill pond at 11:00. Started out at 1:00 p.m. Came past many nice farms and arrived here at 4:00. Stockville, a good sized country town, county seat. A two storey frame house, is the court house. After supper we went up town and visited Mary Black, and after we came back to camp Mary brought papa's cousin's cousin, Mrs. Kronk, over and made us a call.

***

"PASS THE BISCUITS, wouldya there, Anna?" Otto Elling said, walking into the kitchen and sitting down at the dining table.

"Oh, sure. Watch out, now. They're hot."

Anna filled his cup with coffee and handed him the plate of biscuits.

They sat in the kitchen of Lee and Anna Wright, Otto's sister and brother-in-law. Lee had made the "run" for their home here in the Cherokee Strip. The farm was near Cashion, O. T. Otto was here helping with the wheat threshing--making a little extra money.

Lee folded the newspaper he'd been reading while his wife made breakfast.

"Been keeping up on this land deal, down in Comanche Territory?" Lee asked.

"Pretty much," Otto replied. "Why do you ask? Anything new? McKinley come out with his proclamation? Do we have a date for a run--or how are they going to handle it?"

"Who-o-a," Lee said. "No, not yet. Just checking to see if you knew about it. They've ruled out a run, now. It'll be a lottery of some sort. You know you better be sittin' on ready when the time comes."

"I plan to be."

Otto'd already given it lots of thought.

"Don't know exactly how its going to work in with this job possibility in Hays City." He spooned cream gravy over his biscuits and sausage. "They've been talking about this thing--debating it back and forth--as long as I can remember. Guess they're finally going to do it."

"They still don't say when," Lee added. "Gives the qualifications a person must meet to register for a homestead. Want to hear them?"

Otto nodded. His mouth was full.

"First, got to be over twenty-one."

"Wi-tuh." Otto, answered through hot sausage gravy. He was twenty-five.

"American citizen."

"Mm-hmm."

"Must not now own 160 acres.".

"Ha! If I did, I wouldn't be thinking about going down into Indian Territory." Otto laughed.

"Head of household."

"S'pose I'd be considered such."

"How about, 'old soldier with honorable discharge'?"

They got a kick out of that one.

Lee tossed the paper over to Otto, who began scanning through it, sipping his coffee. He turned the paper over.

"This paper's out of El Reno? Exactly where is that?"

"Bout 20-25 miles southwest of here," Lee answered.

Son of German immigrants, Otto Elling had gone from his eighth grade of schooling to college. Eighth grade was the highest grade offered in the Valley Falls, Kansas his eighth grade of schooling to college. Eighth grade was the highest grade offered in the Valley Falls, Kansas community where the Elling family lived. After he'd worked on surrounding farms for a couple of years and accumulated some tuition money, Otto took off for college. He studied for the entrance exam on the train to Manhattan, Kansas. He spent five years in college. After contracting typhoid, he'd been forced to lay out a year, but he'd gone back and finished his degree

He'd been a good student and worked in the Agriculture Experimental Barns for his board and room . Once when some bloomers appeared flying from the smokestack of the girl's dorm, the college president was adamant that the guilty parties be found and suspended. Someone suggested that it was likely that chimney soot would be found in the ears of those who'd helped with the prank. They lined up all the boys in school and checked their ears for soot. Along with several others chimney soot was found in Otto's ears, and he was expelled. Before the day was done, the head of the Ag Department was knocking on the President's door.

"You can't expel Elling, he's the only one who knows the ration we're feeding the experimental cattle herd."

"Well, if we allow him to come back, I've got to let them all come back." It would appear that Otto was instrumental in helping some of his friends not have their college careers terminated.

Otto was certain of one thing. This land deal was something he couldn't afford to pass up. He'd take it a step at a time. When it came time to file the necessary paperwork he could take a day or two; go down to El Reno.

Otto H. Elling, 1901

"Uncle Andrew" Johnson--with grandchildren.[3]

Chapter 4
Uncle Andrew's Tales

<u>June 6</u>
6:05 a.m. Passed through grand farming country. Camped at 11:00 for dinner, 12 mi. N.W. of Cambridge. Started 12:30 p.m. Reached Cambridge at 4:00. Visited Andrew Johnson's in the evening and I stayed all night.

The wagon pulled up in front of Uncle Andrew's white, two-story, frame farmhouse. After the hellos, hugs, and handshaking on the wrap-around front porch Uncle Andrew invited them in for supper. Oliver rubbed his mid-section smiled and said, "I was sure hoping you'd ask. Camp food's all right but after awhile you begin to miss good home cooking. Especially Sara's home cooking." he added, giving her a smile and a pat on the back for good measure.

Stepping through the front door they were greeted by

the mouth-watering aroma of the pot roast that Aunt Sara already had in the oven. Minnie realized for the first time in a long time that she was hungry! It had been a good while since she'd felt really hungry. Surprisingly, her appetite did seem to be improving and tonight she was hungry enough to eat two or three helpings of roast beef. Hope Aunt Sara fixed plenty.

Familiar chatter filled the room during the meal. The dining area took up one half of the big country kitchen. The white lace tablecloth on the table meant Aunt Sara had deemed them worthy of special treatment. It gave the room an added warmth. Much of the talk tonight came in a continuous flow from cousin Tina, seated to Minnie's left.

Midway down the near side of the long rectangular table, with its two extra leaves put in, Minnie was situated so she could listen to the conversation and reminiscences of Uncle Andrew and Papa, as well as attend to Tina's chatter.

Minnie always found the stories about old times irresistible, but she sure didn't want cousinTina to feel that she was uninterested in what was going on here in Cambridge. Perhaps the fact that Arnold was hanging on Tina's every word on the other side would detract from the fact that Minnie's ears were otherwise engaged.

In the middle of dessert–peach pie–Uncle Andrew's whole face brightened. Minnie was pretty sure his next story would be a knee-slapper.

He thrust the last two bites of pie into his mouth, pushed back his chair, cleared his throat, and stuck his unlit pipe into his mouth.

"Did you kids ever hear the story about the Gypsies?"

Papa's face flushed and the handle of his fork dropped with a clank onto his plate.

"An--drew," he groaned, "You aren't going to tell that tired old story are you? Nobody even knows if its true."

"Your own mother verified it, Oliver." he replied, sounding like he was rubbing it in. "Said it was the God's honest truth."

"Yeah, but her mind was slipping–you know that."

Uncle Andrew loved to entertain visitors with his stories. He dragged them out milking them for all the suspense or laughter he could. It seemed especially fun for him if the person on which he told the story was present and found it disconcerting. Papa was obliging on that count.

Overruling Papa's wishes, Uncle Andrew went on. He looked at Arnold, Minnie, and the others around the table, making sure everyone was giving him their attention. After some adjustments–some chairs leaned back, other chairs moved forward, some folks moved around sideways to lean one elbow on the table–everyone was settled and ready. Uncle Andrew began his story:

"It so happened that in the town where Oliver was born–along about 1856–stories got going around that out in Montana there was gold so easy to come by that practically all a man had to do was bend over and pick it up. Now, Oliver–here's Daddy, his name was Halvar–that's Norwegian for Oliver–seemed to take his family responsibilities kinda lightly. A story such as this was more than a man like Halvar could resist.

Along with a couple of neighbors he decided to head out to Montana and pick up his fortune. He just took off, leaving your Grandmother Randina with the sole responsibility of a family of six children. Nellie, the youngest one, was just a baby.

They were dirt poor and through the first couple of years her husband was gone, it was rough! She managed to get a bit of work outside the home, leaving the older children in charge of the little ones. Had some sympathetic neighbors who'd pay her to do some of their chores. She'd work in a neighbor's field or barn during the day, come home and in the evenings knit stockings or fix over clothes best she could.

Months and years went by, no word from her husband. Then her oldest son, John, was taken into the army to do service for the Union in the War between the States. Only seventeen years old. This was an awful blow to Randina. Oldest sons are precious to their mothers and she'd counted on him to be around to help put food on the table. Randina was feeling low--really low.

About this time a caravan of gypsies came through that part of Wisconsin. Someone told them that Randina would sell them vegetables and eggs. Now, these Gypsies were a happy-go-lucky type of people. Oliver, being a friendly little tyke, got right in there playing and having fun with the little Gypsy kids. The Gypsies admired Oliver's dark eyes and hair. Looked like their own. They were smooth of tongue, and it was known they could be persuasive when it served their purposes. Some folks believed it might have been a joke that got away from her; you know how folks'll kid around sometimes saying--about one of their children who is being especially ornery--"You want him? Here, you can have him." or "I'm gonna give you to so and so." Don't know how it happened but one way or the other Randina, in dire financial straits, let them take Oliver with them. Little Oliver,here, not the least bit worried--acted like he was all for it! The little cuss didn't even have the decency to be scared or act worried. So, before Randina called it off he'd scrambled up into one of the wagons with the Gypsy children. Off they went. They didn't get far--not more than a mile or so, I s'pose--before they set up camp for the night. It was still familiar territory for little Oliver. Pretty close to the family's favorite fishing hole.

Well, dontcha knowRandina spent a terrible, sleepless night; walking the floor, fretting, worrying and wondering how she could ever hope to be forgiven for this. Daylight finally dawned and Randina kept going to the open doorway and peering down the road where she'd last seen the Gypsy wagons. After a while, when the sun was up pretty good--way off in the distance Randina spotted a little dust-devil. You know, a little whirlwind. It caught her eye 'cause it looked to her like it was being deliberately stirred up. It was comin' closer and it got so she could focus on it better. She began to tremble with anticipation. Could it be? It had to be--her little Oliver!

Yep and down that road he came just flipping around, taking his time, riding a stick, like it was a horse. I don't have to tell you his Mother fell all over herself running clear out to meet him. Part of her felt like frailing the daylights out of him, but most of her just wanted to hold him tight.

Exactly what happened or how Oliver spent that night nobody knows. Later, Randina said she understood him to say that the Gypsies' food tasted different and the piece of bread they gave him was black (a different kind than what he was used to). The nearest thing they could figure was that he crawled out of the Gypsy camp early, before anyone else was stirring and just started back toward home. Randina said she guessed those Gypsies never went out looking for him; nor as far as she heard ever asked any questions about him." [4]

Everyone had been so absorbed in Uncle Andrew's tale that the room was a vacuum of silence at it's finish. They all sat dumbfounded, wonder and bewilderment careening through their minds. Minnie having never heard the story before tried to picture her father as a little boy, running off with the Gypsies.

Pretty soon questions started popping like corn all around the table.

"Do you remember it, Uncle Oliver?"

"Is that true?"

"Why didn't they...?"

"How did he...?"

Minnie looked at her father. Leaned back in his chair, legs extended, arms folded over his chest, toothpick sticking out of his mouth between his two front teeth, squinted as if trying to see something far out the back door.

"'ell, Andrew, you did it again. If you think I'm gonna hang around answering these questions, you are sadly mistaken."

He sat up and scooted to the edge of his chair, pulled his watch from his pocket, checked the time, and said, "My wouldja look at the time! Arnold, it's too late for this old (*wink*), 'Gypsy' to be out. Take me to our camp, son."

The evening had reached it's finale.

MINNIE WAS invited to stay with Tina while they were in Cambridge and she'd happily accepted.

Before tumbling into her cousin's big feather bed she had the pleasure of indulging in a luxurious tub bath. Life on the trail may have been peaceful, free and liberating for crusty old cowboys but for ladies--it was something else. After four days and nights on the trail, riding in the wagon and walking along beside it, she'd began to doubt if she'd ever come clean or feel soft again.

The tub at her uncle's was especially nice. Not the round style used for laundry but an oblong shaped tub made especially for bathing. Her legs could extend out under the water, rather than having to bend at the knees, leaving her feet out on the floor, as was the case with a "No. 3" tub.

Cousin Tina showed Minnie to their bathing area on the back porch. She helped pull the rose print cotton curtain closed for privacy. The room was arranged by using the back wall of the house and closing in the end of the porch, making a three-sided bathing "room" with a rosy-printed curtain forming the fourth side. Opening the doors to the chiffureau, Tina showed the towels and wash rags, the soap, and the pumice stone. A pitcher of hot water was poured in with the spring water, making the bath a pleasing temperature.

"Here's some rose water that I use on special occasions. You are welcome to use it, if you like. Is there anything else I can get for you?" Tina asked.

"No, I don't believe so, Tina, thank you. I'm ready to sink into that water and soak for a while," Minnie replied.

Tina placed the lantern carefully on the stand beside the tub and went back through the rear door of the kitchen to help her Mother clean up the dishes from supper and make preparations for breakfast.

Minnie modestly removed her clothing behind a screen with her back to the wall of the house. Keeping her body covered with a towel, she lowered herself into the bath water. She placed the towel on the stand within arms reach so that she could follow the same procedure at the end of the bath. Though no one else was present, this process was second nature for Minnie. In keeping with the Victorian propriety of the time, proper ladies weren't usually at ease disrobing nor watching anyone else disrobe. Except for the act of bathing, people pretty much kept themselves covered up.

It was the predominant belief that it was the ladies' responsibility to take precautions in their dress, habits, and manners, lest they should invite unwelcome male advances. Even showing one's bare ankles was considered to be encouraging too much of the wrong kind of attention.

Minnie lingered long in the rose-scented bath water, thinking it impossible to be more content. She vowed that whenever available, she would indulge in life's little plea-sures: a real bed with a soft mattress, clean sheets, long baths in rose-scented bathwater, luxurious shampoos, lotion for her hands, a roof over her head, and--*gravy!* My, she sure missed Momma's gravy.

Plans were to spend a week in Cambridge. Minnie had no intention of learning to enjoy living outdoors like Papa did. Her houghts finally yielded to sleepiness and the softness of the pillow.

At breakfast the next morning Minnie asked some questions of her uncle that had come to mind since last evening's story. He finished off his oatmeal and wiped his moustached mouth. Sipping his coffee he filled her in on a little more of her family history:

> "As your Grandmother Randina's older sons were growing up, their willing hands gradually eased the burden on her some. Soon after the episode with little Oliver, she got the news that her son John had died. It took awhile, but finally the government began sending her an eight-dollar-a-month pension for her son's being killed, and with it Randina was able to buy a milk cow and some other things that helped matters greatly.
>
> One by one the children married and moved to homes of their own, with the exception of Nels who remained a bachelor for many years.
>
> Twenty-five years after Halvar left them--guess who walked back into town with one little old gold nugget to his name?
>
> Halvar offered Randina the gold nugget saying he wanted her to have a ring made of it. She declined with a few choice words. They say she treated him with civility, considering all she'd been through--her being a good Christian woman and all--but she did make it very clear that he was not welcome to move back into her bedroom or her house.
>
> After having a wedding ring fashioned from the nugget for Nellie, who was about to be married, Halvar visited around the neighborhood for awhile. But, it wasn't too long before he'd talked some more folks into picking up and heading back west with him.
>
> Your daddy, Oliver, was one of them!
>
> He quit the bunch, though, when they got as far as South Dakota. He settled there, built a sod house and went back to Wisconsin and moved your Momma and you and your sister back out there with him." [4]

AFTER HELPING Aunt Sara with the breakfast dishes Minnie and Christina went out on the front porch to sit in the sunshine and fresh air. They chatted catching up on each other's families, schooling and the like.

"Why are you going to Indian Territory?" Tina asked, suddenly. "Looks like your father and brother would've gone without you. I–I'm not being critical, but isn't it sort of rare–a daring thing–for a young woman to do?"

Minnie smiled wryly and gave her head a shake. "You don't know my Papa very well, do you?"

"Guess not."

"First of all, Papa doesn't give two hoots an a hollar about what other folks might think. He figures he can take care of me without worrying what others might think. The second thing is he is convinced he needs me along–he doesn't read you know. He believes I'll be able to help him in that respect. Arnold could do that,. I suppose. It's partly for my health. I haven't been in first rate condition for over a year now," Minnie went on. "It started with typhoid–"

"My goodness, Minnie, I had no idea! Are you all right, now?"

"The infection seems to be gone but, the doc says my body just isn't regaining strength like it ought to. Papa believes the trip will be good for me. He's convinced that fresh air and sunshine will cure anyone of anything."

"How do you feel, now–after a week on the trail?" Tina asked.

"You know," Minnie said, a sparkle beginning in her eyes, "just last night I realized, my breathing sounded clearer than it has for a long time and my appetite is improving.

"That's good, Minnie, I'm relieved to hear it." Tina said. "I've hoped you might want to meet some of my friends, this week."

"Oh, I'm sure I'd like that."

"Tell you what, ever had an ice cream soda?"

Minnie shook her head.

"After dinner let's see if Mom can do without us for a couple of hours. We'll take a stroll downtown. Sound good to you?"

"Sure does."

Chapter 5
The Week at Cambridge

Cambridge, Nebraska, was a lively, lovely place in June the summer of 1901. Minnie just beamed, reveling in the many occasions to socialize with other young folks her age. In the town itself there were several large, beautiful Victorian houses to admire. Downtown there were businesses never even heard of back in their hometown of Gordon. In her cousin Tina, Minnie found–if not a soul mate–a chum, someone with whom to pal around.

Saturday forenoon the girls spent fishing–sort of. With Tina's friend, Addie, the girls rowed out to the middle of a pond at the east edge of town, and threw their lines in the water. Minnie loved to fish, but today, the girl talk was more interesting than the fish. Seated leisurely in the rowboat, the young ladies chatted about everything–girl things–personal things.

"Do you believe in love?"

Tina posed the question.

"You know, the kind you read about in novels. The kind that makes your insides do flips, wanting to be with a certain guy. I might as well tell you, what I'm saying is: I think I'm in love with Warren Latham," she finally blurted out.

"Really?" both of the other girls said at once.

"What makes you think so?" Addie squealed.

"How does it feel?" was Minnie's question.

"Oh, gosh, let me see...it's...well, it's hard to describe."

Minnie got a nibble on her line, but reached for the pole too late. Quickly she put fresh bait on her hook, plunked the line back into the water, and turned to listen to Tina. This should be good.

"I think about him all the time–when I get up in the morning, when I go to bed at night, when I'm cleaning house. I burned my thumb on the iron yesterday, just because I wasn't paying attention." Tina went on, "It's an obsession; thinking about him is something I just have to do, all the time. I get these little twinges in the middle of my chest. Right here," she pointed to the spot, "when he looks at me or touches me, or even when I just think about him. They are quick little 'zings'. Kind of like an ache."

"Maybe that's what they call a 'thrill'?" Minnie said, "No, I've got it. It's Cupid's arrow piercing your heart!"

All three busted out into self-conscious giggles.

"Now, Tina, you know you should never let Warren know that you are so smitten with him. They say it's the quickest way to make a man turn around and head the other direction. If he thinks you're 'gah-gah', he'll 'go-go'." Addie said later as they pulled the boat up onto the edge of the pond.

"Where did you hear that?" Minnie asked.

"Well, I have this friend, Esther, who got married last Christmas and I asked her about it. Well, she said it was true. Said she finally had to act like she didn't even care for Lars at all, for him to get interested enough in her to propose. See, it goes like this–first you attract them, then you act like you don't really care one way or the other. You just keep them guessing."

Minnie eyed Addie with one eyebrow raised. "Bunk." Minnie said, "Your joking, right? That sounds dreadfully contrived to me. I can't imagine planning in advance how to act with a gentleman each time I see him."

"I've heard it too, Minnie," cousin Tina said in a wide-eyed, innocent tone that translated into "So there you have it."

"Well, that makes it the majority opinion, I guess," Minnie acquiesced. She chose not to have this debate this day. She would just file it along with the advice her Mother gave her under "phenomena-yet-to-be-observed."

***

IN THE AFTERNOON Tina and Minnie strolled uptown for Minnie's first ice cream soda. Although Tina's agenda for the afternoon *was* slightly different. She was hoping Warren would be around. He worked at the livery stable and wasn't usually there on weekday afternoons. There were usually several young people at the Soda Shoppe.

As they turned the corner, Minnie beheld the striking pink-and-white-striped, dome-shaped awnings adorning the windows of the establishment. They flapped in the breeze. Inside, a "Gay 90's" decor of pink and white stripes decorated the walls and the seats of the chairs. The "look" was something the owner's wife had seen on a visit to St. Louis the previous summer.

In the Soda Shop, Minnie and Tina sat at the counter, behind which was the most handsome young fellow Minnie had ever laid eyes upon. Tina immediately gave her usual order and spying a trio of girls at a round table in the back corner she quickly introduced Minnie to John Perdoux and hurried away.

Turning his attention to Minnie he said, "Well, hello, Tina's cousin, what can I fix for you?" He wiped the already-shiny-clean counter in front of Minnie in slow circles. When Minnie looked at him, she found John's eyes looking straight into her own. For a long moment, it seemed as if he held them hostage.

"Well, let's see--" Minnie stalled, unable to think of anything but those eyes. She was aware that she was, now, to indicate a flavor. But she couldn't think of a flavor--any flavor!

Easing her eyes away from his, she managed a lame,

"Um, what are my choices?" My, she was enjoying John's attentions enormously. But her face! Why was she suddenly so warm? It seemed as if his eyes had heated up the area around them.

As he spoke the list of flavors, his eyes again flirted with her. He had a way of saying the flavors of ice cream that made Minnie feel like he was speaking sweet words to her. She'd never experienced anything like this!

Finally noticing the silence that meant he'd finished listing the flavors, her mind jolted toward an attempt to think--to speak.

"A-hem," she cleared her throat, "let me see. I'll–have–a..." she reached into her bag, fumbled, found her fan and opened it. Casually she began fanning herself. "Is Cambridge always so hot this early in the year?" He just smiled.

"Take your time," he said, then asked, "Where are you from?"

As if in answer to his question, Minnie, having thought of a flavor, blurted out "Strawberry."

"Strawberry?" he cocked his head sideways like a confused puppy.

"Oh, I'm sorry," she placed her hand over her mouth–"Gordon."

"Gordon? My name is John."

"Gordon, Nebraska," she clarified.

"Hm-m-m, Strawberry–Gordon–Nebraska?" he said the words slowly as if trying to make sense of them. He was kidding her now--and she knew it. Happy half-laughs came from each of them. She decided to start all over.

"Hello, John. My name is Minnie Johnson."

"Oh?" he said, surprised at her change of pace.

"And, I will have a *strawberry* ice cream soda." Now she raised one finger and gave the air in front of her a quick chop for emphasis, "and I'm from Gordon, Nebraska."

Satisfied with the correctness of her performance–stiff though it may have been–she relaxed and waited, on the very edge of a giggle, for his reply.

"Never heard of it," was his suddenly aloof response. He concentrated his gaze on the soda glass he was drying, holding it up to the light, squinting at it, and shining some more.

"John!" Minnie said in exasperation, "What have you not heard of? Gordon?"

"No, strawberry ice cream soda--never heard of it."

She slapped at his arm with her fan, "YOU are incorrigible!" What a fun guy to be around she thought.

John dodged the fan, turned, and giving her a quick wink began making the soda.

Minnie was simply not used to this.

Basically in her lifetime Minnie had: lived at home, gone to school, taught school, got typhoid, recuperated for a year, and now here she was in Cambridge at twenty years of age being seriously flirted with for the first time in her life.

"Do you like it?" John said returning to the counter. He'd fixed Tina's soda and delivered it.

"It's very good."

"Don't s'pose I could interest you in a buggy ride with me later this evening? I can give you the grand tour of our wonderful town."

Minnie quickly looked out the front window trying hard to keep the composure she'd finally regained. But, she realized she was warm again, and her heart had suddenly started pounding.

"Well, I'd love to, but I–you know–I can't go out with you alone. You're a strange man. It wouldn't look– perhaps Tina could join us?"

"Me, strange?" He smiled at her.

"Very."

<u>June 8</u>
Went boat riding and fishing, also buggy riding and took
supper at Babcock's. Ice Cream soda.

When she told Papa about the buggy ride with John and Tina, Minnie got the impression that he wasn't very pleased about it. He asked her a lot of questions about the young man; who was he, what did his father do? She *wanted* to say, "Papa, I'm old enough to make decisions like this for myself now." But she didn't dare. Papa wasn't ready for that yet.

Next day he urged her to go along with him to Henry Thompson's for Sunday dinner so she did. To her chagrin they stayed all day.

<u>June 9 -- Sunday</u>
Took dinner at Henry Thompson's and stayed all day.

<u>June 10</u>
Washed clothes in the fore-noon, went up to Babcock's after supper and Tina came down and we six went down to Elmer and Martha Kronk's and spent the evening.

<u>June 11</u>
Spent the day at Tom Thompson's. That is papa, uncle, and I. It rained while we were there and we came home after the shower. Persons I have met during my visit at Aunt's and Uncle's:

> Addie Swalley
> Susan Moriarty
> Mr. & Mrs. Babcock
> John Perdoux
> Mr. & Mrs. Elmer Kronk, Henry and Della
> Earl Murray
> Stella Eulow
> Henry Thompson & wife
> Tom Thompson & wife
> Clarence Minnide (Minnick)
> Warren Latham
> Ollie Murray
> Hazel Brown
> Bertha, Ada, Ernest, Hattie, Ella, Tom,
> > William, and Herschel Thompson.

<u>June 12</u>
Babcock's gone to Crete. I stayed with Christina while they were gone.

***

CHECKING IN AT CAMP on Wednesday evening Minnie found Myrtle Hawp worked up into a real tizzy. At first she merely questioned Minnie about where she'd been and with whom for the last few days. As she listened to Minnie's responses she would squint disapprovingly over the rims of her spectacles. At length, Myrtle Hawp, like a pressure cooker releasing a head of steam, vented her frustrations on Minnie. She gestured and punctuated her statements with the meat fork she was using to fry potatoes.

"Minnie Johnson, I'm not your mother, and if your father allows you to go galavantin' all over town doing heaven-knows-what with heaven-knows-who, I'm sure it's none of my business."

Minnie started to reply but was cut off. Myrtle was fired up.

"Oh, I understand it's a whole lot more fun runnin' around with folks your own age, but just *what* about the arrangement we have with your father? With you staying over at your uncle's house, I never see you. I thought you might at least come down to the camp and... "

When Myrtle's tirade finally wound down, Minnie wasn't sure how or if she should answer.

She decided not to. She'd chalk it up to Myrtle's "change of life" problem and let it go at that. She was much too happy to let Myrtle ruin her evening. She turned to go on over to Uncle Andrew's house.

Papa, who'd been unharnessing the team, heard every word of the tongue-lashing Mrs. Hawp had just delivered. She'd just crossed over several of his sacred boundary lines. He stepped into the kerosene lamplight of the camp area. With every step bringing him closer angry words reeled through his head. He searched for words that weren't curses to use. Minnie was his daughter, and it dang sure wasn't Myrtle Hawp's place to fly into her like that.

"Mrs. Hawp," Papa addressed her in a carefully controlled tone from the opposite side of the campfire. Minnie could tell he was maintaining a tenuous grasp on his temper. Myrtle Hawp had best mind her p's and q's.

"You're way outta line shootin' off your mouth at Minnie like that! Way outta line! In the first place, she is my daughter and as her father, if you have a problem with her behavior you need to take it up with me. Now, about the agreement you spoke about. Isn't it obvious that it applies only when we are all in camp? Arnold and I haven't eaten a meal here since we've been in Cambridge. There is absolutely no need for Minnie to come over here and help you cook, wash and clean if her family has had nothing to do with the eatin' and the messin' up."

Papa waited for that to sink in or for her to reply. She mumbled and played with some hair that had escaped her bun and was hanging down the side of her neck. He walked around the campfire to stand closer to her.

His voice became lower as he said, "You will not be jumpin' down Minnie's throat like that again."

Another long pause.

"Now, we're goin' to be travelin' and campin' together for the better part of the summer." Papa's voice was much calmer now. "So for everyone's peace of mind we need to maintain a peaceful camp. We *will* do that. We are going to have a friendly camp. Any differences of opinion can be talked out as respectful adults."

Oliver's tension had gradually lightened. He'd laid the ground rules.

"Do you understand what I've said here, Myrtle? Can you do what I'm asking?"

"Yes sir, I can, and I agree with you–but she..."

"Myrtle," it was Earnie, now. He'd jumped in the very second he heard his wife say *"but she"*. At this point those two words and *whatever* followed them would be the worst thing she could say. He spoke in a tone they'd never heard Earnie use before. It was a low, serious "come-to-your-senses-NOW" tone. Then he said one word and he only said it once.

"Hush." It was almost a growl.

And she did.

<u>June 13</u>
I helped Tina nearly all fore-noon in order to get ready to go to Indianola at one p.m. to see a ball game played between Cambridge and Indianola. We reached Indianola at three and the game commenced at four. During the

> *game, a foul ball struck Clarence in the eye and hurt him badly. Warren took his place. The game stood 5 to 8 in favor of Cambridge. We had supper at the Commercial Hotel and started home at seven and drove it in 2 hours. 15 miles! Passed through Bartley about 9 miles west of here.*

As far as the incident with Myrtle was concerned Minnie decided it was like her Momma used to say, "Some folks are kinda like puppies and kids–you have to give them plenty of attention or they'll act up." Minnie would go and give Myrtle Hawp some attention tomorrow. She thought a lot about Papa's defense of her. Had he done it because he thought her incapable of doing it for herself? Was she capable of doing it for herself?

> <u>June 14</u>
> *I came down home and helped Mrs. Hawp bake cookies, and washed. In the evening about six, Elmores, Jim and Reeds came. Also, Babcocks and Anna and Ruth. After supper Tina came down and we went downtown, and Warren and John came home with us.*

Two more wagons and a buggy had now arrived in Cambridge to join the group from Nebraska headed for Indian Territory: Mr. and Mrs. Elmore and Shirley, Jim and Gus Reid, brothers, and Sam Joice, a friend of theirs who together made a threesome that would stick together during the trip. Their little wagon train was taking shape. After greeting the new campers and sharing supper with them, Minnie and Tina walked to the soda shop where they found Warren and John, hoping the girls would drop by.

> <u>June 15</u>
> *Baked 16 loaves bread, put away clothes and prepared for Monday's journey. In the evening all of us young folks went boat riding and didn't get home till 10:30 p.m.*

The good times in Cambridge were rapidly coming to an end. Monday, the 17th, was the date set for leaving.

The people joining them for the trip down to the land opening were anxious to get on the trail.

Minnie had met so many new friends here, stayed out late, found out what fun there could be in being young. She'd never enjoyed life as much as she had in these last few days. Her mind fairly waltzed as she thought about it all.

The best of all was yet to come. John Perdoux had invited her to go with him to church tomorrow. And–she still couldn't believe it–Papa had agreed.

> <u>June 16 - Sunday</u>
> John and I went to Congregational Church. After dinner John, Tina and I drove clear in sight of Holbrook, 9 mi. east and came home in time for supper. We also had our stamp pictures taken in the afternoon. In the evening Elmer, Martha and Warren came over and Warren spent the evening with us.

Happier than she'd been in her life, Minnie strolled dreamily into camp before dusk Sunday evening.

"Girl, where have you been?" Papa asked in a tone though not angry still carried an edge to it. Startled by her father's question, she said defensively, "Papa, you knew where I was going. We talked about it yesterday. I said that after church we would be spending the day since it was our last one here." Minnie couldn't help but be peeved with Papa to think that he would suddenly have a problem with her plans–after the fact.

Papa wasn't conscious of it, but his *problem* was that his little girl was looking so durned attractive lately. She was becoming a young woman and he was having trouble dealing with it. Especially tonight, her face fairly glowed. He hadn't noticed it this morning when she left for church. But tonight, in her white blouse with those puffy sleeves, she looked quite so fetching. A feller'd be crazy not to notice. Oliver wasn't ready for his daughter to be spoken for.

"John Perd-o-u-x." Minnie breathed into her pillow after she'd crawled into her bed roll. Sitting in church beside him this morning she'd felt like "God was in his heaven and all was right with the world." Then their unforgettable afternoon. Remembering it now gave her chills.

The Reuben E. Pool Family: Garfield, Reuben, Clarence, Hellen, and Lydia. *circa 1888*

Chapter 6

Crossin' Kansas

"Good-bye, Minnie."

"Bye, Tina. You better write me," Minnie called from the wagon seat.

"I will. I promise I will."

"Tell everyone goodbye for me. I wish I could've stayed longer."

"Yes, yes, I will."

The wagon was already moving, slowly. Minnie and Tina's goodbyes had been said the evening before. Nevertheless they were repeating them as Uncle Andrew's house diminished in size.

Minnie hated to leave. She'd had a great time; learned a lot about life and herself in one week.

At least she had a lot of addresses and people to write. There would probably come a time when she'd be happy to receive a letter from anyone.

When they arrived at the south edge of town, Minnie gave a welcoming wave as the Elmores, the Reids and Sam

Joice pulled their rigs into line behind the Johnson and Hawp wagons. They were leaving Cambridge, early Monday morning, June 17; headed south toward the Kansas border.

<u>June 17, Monday</u>
Ready to start about 6:40. Bid the folks all good-bye at camp. Crossed the Republican River first, then passed through lovely farming country. Camped at Wilsonville at 10:30 for dinner on Beaver Creek. After dinner we crossed the Nebraska line into Kansas. 30 miles from Cambridge. Followed a beautiful creek valley and camped on a hill. Just as we were eating supper in the tent a storm came up and it rained and hailed until the water came thro' the tent and everything was wet except our beds. Elmore's tired of the trip but stood joking yet. Some of our horses sick. Fifteen miles from Norton. 35 miles from Cambridge to Norton.

✳✳✳

CLARENCE AND HIS FATHER, Reuben, sat in the morning sun on the east porch of the family home on the outer edge of Corning, Iowa. Shining through the leaves of the hackberry tree in the front yard the sun hadn't yet become unpleasantly warm. Lydia's, beautiful blue morning-glories crept up and over the white picket trellis at the front gate. Clarence sat on the front porch steps, holding a copy of the *Des Moines Register*. His father, behind him in the rocking chair, listened while Clarence read from an article on the third page:

> "...and it is still not known at this time, when the President's proclamation announcing plans for the opening of the Kiowa-Comanche-Apache ceded lands in Indian Territory will be made public. Some sources around Washington say that he will choose to do so soon, as further delay will make it impossible for the process to be completed this summer. Plans for a strictly controlled system that will be fair to all parties concerned is being drafted by the Department

of the Interior, under the guidance of the new
Secretary of the Interior, Ethan A. Hitchcock. In
addition, th--"

"Aw, thunder, Clarence!" Mr. Pool interrupted in exasperation, jerking his freshly lit pipe from his mouth and leaning forward in the rocking chair. He felt so aggravated with Clarence lately. His oldest son was being so pigheaded about this land opening thing.

"The papers have been saying the same blame thing for the last month. McKinley'll announce the opening when he's ready, and it'd behoove a fellow like yourself to be ready when that time comes." He sat back and puffed a few times in silence.

"It all boils down to this," Mr. Pool said finally after he'd rocked a couple of times, "are you interested in taking advantage of the opportunity or aren't you?"

"Well, of course, I'm interested--but that doesn't decide the thing, now does it?" Clarence returned defensively.

"I want to be absolutely certain of what I'm getting myself into. If it turns out to be another one of those horse races for land, you know darn well, I wouldn't stand a chance, bony as I am now. You don't seem to understand, Dad. Look at me! I'm not the same as I was when I left for the Philippines."

He stopped for the moment. Why, didn't his father understand? Could he not see?

The debate went on about the same everyday. Reuben prodding. Clarence defending.

Rueben E. and Lydia Pool
circa 1920

Next to the porch more of the big, blue morning-glory vines wound their way up the wires attached to the roof's edge. Lydia, Clarence's mother, had early this spring enlisted his help in placing the wires at just the right intervals. Now, looking out the window at her husband and son in intense conversation, Lydia admired her morning-glories, as she did every morning.

"Hel-len," Lydia called to her daughter, Clarence's younger sister, "come look at the morning glories. I swan, they get more beautiful every day." Her daughter came into the front room, drying her hands on her apron. She leaned toward the window and looked in the direction Mother was pointing.

"Yes, Mother, you're right. They are at least as gorgeous as they were yesterday when you pointed them out to me." Hellen said in mock surprise. She was kidding her mother--they both knew it. As she looked dutifully out the window, her curiosity turned to Clarence.

"Do you think Clarence is ever going to get married? What is he now? Twenty-six?"

"Oh, Hellen, for goodness sake. He doesn't need to be in any hurry to get married." One of Lydia Pool's pet peeves was the subject of her son's needing to be in a hurry--trying to rush him off.

"No I believe he changed a lot since his time in the Philippines." Hellen seemed bound to push the point further this morning. "Haven't you noticed? It's as if he's lost his confidence. Or, maybe, losing so much weight and strength with the dysentery...I don't know... It just seems like its taken away his feeling of being worth anything."

"Now Hellen, that may well be; though I haven't noticed anything of the sort. But what he needs more than anything else is his family being more considerate of his feelings; not bringing up touchy subjects.

After a bit, Hellen went on, "Have you noticed how the widow Kirby always seeks him out after services on Sunday? I think she's sweet on him. And those cute little twins of her's do so need a father. I think Clarence and she are about the same age. Aren't they?"

"I hadn't noticed." Lydia's daughter was coming awfully close to overstepping herself today. "Clarence is doing just fine. I *wish* you and your father would quit worrying him. He needs our support and concern and enough time to recuperate properly."

Clarence Pool never did anything anymore without first thinking it through from every angle–since the dysentery. He was less free in his actions and decisions. He took time to picture himself in every possible situation that might arise and foresee how he would handle it. Before leaving for the service, Clarence had attended college in Ames, Iowa. He completed his study of law, took and passed the bar exam. George Corvah, a friend from college days, had begun lately, to suggest that Clarence give up his aspirations for a career in law and move to a drier climate. He respected George's opinion and for that reason alone was considering it.

Clarence O. Pool
Before and after his time in the Philippines.
***

June 18
Started 6:30 and drove Norton, Kansas for dinner.
A beautiful town of 1500 inhabitants and county seat.
Many large brick buildings. Left camp 1:20 p.m. and
camped about 5 mi. from Edmunds (west) for the night.
Thundering and may rain. Papa lost his rifle right after
dinner. Norton 35 miles from Hill City. On Salmon
River.

June 19

Started 6:07 cloudy and cold. Papa killed two jack rabbits for the dogs. Crossed the Missouri-Pacific at 8:00 and camped 6 mi. N. of Hill City for dinner. Started 1:10 and came through Hill City, a dull town, but has so many pretty Kansas stone buildings. Crossed the Union Pacific, and a river. Twenty-Five miles to Wakena. We are camped in a place similar to Stinking River, but no valley on either side to speak of. Mrs. Hawp and I washed clothes down at the creek, our faces and ears and combed. Our bed springs being broke we made our bed down on the Green moguette but haven't hurt it any yet. Hot this afternoon and saw men harvesting for the first time on this trip.

June 20

Started 6:20 and drove to Wakeeney by 11:00. It was foggy and cloudy all forenoon. This town is over twenty years old but small and on a flat. The courthouse is a large stone structure two stories and a half high with basement. Union Pacific railway passes through. 55 miles from here to Ness City. Camped at 5:30 on Smokey Hill River. Before reaching the river we drove down a gradual slope about seven mi. long, and river at the foot was very shallow with red sand on the bottom. Mrs. Elmore and I went wading and the men went in all over. The water wasn't very good.

June 21

Started 6:08. Crossed the river and drove about 5 mi. up a canon where the rocks projected out of the banks in many shades. Just before dinner we came through heavy grain country and where wheat was being harvested. 9:00 a.m.--we passed 2 mi. east of Ransom and crossed the Missouri-Pacific. We camped for dinner at 10:30 on a spring draw. Water just fine, also the feed. Are now about seven mi. from Ness. Started 12:40 and arrived in town at 3:00 p.m. Sam Joice's horse has the scours and we decided to wait a day or so to see if he

would get well. Mr. Olson rode with us this afternoon.
Went to a ball game.

<u>June 22</u>
Mrs. Hawp and I washed clothes all morning. Add two
tubs and two wash boards, and did a big washing. The
men carried water for us. After dinner we cleaned up and
Mrs. Hawp and I went up town and mailed some letters.
After supper Mrs. Elmore, Mrs. Hawp and I walked all
over town and saw so many pretty yards and houses.
Honeysuckle, Jasmine, Peaches, Pears, Mulberries,
catalpa, cherries, and so forth in the yards. One bank
(Ness County) three stories and a basement, of stone cost
$37,000. Nearly vacated, the grandest sculpturing I
ever saw. Also, the State Normal; stone. Sugar Corn
factory $140,000. burnt down on account of $90,000
insurance. The town built mostly of stone, looks like the
ancient ruins of Jerusalem. In the eve about 8 p.m. we
went to an ice cream social, given by the W. R. C. in the
G. A. R. hall. It was decorated beautifully with garlands
of honeysuckle and one table the length of the hall. We
were there first and too tired to stay for programme.

The day's layover in Ness City allowed the women
time to catch up on laundry and baking. After they
finished, they ladies around the town to see the sights. On
their walk they noticed a sign inviting "one and all" to an
ice cream social. They told the men about it and decided
to go. They might meet some interesting people.
Waiting around for Sam's horse to get better wasn't
sitting too well with Papa Oliver. He wasn't very good at
sitting still. He needed to be in control and moving. Not
good at niceties and diplomacy anyway, he was also
having fears of arriving too late for the big opening. As
the thoughts nagged at him and he–in turn–sorta nagged
at the other folks. It was becoming irritating for everyone.
Finally he told the others, "I'm sorry folks, we've just got
to move on." The Hawps went along with the Johnsons.

The men, H & O.H., decided we would go on and Elmores & Reeds stayed on account of the sick horse. It was hard to part with part of our crowd, but we said a last adieu at 6:20 a.m. and departed for Jetmore, 28 mi. south and 2 east. This has been a hot, windy forenoon. Camped in a draw for dinner at 11:00. A strange dog (scotch collie) fell in with us on the prairie, evidently lost. It went through a pasture from where we found no outlet. The men loosened the wire from the stone posts and drove over. An Irishmen caught up with us soon after and cussed a blue streak. Said he would have us arrested. I'll not repeat the reply to his uncouth words. Left dinner camp at 1:00 and drove till 5:30. Came through Jetmore 3:00 and watered at the court house. Came on 6 and a half miles and camped near a farm. The man was a merchant at Jetmore. Mrs. Hawp and I went up to the house and spoke with the family and shortly they all came to camp and made us a call. Real nice people. Santa Fe R.R. through Jetmore. Saw Log Creek. 22 miles from Jetmore to Spearville.

This wasn't one of their better days.

Minnie wasn't happy at having to leave the rest of the group. They'd been traveling with them only a week, just long enough to get to know everyone and become accustomed to their company. She really didn't see what it would've hurt to have stayed another day.

Then, there was the cussing they got from the Irishman in the afternoon. She tried to put it out of her mind–to let it roll like water off a duck's back. But, a cussing was something Minnie'd never experienced--it kind of hurt-- stirred up those mean juices in a person's gut. They'd been doing the only thing they saw to do, to get out of the fenced pasture. They took the wire down, rolled over it and were in the process of putting it back up. Just look at the thanks they got.

<u>June 24</u>
*Started at 6:18. Clear and windy. Passed through
Spearville at 10:15. Crossed the A.T. & S.F.R.R. and
camped (dry) a few miles this side of town, at 11:00.
Started at 1:00 and crossed the Arkansas River. Camped
for the night in the suburbs of Ford. Camped at 4:30.
Crossed the river on a bridge as it was up. There was
water in it, but usually dry. Little timber in this part of
the valley. We came into a sort of sand hills north of
here 8 mi. and cattle country through this belt of sand so
far. Twelve miles to Kingstown from Ford.*

Rolling down the plains of Kansas, Minnie had a lot of
time to think. John Perdoux, of course, was on her mind
and in her daydreams. He'd been part of her exciting
adventure–the week at Cambridge.

She wondered if what she was feeling was love or
what her Momma would call lust. There wasn't one soul
traveling with them she'd dare ask.

<u>June 25</u>
*Started 6:03--came through farming country & crossed a
branch of the Rock Island R.R., camped for dinner at a
country school house 10 to 11 and pulled out at 12:35.
Soon after crossed Bluff Creek and later came in sight of
Ashland about 10 miles away. Came in to camp about
5. Camped just across from the court house in a vacant
block. Court House is brick and three stories, a beautiful
structure. We came through so many brick colored hills.
Some blue, quite hilly. Clear & windy, very. Bus met
the train and is taking the passengers to the hotel.*

They hadn't seen a "bus" before. These newfangled
conveyances had come into being in recent years with the
expansion of the railroad system. An elongated cab
enclosure, mounted on a wagon chassis, there was a rack
on top for luggage and travel trunks. Unlike the
stagecoaches of yesteryear, the passengers sat in benches
that ran along each side under the windows.

When the Johnsons and Hawps crossed over the
border into Oklahoma Territory, it seemed their dream
took a huge leap toward becoming reality. They stopped
the horses for a few minutes, just to breathe in the new air
and celebrate the fact that they were now in Oklahoma
Territory.

Arnold, half-expecting to see Indians in war paint as
soon as they crossed over the line, was most excited.
Finally, after a couple of hours, he rode up to the front of
their wagon where Papa and Minnie were riding on the
padded leather, spring seat.

"I thought this was Indian Territory," Arnold said.

"It is," Oliver replied.

"Wull, why haven't we seen any Indians yet?"

"We probably won't for a ways yet, son. Might even
be a couple more days." His father answered.

"I think this part of the land was settled by a run in '93,
which would make it Oklahoma Territory, officially."
Minnie said, sounding more "teacherish" than she'd
intended.

"I wish it'd be a run this time." Arnold said, seeing
visions of himself on Red, the feisty sorrel, riding like the
wind, faster than anyone to the best 160 acres to be found.
Then, he would bravely stand his ground, fighting off
interlopers, till Papa and Minnie got there with the wagon.

"Not me," Minnie said, "I'll be perfectly happy with a
lottery. I've heard too many awful stories about wagon
wheels breaking when they hit coyote holes at top speed.
The wagon, horses, people, and all their belongings go
flying end-over-end. There are stories of horses breaking
legs in prairie dog holes or being run to death. Runs seem
to invite cheating and violence, too."

"I imagine there will be some cheating and violence no

matter how it's done," Papa commented.

"Well, it just doesn't sound like the kind of thing I'm cut out for," Minnie said.

"How about you, Papa? Which one'd you ruther it be?" Arnold asked.

Papa wrinkled up his face and thought for a while before replying, "Oh, I'd feel more comfortable racin' for the land. I know I can hold my own, man-to-man or horse-to-horse, but this paperwork is another thing altogether. It appears to me, that a land lot'ry would involve a lot more signin' up and linin' up and you kids know how I am with readin', writin' and dancin' to somebody else's music. Never had to, don't like to, an' don't do too good at it."

June 27

Started 6:20 and soon reached the old Salt Trail and went south, passed no houses, but came to a canon where we found good water and an elderly gent, who had just located with a small bunch of cattle. Left 1:25 and drove to Salt Marsh on the Cimarron River for the night. The marsh, 2 mi. by 12, was a very pretty sight.

The wagons jolted along over dried ruts in the road made by other wagons after a rainy spell on some long ago day. In places where the prairie grass was tall enough, it waved in the warm, south wind. Minnie was amused by the prairie dogs who sat up on their rear haunches and yapped at people going by.

June 28

Next morning we left at 6:15 and soon overtook Salt haulers whom we saw the evening before at the Marsh. We came on through ranch country and met a minister, Rev. Ross, a great talker who lived near Ft. Supply Res., Formerly of Olvis, and this morning we are camped on Beaver Creek in Sand Hills--red sand. Just a mile from town. I have had a severe headache all day.

June 29

We hitched up and drove to town at 6:20 and camped a day in order to rest the teams. The town of Woodward,

1000 inhabitants on the main line Santa Fe is a cowboy town--very lively.

The Johnsons and the Hawps enjoyed the lay over in Woodward. They located a general store in which to obtain some necessary items. Minnie got a powder for her headache. Walking along the boardwalk, near noon, they decided to treat themselves to dinner in an eating house.

"What looks good to you, Minnie-girl?" Papa asked after they sat down at a table with enough room for six. Minnie found the menu on the wall written in chalk on a small blackboard. In the center of the table was a pitcher of water and a stack of glasses turned upside down.

"I've been craving mashed potatoes and gravy, Papa. I don't care what else, as long as there's lots of mashed potatoes and gravy on the plate."

Arnold agreed and added corn to the list. Leaning over he told Papa quietly, "The meat-for-the-day is roast beef."

"We'll have three roast beef dinners with corn and mashed potatoes and gravy," Papa said to the lady who came out from behind the counter. Mr. and Mrs. Hawp agreed and Myrtle inquired if they happened to have any fresh radishes.

"Yes, Ma'am, sure do," answered the lady. "I'll put a bowl of them and some green onions on your table."

Papa leaned over and asked Minnie the price of what they'd ordered. "Looks like dinner plates are twenty-five cents a piece," she whispered. Papa's eyebrows didn't raise or anything obvious like that, but Minnie could tell by the way he nodded that he thought that was enough.

"Guess that'll do it for us," Papa said.

The lady looked over at Mr. Hawp who looked over at Myrtle. Myrtle nodded her head giving Earnie permission to agree to the order. Minnie winked at Arnold. They enjoyed finding humor in the things the Hawp's did.

"A dessert comes along with that dinner plate. You can have your choice between peach cobbler and lemon meringue pie," she said. Minnie and Arnold wide-eyed each other. What a nice surprise.

June 30, Sunday

Started 5:53, crossed Indian Creek and camped for dinner at Hackberry and after dinner drove to Persimmon and camped for the night. Joe Jordan lives 2 mi. west of here, but we were expecting him in to church and did not get to see him. Mrs. Hawp and I attended Epworth League in the evening and heard a very interesting meeting over 50 young people were assembled Mr. Osborne Merdraft (?)

July 1st

Started from Persimmon at 6:10 drove through Bloomfield P.O. and camped in the shade of a big elm about 1 1/2 mi. this side, east. We have crossed about 16 little creeks this morning, about 1/2 had running water in them. Country mostly farmed through here and the best crops we have seen so far. The fields are mostly planted in corn and castor beans which bring as high as $1.50 a bu. Camped 2 hrs and left camp at 2:45 p.m. We came through Lenora and camped near the Canadian River for the night 5:15, back of a school. Mrs. H. and I took a bath within its walls.

July 2nd

6:00 a.m. We came through a strip of lovely timber just before crossing the river, in which we saw the first oaks (jack), walnuts and hackberry trees. The river bed is about 3/4 a mile wide, no water running. Raymond P.O. north side of South Bend. We passed through Burmah where we saw the 1st cotton gin, camped for dinner at Elm P.O., at 10:50 in an Elm grove where a number of people were assembled and held Camp meeting. After camping about 2 hours, we passed on through Gip P.O. and camped on Barnet Creek for the night, farming country. The fields are all planted in corn, cotton, sweet potatoes and castor beans. Once in a while we see small grain, now threshed & being threshed, hay cut and being bailed. Orchards all through the country and vegetation in general very extensive.

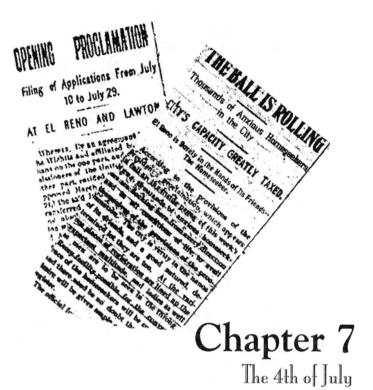

Chapter 7
The 4th of July

Wagon after wagon of Indian families joined with those on route south to Cordell. The dusty trail ahead and behind was filled with Indian vehicles. Arnold was fascinated.

"Guess they're going to celebrate the 4th of July, too."

Something about it seemed strange to him, their wagons rolling along the same stretch of road with the Indians. He wasn't quite sure exactly what it was. Arnold's dream of seeing Kiowa and Cheyenne (who lived farther north than the Comanche) people up close had come true but he had the feeling there was something unexpected about this. Riding closer to the Johnson wagon, it suddenly occurred to him it was the *wheels*.

Indians on wheels! This wasn't the picture he'd learned to expect. The north American natives had for centuries dragged their belongings behind horses on *travois*. The native Americans hadn't been using "wheels" for transportation until recent years.

Didn't wheels come to North America with the Europeans? Arnold tried to remember his history lessons. Ah, yes, and so had small pox and typhoid. Along with the good things the white man brought came the bad as well.

<u>July 3rd</u>
6:00 a.m. *We passed through a busy country town and county seat, Arapaho and on south, crossed the Washita River right where a number of men were building a railroad bridge on the new railroad A.T. & S.F. (Atchison, Topeka & the Santa Fe). This stream not much more than a good sized creek, very pretty valley, lovely timber. Indians farm all along the river bottom. Live mostly in Teepees. Camped between two fences, and got water in a slough nearby. 1:05 started on for the town of Cordell, County Seat, where we intend to celebrate. Many wagon loads of Indians were both ahead and behind us going to town. On reaching town we could find no place to camp except on some vacant lots which we accepted, as the Indian teepees were lining both banks of the creek. We arrived here 4:00 p.m. After teams were unhitched I patched one of our comforts, washed and combed and started to help get supper.*

"Look for a newspaper!" Minnie reminded her father as he stepped briskly away from the wagons, headed toward the bustling center of town.

A wave was his reply.

Almost everyone they'd spoken with in the last week had repeated the story that McKinley's proclamation would be in the papers on the 4th of July. Certainly, if the opening was going to be done this summer, it was high time the White House announced the particulars.

For Arnold, this 4th of July celebration was the high point of the journey. Indians dressed in their colorful dance regalia filled the square in the middle of Cordell. He roamed all over the grounds, studying everything he saw. When he smiled at a pretty young Indian girl who looked to be about his age, she'd slowly returned his smile, and looked downward, giving him a curiously happy feeling.

For Minnie and the rest of the group, it was a celebration of more than just Independence Day. Having the major portion of the miles behind them was an immense relief. They were now within an easy two and a half, maybe three day, drive of Fort Sill. It was comforting and exciting being here. Comforting, because they'd gotten this far, and exciting, because they were celebrating the 4th in a new, unexplored land–with a different culture from their own.

The Kiowa people danced in the afternoon. Their colorful regalia and dancing skill was something to see. Some wore brass rings in their ears, copper bracelets, silver arm bands, and silver disks attached in long strings to their scalp locks. The clinking rhythm of little pieces of metal attached to the dancers clothing ankles and arms kept time with the steady beat of Kiowa drums. There were always at least three singers beating on the drum. The songs, the sounds, and the rhythm had an enchanting, almost hypnotic, effect. Minnie got goose bumps, feeling a sense of adventure at being part of this celebration. If she closed her eyes, she could picture the land before the white man and "civilization" came calling--feel at one with the prairie--Mother Earth.

"Hey-Yah, hey-yah-anh-ah-hey-yah-yah-nah. Anah-hey-hanh-nahn-nah-ney." Along with the regular beating of drums, the dancers made skipping movements first on one foot and then the other.

"Look," Minnie whispered, indicating with her chin, "over there, to the right of the drum and singers--see that little girl. Isn't that the most endearing sight you've ever seen."

It was mid-afternoon. Minnie, Arnold, and the Hawps had been strolling around, taking in as much of the celebration as they could. Minnie watched as Arnold found the child to which she referred. He smiled in agreement. Mrs. Hawp took it up, and pointed out the little girl to her husband. By his smile, and the twinkle in his eye, Minnie could see that the little tyke had melted his heart, as well.

She was a tiny, tan-faced girl–about three years of age–with long, black braids and feathers in her hair. She was a perfect vision of innocence and beauty. Her garment was made of soft leather–perhaps deerskin–and had colorful beading and fringes on the sleeves that swayed when she did. With tiny moccasins on her feet, she bounced her precious little body to the rhythm of the drums. Two big tears welled up in Minnie's eyes and rolled slowly down her cheeks.

A merry-go-round, food and carnival booths, foot races, horse races, a parade, some gambling and other festivities went on throughout the day. In the evening came the fireworks. With each one there was the exciting first rush-sh, a hiss, an explosion, a burst of colored stars, and the long ah-h-h-h! of blissful satisfaction from those watching. It was a good day.

<u>July 4</u>

As soon as breakfast was over, I scoured up our silverware, made some lemon pie and nut cake. After dinner was ready, Papa brought some beef which was a fraction of the 8 beeves that were cooked Barbecue fashion. Dishes washed, Mrs. H. & I went down and watched the dance all afternoon. After supper we stayed at the bowery till 10:30, watched the merry-go-round & fireworks. Over two thousand people were assembled and a better behaving crowd the writer never saw, and enjoyed the exercises very much for a stranger.

***

IN ACCORDANCE WITH the Jerome Agreement, tribal members had already selected their own piece of land. Each Kiowa, Comanche, and Kiowa-Apache man, woman, and child had been allotted, one 160 acre tract of land. Though some of the elders had proudly refused in protest to select their parcel of land, the U.S. Land Office simply assigned a piece to them.

It was reported in an Altus, O.T. newspaper of the time that a man called Kiowa George, the father of twelve children, had shrewdly staked all 13 claims near Mountain

View and got 2,080 acres of the best land in the area. Now, *that* was the intent of those Indians who were in favor of the agreement.

"The white man is going to come. If we like it or if we don't like it. Nothing you could do will stop it. Might as well get you a good piece of land–big as you can."

Grass money–a twenty dollar gold piece–had been given twice a year since 1893, to each Comanche and Kiowa, by the Texas cattlemen to pay for grazing rights to the southern portion of their land. Comanche Chief Quanah Parker, with his portion and some extra paid him as arbiter–the same pay as if he were one of the cowboys–built a very nice, large, white frame house. There was a room for each of his wives and her children.

Quanah Parker's Star House

"Star House," people called it, was located south of the Wichita Mountains, fifteen miles west of Fort Sill. It had five, huge, white stars painted on its red roof. Quanah had directed the workmen to do this, noting that U.S. Army generals wore many stars--the more stars, the higher the rank. It was said he liked the symbolism.

One particular Indian Agency official had a problem with Quanah Parker's having several wives. He suggested to Quanah that he should make a good example for his people by selecting only one wife to live in his home. Quanah had been asked many, many favors "for the good of your people" and to be a "good example to your people". But about the third time this particular man made this particular suggestion, Quanah answered him saying, "Okay, this way, I tell you and maybeso you couldt understand. YOU couldt pick the ones that has to leave. And, than YOU couldt towl (tell) them." Everyone laughed except the official.

Quanah had been of great value in helping his people see that in many respects the road of the white man might be a little better than life the way they were forced to live it–without the buffalo, nor being allowed to roam. At any rate, he told them it was inevitable and they might as well make the best of the situation. They got us outnumbered.

There were three things from the old way that the Indian Agents would never convince Quanah to give up. One was his braids–he would never cut his hair. Second was his practice of polygamy–he kept many wives. The last was his use of peyote. He held strongly to the belief that answers to life's questions came from the Great One, when sought through prayer within the veil of peyote medicine and ritual.

In the nine years since the the signing of the Jerome Agreement, Quanah had made eight trips to Washington D. C. with other Kiowa and Comanche elders. These were made in efforts to delay the implementation of the agreement and in so doing hold back the encroachment of the white man as long as they could.

***

"You find a paper, Papa?"

"Yeah."

"Where did you put it?"

"Tossed it in the wagon. 'Bout an hour ago."

"Okay, I see it." Minnie picked up the newspaper and rapidly scanned through it. No proclamation here. She went through it again--slower this time.

"Nope, looks like we wasted our money on that one."

The proclamation wasn't in the July 4th edition of most newspapers in Oklahoma. The Whitehouse had neglected to make sure the copy was sent in time to have the huge article typeset.[6] Consequently, the July 5th or later issues of most newspapers was the one landseekers would carry around with them all summer.

ARRIVING AT THE PLACE where they intended to ford the Washita River, Papa eyed it warily. The decline near them looked awfully steep. Minnie sure hoped Papa wouldn't be careless enough to try it.

Slapping the reins on the horses backs, Papa hollered, "Hold on, Minnie, we're goin' for a ride."

"No–o–." Minnie grabbed the seat beneath her. She could not believe Papa was doing this.

The horses took the first couple of steps down the embankment just fine, then their feet began slipping, alarming them and causing their usually balanced pull to be at cross-purposes. A step or two more, Cole reared up and the wagon began to tip.

"Pa-pa!" Minnie yelled, unable to find anything to hold onto. Her side of the wagon was going down.

Oliver had his hands full with the reins and the horses. Minnie couldn't hold on any longer. She turned, slipped off the seat and dropped to the ground, hoping to roll to safety. She landed on her feet, but not for long. Papa fell against her knocking her to the ground. The wagon came to rest, leaning perilously against the red soil of the bank.

Papa and Minnie were beneath the spring seat. Since the weight of the wagon was not resting on her, Minnie was able to squirm out. Seeing that Papa would also be able to wriggle free, she began looking for a way to get up the muddy bank--out of the way.

Still holding the reins, Papa never seemed to lose his composure. He scrambled to upright himself while trying to calm the horses whose legs were still slipping as they tried to gain a foothold.

Arnold; up on level ground, had dismounted, dropped Red's reins, and was scurrying down the incline where the left side wheels of the wagon still turned in the air.

"Want me to unhook 'em, Papa?"

"Not yet," Oliver said out of breath and covered with mud.

"Easy, girl, e-e-easy," Arnold said calmly. He was in front of the team, stroking Neg's nose as he grabbed Cole's bridle attempting to soothe him as well.

Minnie still fighting the slick mud in her attempt to ascend the steep bank, saw Mrs. Hawp hustle down off their wagon and grab the reins of Arnold's horse. The last thing they needed now, was for Red to get spooked and run off. But bless her heart, she simply could not keep from squawkin' and squealin'.

"Oh, my Lord." "OH!"

"Oh, Minnie-girl, are you all right? MIN--NIE?"

Minnie couldn't answer. Her heart was pounding, her hands shaking, and her legs felt like they were made of putty. She could see and hear Mrs. Hawp but was much too busy crawling up to level ground to answer her.

As Minnie reached the edge of the sod at the top of the embankment, she gathered all her strength and gave one final lunge putting herself halfway over on it. Legs dangling she lay there trying to catch her breath and feeling her heart pound as if it would escape her chest.

Head still on the grass, Minnie watched Papa allowing several minutes for things to stabilize, and taking stock of the situation.

"Arnold," he said finally, "I'm going to try to get in between the horses and the wagon and unhook 'em. You keep doin' what you're doin'. Just hold 'em easy like that."

Finally the team was released from the binding pull of the twisted wagon behind them. Arnold and Papa led them separately back up the narrow opening in the river bank.

A couple of wagons following the same trail pulled up behind them. The menfolk got down and walked toward the tipped wagon.

"Need some help?" one of them asked Minnie who was now sitting cross-legged on the bank.

"Yes, sir, we sure do. Thank you." Even now her chest was still heaving and her words were clipped.

It would only be a matter of time now until the men could set the wagon upright and they could be on their way. She could breathe easier now.

<u>July 5</u>
Started 6:20 and came through grand farming country--
corn stalks 8 & 9 ft. high. Came 3 miles west of Cloud
Chief and camped a little this side of a creek for dinner at
10:30. Started 1 p.m. and as we came back to the

Washita River we started to ford it and upset, just at the foot of the first bank. We slipped just 1/2 over against a bank, and there being four men in our wake they soon set it on wheels again, nothing was spilled or broken and nothing fell out of the wagon. After reaching Mountain View and searching for a suitable camping place, who should we come across but Mr. Reed and Sam Joice. What a surprise! They told us where we might find the remainder of the crowd, and we went straightaway thither. What a pleasant surprise to find them all in good spirits--and glad to see one another. They'd traded their sick horse off and came on just a day and a half behind us, but us lying over gave them the start on us and they drove in here just a few hours ahead of us. Cloudy, very, this eve and may have rain. No rain has fallen on us since our first night in Kansas. Our camp is on the bank of the river, Washita.

"Five days?" Papa repeated in shock.

Minnie had finally gotten her hands on a newspaper and was briefing Papa on the information in the proclamation. The date for beginning of registration for the lottery had been set for July 10.

When the proclamation finally came out, this little piece of information threw many in Oklahoma Territory and surrounding states into a whirlwind of activity. They had five days to decide whether to go or not; and if they were going–did they want to purchase train tickets or drive their own rig?

The railroad companies rushed about, attempting to book everyone who wanted it, some kind of passage. It all caused a great deal of mayhem. Cheap tickets were sold for floor space in the aisles and in cattle cars. Some would even ride on top of cars–*without a ticket*. El Reno and Fort Sill had been named as the two locations for registration. El Reno was accessible by train--Fort Sill was not.

<u>July 6</u>
Mrs. Hawp & I washed clothes this morning. The men decided to move camp after dinner to a cooler place.

Right after dinner we pulled out across the river on the Kiowa Reservation about 2 1/2 mi. Camped at the mouth of a horseshoe in the shade of some oaks, and we all took turn about and dug out a spring. In the evening, Mrs. Elmore & I washed some more under the creek bank. Papa got supper.

July 7, Sunday
Sunday, and everyone after breakfast arranged things and fixed their toilet, then wrote letters. Papa got breakfast this morning and I washed the dishes. Mr. & Mrs. H. were both sick today. Sam washed clothes.Shirley read my book, "Romance of Gilbert Holmes". This eve the men hitched to Mr. Reid's buggy and went to town.

July 8
After breakfast I picked up a few dirty things besides the sheets and pillow slips, and washed them. Then, Shirley having finished that book, I laid down on my cot (composed of my wool mattress and an upright chair) reclined & read awhile. Then got dinner & helped wash dishes, after which I took my former position and read a while. Stopped and washed my head, visited awhile at the neighbors and resumed my seat beneath the tree. Sam and Reid let their horses get away so Jim went horseback on one of the blacks to look for them, and four of the other men went in the buggy to town to look for them. Later, Jim found them.

Papa was fit to be tied! They'd laid over here in Mountain View for three days now! He couldn't understand what was holding these other Nebraska folks back. He was getting fidgety and irritable. Minnie could tell he just *had* to get moving--or explode.

After supper while the ladies were cleaning up she watched him address the men, "If it's all the same to you men, I'm ready to pull camp and get on down to Fort Sill."

There was an awkward silence for a few moments. Some of the men who hadn't finished eating kept on chewing and looking down at their plates. Jim Reid and

Sam Joice looked at each other. Then both started to speak at the same time. Sam deferred to Jim.

"Well, Mr. Johnson, we sure don't mean to be rude or nothin' like that but we'd kinda like to lay over here at Mountain View for another day or two. You know we've got word back that the trail to Fort Sill is just thick with wagons and we'd like to avoid that mess if at all possible."

Sam took it from there. "According to the newspaper, Oliver, the proclamation allows for a twenty day registration period for this lottery with the last person registering having equal opportunity with the first. So, we can't see as we need to be in any hurry."

"You sure about that?" Papa asked appearing to be ill-at-ease but still looking Sam in the eye. He'd known him a long time. "Seems to me the earlier a person gets registered the earlier number he'd oughta get."

"Well, that's not the way the paper reads, Mr. Johnson," Jim replied, his tone reproachful. "They's doin' it a whole lot different this time. In fact it just could be that the last cards thrown on the stack might be the ones on the top when it comes time for the drawing."

Papa was taken aback by Jim's reasoning. He hadn't thought of it like that. He glanced at Jim sideways. Minnie had tried to explain this to Papa but there was no way he'd believe it coming from her. She felt a little sorry for him now, though. Sometimes, his know-it-all attitude got him into embarrassing situations.

Gus Reid, who seemed to be on the shy side, got up and walked over to his brother Jim. He said something to him that the rest couldn't hear.

"Oh, okay," Jim said with a chuckle. Then turning and speaking to the others he smiled as he said, "It seems that some of us have left our laundry in Mountain View, so we'll be needing to pick that up before we leave here, as well." The laughter over Gus's predicament helped to ease the tension.

"Well, looks like we'll just agree to disagree on this point, Jim, if that's all right with you and we'll be on our way in the mornin'." Papa was speaking in his most congenial manner.

"I sure don't want any hard feelings between us but I just got the feeling that we need to be gettin' on down to

Fort Sill," he added.

"Oh, no, Mr. Johnson, no hard feelings at all. If you feel like you need to be down there that's where you need to be. I'm sure we'll be running into you there in a few days. Maybe we'll be able to squeeze into a camp next to you."

Papa nodded his head and turned to where the Hawps were seated, "Mr. Hawp, will you be leavin' with us? I'd like to get started in the morning about–oh–say, six, six thirty."

"Yes, sir, we will. We'll be ready." It was Myrtle who answered leaving Earnie's mouth gaping open ready to reply. He closed it, turned and gave her a look. Minnie could tell how much he wished she wouldn't do that.

> July 9
> Hawps & us left camp for Lawton at 6:40. Reids left their washing in town and could not come on that account. We had not been on the road but a short time until the road was lined with wagons and buggies going to Ft. Sill to register as the 10th was the day set for it to begin.

Heading southeast, toward Fort Sill, they watched the north side of the Wichitas all morning. Minnie thought how they seemed to grow larger as the wagons came closer to them. By mid-morning they reached the foothills. The trail was indeed thick with wagons. One behind the other they formed a continuous line. The trail through the mountains was filled with covered wagons, buggies, buckboards, a cart or two, an occasional bicycle and several men with packs on their backs were walking.

They'd topped a rise and gazed down at the long, curling white ribbon of wagons winding between the mountains.

"What a sight." Minnie's mouth dropped open.

"Would you look at that!" Papa said in astonishment.

The Wichita Mountains were impressive. A small range, they ran east to west for a distance of about 40 miles. Alongside the Rockies these mountains would have looked like mere piles of rocks. The impressive thing about them was the fact that they were here protruding up out of a vast prairie. Giant, granite boulders seemed in places to have been precariously stacked one on top of the other.

Minnie took in every inch of the beautiful scenery. This was the first break from sheer prairie and farm land they'd seen since leaving Gordon.

> <u>July 9, continued...</u>
> *We soon reached the foothills of the Wichita Mountains, passed between Mt. Scott and Rainy Hill. We camped for dinner in a valley between the mountains at 10:30 and left camp again at 12:20 and at 5:00 p.m. drove within 1/4 of a mile of an eating-and-store house, where a large no. of people camped. Campers all around us. Part of the campers were very noisy, mostly men which accounts for it--singing and mouth harp music.*

Because of the worry brought on by thousands of people, horses, and other livestock camped together in such close proximity, Minnie and the others realized that their days of peaceful camping were probably over for awhile. That evening, they made camp nine miles out to the northwest of Fort Sill. Nonetheless, the number of camps surrounding them kept growing, and so did the clamor.

The air was filled with sounds of revelry. Everybody seemed to be anticipating wealth and good fortune.

Part of the crowd at Fort Sill for registration

Photo courtesy of Fort Sill Museum

Chapter 8

Registration

> July 10
>
> It came very near being the 9th as we arose, wagons kept
> coming in all night, and such a noise! We couldn't sleep,
> so we arose at 1 a.m. had breakfast, washed dishes,
> packed and were on the road by 1:45. The moon raised
> at one, so it was light as day. Many teams had already
> pulled out but the road was taken by teams both ahead
> and behind. My rest being broken, I put Papa's coat on
> and laid down in the back part of the wagon and slept
> until daylight as we were crossing a creek.

Like a giant swarm of locusts landseekers descended
upon W. H. Quinette's Post Trader Store & Post Office at
Fort Sill the morning of July 10. The size of the crowd far
exceeded all projections and the small army installation
was not equipped to handle the invasion–peaceful though

it might be. There were plans to start a new town just south of the Fort.

"Saints preserve us till that small feat is accomplished." Mr. Quinette the Trader Store owner said, shaking his head in disbelief.

At 5:00 a.m. the bugle sounded and the cannon boomed, alerting anyone who might have been sleeping of the beginning of another day at the fort.

Small groups of men gravitated near the front door–had been there since the evening before. Some spent the night there–playing cards, telling stories, swapping lies and making durn sure they'd be one of the first through the door. Their numbers kept increasing, believing it seemed, like Oliver Johnson, "the sooner the better." Every man in the 10,000 man crowd around the store, had done his dead-level best to be among the first to arrive and would defend his position in line by whatever means it took. If a man had to leave his place for any reason, asking another to hold it for him, there would be a vicious verbal exchange on his return. The man didn't always want his place back, having had life and limb threatened.

By 9:00 a.m. the line coiled around the quadrangle of the fort and down toward the corral. If things had been allowed to continue in this way, eventually the line would have been miles longer and worse than that tempers and perhaps guns would have been flaring.

El Reno too, was jampacked with people. Complicating matters there was the fact that all who'd arrived by train were expecting to be put up in a rooming house or a hotel. But all rooming houses and hotels were full and overflowing. A bed of any sort–a pile of hay–was soon in great demand.

***

The eastern-thinking advisors to Secretary of the Interior, Ethan A. Hitchcock, had grossly underestimated the number of hardy souls who would be willing to make the long haul south to the old army outpost established during the Indian wars in early 1869. The fact that it lay deep in Comanche lands, unaccessible by railroad hadn't discouraged those here today. The planning committee had projected that only a tiny fraction of the land speculators would be apt to go so deeply into Indian Territory (to Fort Sill) since El Reno was much more accessible. Consequently only one registration site was provided at Fort Sill while in El Reno they set up six sites around town.

On opening day the implementation of their plan hit a snag. The sheer numbers of landseekers at Fort Sill and El Reno was shocking. With each wire transmission to Washington the new estimates of the size of the crowds went upward.

Had there been any method at all to their madness? The planners had simply underestimated the extent of hunger for this land. The proclamation had been sent out on the 5th of July–the 10th being the day registration was to begin. Newspaper editors had no lead time to make interpretations nor to condense the lengthy, legally-worded proclamation with all its whereasing, whereforeing and heretoforeing into a more readable form. In some cases the proclamation hadn't even been printed until Sunday, the 7th. There was only time to set the type, press it and hit the street with it. In the absence of genuine knowledge, half-truths, rumor and speculation spread like wildfire. The fact was it didn't matter when or where (El Reno or Fort Sill) a person registered. A generous span of time in which to register–July 10 through July 26–had been allotted in the belief that this would prevent over-crowding.

There was an elaborate plan for making sure every registrant's card had equal opportunity to be drawn.

The proclamation outlined other particulars of the land lottery and drawing process as well. It stated that no matter where a person registered, his name could only be entered in the lottery for one of the districts. Applicants would be asked to designate, at the time of registration either the Northern District–El Reno area–or the Southern District–Fort Sill area. At the end of the registration period all registration cards from both El Reno and Fort Sill would be placed in plain, white envelopes combined in one large container, and given a good shuffling. The envelopes would then be separated into two large

specially made shuffling bins to await the "Big Drawing."
It was to be held in El Reno beginning as soon as possible
after registration. Each person's notarized affidavit would
be kept in the land office files.

***

AN ARMY OFFICER AT Fort Sill this morning, seeing
the extent of the predicament of lining up the people,
conceived a wonderfully army-like solution. It was
approved by Mr. L.K. Ross, the receiver-in-charge, and
announced to the eager homesteaders within hearing
distance. It would then be spread among those at greater
distance by officers on horseback.

Oliver stood beside Mr. Hawp near the back of the
crowd. Squinting against the sun, his face wrinkled
disapprovingly as he listened to the gentleman shouting
directions.

"Gentlemen, we have decided to ask your cooperation
in organizing a better system for registration."

"First," his voice echoed off the stone walls of
buildings on the post, "we ask that you form yourselves
into companies of 100 men each. Not 102 or 103, or even
99, but exactly 100."

Naturally, a few men began to attempt discussion and
implementation of the first instruction before having heard
the whole thing. They were soon shushed by those
standing around them.

"Then, gentlemen, when you have accomplished that
the next thing that you will do is--the speaker coughed,
cleared his throat and took a deep breath; he was talking as
loud as he could--each group will elect a captain from
within its ranks."

"You will then send that man up here to the Trader's
Store to report to the land office officials. Each captain will
be given a number for his company and other instructions
at that time. He will then return to you–his company–and
give the number to all members of his group."

"By keeping track of the number of the company
currently being registered at any given time, you will

easily be able to determine the approximate time that your company will need to gather here."

The plan worked splendidly!

The men were free to go back to their camps and relax in the shade along East Cache Creek and Medicine Bluff Creek while they waited. They were given one last caution–that they were *individually responsible* for keeping themselves apprised of which company was register-ing–thereby estimating their own approximate registration time.

And the ladies? They could walk up at any time and be registered. Once at the registration desk they had to meet the same criteria as the men and swear they were the head of their household. Twenty-one-year-old unmarried men and women were considered heads of household.

> diary continued--July 10
> Just sunup at 5:00 we drove into camp near Fort Sill. Heard the bugle blow as the soldiers were answering to roll call, and then the cannon boom. Six o'clock I seated myself to write and keep an eye on the horses while the men went up town.

"MORNIN', MA'AM."
Minnie jumped as if she'd been bitten. The voice came from behind her. It had been very quiet, because Papa had been able to locate a space with no other campers near.

Minnie had been totally absorbed in her reading. Earlier in the day she'd put her wool mattress out under the trees and curled up to read. If the sound of the soldier's voice unnerved her; the sight of his official looking, gold-trimmed blue shirt and infantry cap, intimidated her further.

Of course, she'd known there would be soldiers here. It was a fort, after all. This just happened to be the first one she'd seen.

"G-good morning, sir." Minnie replied in a proper almost curtsying manner, hoping to give the impression that she wasn't as alarmed as she was.

"Private 1st Class August Anderson, Ma'am", he said, touching two fingers to the bill of his cap–not as a salute–but because gentlemen do tip their hats to a lady.

"Sorry. Didn't mean to startle you. You all right?"

"Oh, yes," Minnie smiled nervously. "I'm all r-ri... You mere-simply caught me by-off-*uh*-surprise. I-*um*-just didn't-hadn't expected an army s-soldier."

She kicked herself for sounding like a blithering idiot. Locking her hands together she tried again. "Is there anything wro-- have we done something against regu-- or...?"

"Oh, no, ma'am. No. I mean-*wull*-not really. I'm here because I have orders to ask you to move your camp. I mean, not you personally, you understand. Are your menfolk around?" he asked looking around the camp as if he'd rather be telling this to a man.

Seeing that the soldier was as flustered as she was, helped Minnie relax a bit. She smiled, took a deep breath and slowed herself down.

"No, sir. No they're not," she said in a most cordial manner. "They aren't here at the moment. They went up to the Trader's store early this morning to see about getting registered."

"Oh, be glad you didn't have to go with them." Private Anderson said shaking his head. "It is a gen-u-wine mess up there, let me tell you that."

"It is? I'm glad I'm not there then." Minnie said, realizing she should perhaps offer the man a drink of water.

"I'm sorry, Private Anderson, I seem to have lost any manners I may have had. Would you care to sit down or may I offer you a drink of water? Our water came from a spring in the mountains and it is sparkling clean," said Minnie, recovering well.

"Yes, ma'am, I *am* thirsty. If you don't mind I will accept a drink of water."

Minnie filled a glass of water while she listened to what he was saying.

"Y'see, our orders are to keep this area clear of campers because of the work being done on the new railroad grade over behind you there," he went on to explain.

As Minnie brought him the glass of water he pointed

The photographer's caption on this photo reads: Fort Sill, O. T. "Company fighting to march in and register." "Sometimes we were compelled to stand in line for 8 hours to get our turn at the P.O. window.
--W.R. Sharks, July 1901
(Note what appears to be a scuffle on far left--background.)

Courtesy Oklahoma Historical Society

to a spot over her left shoulder where the ground had been graded up to a higher level.

"Oh, yes. Yes, I do see it plainly now. You know–it was still dark when we arrived this morning and I suppose Papa didn't notice there was work being done over there."

"I understand. Thanks for the water. Yes, Ma'am. I do understand. A person wouldn't notice it in the dark," Private Anderson said, handing the glass back to Minnie having tipped and drank it in big swallows. "Thank you very much, ma'am."

"You are quite welcome. I expect my father and the others will be returning here around noon for dinner. Will that be soon enough for us to move?"

"Yes, ma'am. I'm sure it will," He said with a nod and another touch to the bill of his cap. "I'll report that to the First Sergeant immediately. Good day."

Doing an almost regulation "about face," he turned and headed back up the slope in the direction of the guardhouse.

"Who was that, Minnie?" Myrtle Hawp called from inside the Hawps' wagon where she'd been napping.

"A soldier," Minnie answered–preoccupied–as if she were saying, "A fly." Her arms folded in front of her she watched the young soldier walk back up the long slope toward the quadrangle.

> _diary entry continued--July 10_
> _A soldier just now kindly asked me to move our camp across the creek to the other side of the railroad. Which we did just before dinner. In the evening we, Mr. Hawp and I went to the post office, one and a half miles from camp._

Lawyers were arriving by the dozen. Many, like the Johnsons, had unknowingly placed their tents on grounds designated "off-limits". In their eagerness to learn the process of registration, "chat-up" customers, and initiate work for themselves they hadn't paid much attention when the announcement was made to move their tents.

Finally, the exasperated officer in charge of the detail gave the order that all tents not moved in ten minutes would have the job done for them. Consequently, mounted enlisted men soon attached ropes to a couple of tents and pulled them down. Seeing this the lawyers realized the seriousness of the Army's request and scurried toward their tents.[7]

> July 11
> *As soon as the breakfast dishes were done, Mrs. H. & I went to the Fort with Mr. H. & Papa. Arnold stayed in camp. We saw the soldiers, 8th Cavalry, in their uniforms performing their different duties. All were young men from 18 to 23, and good-looking, polite & very gentlemanly. We stayed all forenoon, sat on the front porch of one of the soldiers buildings, were very comfortable, and watched the mass of people--about 15,000 in all. Two companies of soldiers. After we walked back to camp, and had dinner. I read all afternoon.*

At Fort Sill the morning of the eleventh, the Hawps, Papa and Minnie watched the soldiers going about their daily routine. From their vantage point on the porch of one of the soldiers' buildings they were able to look out across the post quadrangle. Across the square to the north were the officers' residences. They were nice, large, solidly built stone buildings.

Sherman House, the one in the middle, was always reserved for the commanding officer of the post. It had been named for General William Tehcumseh Sherman who, though he'd never lived in the house, had once been in mortal danger on its porch when speaking with a group of Kiowa Indians.

Following a raid into Texas, in 1871 Satanta, Satank, Big Tree and Maman-ti, the medicine man, were asked by the Indian Agent, Lawrie Tatum, at Fort Sill if they were responsible for the raid in which four teamsters of a line of ten freight wagons were killed and another wounded. The tall, imposing Satanta not only admitted that he had led the raid, but boasted of the efficiency with which it was carried out. The group then demanded guns and ammunition for further raids saying they weren't being furnished enough food and clothing as had been promised.

Upon hearing this, Sherman sent out word that the Indian leaders should meet him in council on the front porch of Colonel Grierson's residence at Fort Sill.

Satanta, Big Tree, Satank, Lone Wolf, Kicking Bird and Stumbling Bear kept the appointment. Kicking Bird was a worker for peace and tried to restrain his fellow chiefs from telling about their part in the massacre, but Satanta again proudly told the story. Sherman then stated that Satanta, Satank and Big Tree would have to be taken back to Texas to be tried in civil court for the murders. In addition, he said the tribe must make restitution to the owners of the wagons and mules.

The Kiowa's hatred of Texans was implacable. They perceived the Texans as being responsible for driving off and killing the buffalo–the Kiowa's means of existence, and a big part of their religion. The treaty of Medicine Lodge didn't say they couldn't raid the hated Texans.

This being a time when the U. S. hadn't been keeping it's promise to provide the Indians with all they needed to live on the reservation was not a time that the Kiowas were feeling receptive to the any idea of restitution. They were being kept poor. Sherman, whether the Indians knew it or not, was as much responsible for this as anyone. His charge from Washington D. C. was to get the Indians under control, by whatever means it took.

Satanta started to draw a pistol, saying that he would rather be shot than return to Texas to stand trial. He was quickly covered by the carbines of the soldiers. Kicking Bird tried to plead for the accused chiefs, but Sherman was adamant. Stumbling Bear, who was an advocate of peace, upbraided his men and then surprised everyone by announcing that he would kill Sherman himself. He drew his bow, but some of his friends grabbed him and the arrow went wild. Then Lone Wolf aimed his gun at the general and was tackled to the ground by Grierson.

Sherman reiterated his demand that the three chiefs of the wagon train raid must be taken to stand trial. They were taken into custody on the spot.

***

DURING THE LONG hours of waiting, campers would congregate to watch the soldiers and learn more about the historical old fort. Stories went from one group to another:

Lt. Colonel George Armstrong Custer, the impetuous and eccentric former Civil War brevet general, with his long 'yellow' hair and swashbuckling appearance, had assisted General Sheridan in selecting the location of Fort Sill, in January of 1869.[8]

In November of 1868, Custer directed the pre-sunrise attack of a winter encampment of Cheyenne on the Washita River. Black Kettle, his favorite wife, and most of the other inhabitants were killed.

Geronimo, the wily-spirited old war leader of the Chiricahua Apache was kept here. It was he who had so long defied attempts by the U.S. Army to bring him and his small band in. It had not been until 1886 they surrendered to the U.S. Army. Nowadays, living as a much-esteemed POW at Fort Sill he was allowed much freedom. Currently, he was on tour accompanied by soldiers. Having been given quasi celebrity status, he was paraded as an attraction at fairs and expositions. Newspapers loved to report that he had nine white scalps attached to his belt and was looking to make it an even ten.

Quanah Parker lived nearby. The half-Comanche, half-white son of the late Comanche Peta Nocona and his wife, white captive, Cynthia Ann Parker; he had risen in respect, despite his half-white heritage to the level of Chief of the Quohada band. Now, he was a much respected spokesman for the Comanche people and the native Americans in general. Friendly and wise he lived in his huge Star House in the foothills of the Wichita mountains.

It was with Quanah and other Comanche and Kiowa elders with whom the government had met when dealing for settlement of their territory by non-Indian people. In talks with the Jerome Commission, in November of 1892,[9] he had been the only Indian who by questions asked and the words he spoke conveyed an understanding of what the government was proposing to do. It was Quanah who day after day stood and asked, "How much for one acre are you going to pay?"[10]

"You say that our land–some of it–is rocky and useless for farming, but we see that your white soldiers and settlers build houses out of these useless rocks and that some of the white people believe there is gold in our useless mountains."

Quanah had many friends among north Texas ranchers and in Washington, D.C. among senators and representatives. He entertained many non-Indian people at Star House, as well hosting many of his own band. There were always several Comanche tepees set up around his house. His own people were welcome to eat from his kitchen, and loved to socialize there.

Most of the stories circulating on the parade grounds among the settlers were true. But, some had gotten all mixed up in the retelling.

The whispered gossip and overheard tidbits sometimes got so mixed–up, it became ludicrous. For instance; one told that the Indians chewed the buttons of a cactus plant and it made them so crazy they spoke in tongues and practiced polygamy.

Anything for a good story.

Oliver listened to the bits of talk here and there, and brought pieces back to his group.

Some of the more prudish believed every word and were shocked by the stories going around.

"Why, I never! The heathens." Myrtle Hawp gasped in disapproval. She probably didn't know what polygamy was.

***

"WHAT COMPANY you in?" one man said to another.

"Sixty-five," came the disgusted reply, "I won't be up till day after tomorrow."

Several times Oliver heard this exact same question! "What company are you in?" About the third time, he started getting uneasy. He got the feeling he'd missed something, somewhere along the way.

From then on, if anyone asked him, "What company

are you in?" he managed some kind of an answer, but he was worried. Was he supposed to have remembered something? A number? Dat-gum the luck, anyhow. When did they give out numbers?

Yesterday, Oliver had been with his company of 100 men when their "captain" returned to report to them. Oliver was on the far outside edge of the group, his having a phobia about being in the middle of a crowd. He just couldn't stand it! But, stand it or not, he hadn't heard his company's number. Probably the most important little piece of information, yet.

Since the families from Nebraska were still separated this left Mr. Hawp and Oliver, the not-so-fluent reader, responsible for figuring out when they were to show up at the Trader's Store again. Papa was no idiot, mind you. But his lack of ability to decode the written word put him at a severe disadvantage for this particular task. He'd never felt so useless.

Later that evening, after supper Oliver asked, "What's the number of your company, Hawp?" He studied Earnie's face across the campfire.

"Wull now, that's a good question, Oliver. I'm pretty sure he said seventeen. But, thunder! It might've been seventy. I didn't have time to study over what it was he was a-telling us. How 'bout you? What's your number?"

"Hell, I don't know. Couldn't hear from where I was standing. I was in a group that counted off to a hundred. I didn't know it was going to be all that important. Seem like it happened too fast. When our captain fella came back out of the store he wasn't talking very loud. Seem like he was just talkin' to the ones up around him. When he finished talkin' to them, he just starts walkin' off. Some of the other gents standing around me chased after him, but I was so aggravated by that time, I walked off, too."

"Why didn'tcha let your son go up there with you, Johnson? He might coulda helped out."

"They just asked for the men wanting to register to get into the groups." Oliver said, and then was silent. Why hadn't he let Arnold go up closer to the store with him? He'd certainly thought about doing that, but was afraid of an argument arising if someone thought he was trying to pass Arnold off as being twenty-one years old or a head of household. Oliver didn't like trouble, but if it happened he darn sure wouldn't back up from it. That didn't always turn out so pleasantly. Besides Oliver's pride just wouldn't allow letting it be known he couldn't read. He cursed himself, now, for not paying better attention yesterday.

"Maybe I could get in with you on your company. You spose?"

Hawp shrugged his shoulders. "Guess you could give it a try. But, they's only supposed to be a hunderd in ever group."

"Maybe some won't show up."

> <u>July 12</u>
> I read all forenoon and right after dinner prepared to go up town. I was ready and waiting for Mrs. Hawp when a gent told us a man had small pox in a camp right below us! So, I rushed to the Fort and found Papa and Arnold and went back. When I reached camp, everything was loaded so we hitched up and pulled out. On going a little ways we met Reids and Elmores and followed them to their old camping place about four mi. N.W, of the Ft. where we found plenty of shade along the Creek and a good spring. We never as yet have learned whether that boy had small pox or not. But two officers and two privates set out after them. A man trying to steal a valise was shot and killed about 12 mi. from here. Mr. Hawp registered but Papa was thrown out. Hawp was Co.17, No 2.

"Pardon me? Papa was *thrown out!*" Minnie responded to Arnold who had been explaining what happened at the registration today.

"Yeah, he was trying to get in with Mr. Hawp's company and everybody in that bunch knew he wasn't in it when they numbered-off the other day. He was hoping somebody wouldn't show up."

"Oh, my Lord! Was he embarrassed?"

"Shoot. Papa? Embarrassed? Like a rock. I was the one that was embarrassed."

FORT SILL WAS THE ONLY settlement for miles around. East Cache and Medicine Bluff Creeks were about the only water sources for the campers. There were no hotels, rooming houses, nor private homes in which people could rent a cot, as was being done in El Reno. Right now, the people who had come to settle here in the southern district were obliged to camp out. Many were along Medicine Creek. But, with every day, there were more people camping farther south along East Cache Creek. The encampment now came from the north and ran east of Fort Sill and on down past the new town site. Over five miles in distance. Hundreds of tents covered the area for miles along it.

In the evenings, crowds would gather around the parade ground to watch "guard mount and retreat." Most of the people were in good spirits. The whole affair at times seemed much like a gigantic picnic. People were happy. They had high hopes for themselves in the lottery and hope always seemed to make folks happy.

Soldiers patrolled the area. If need be, they would break up drinking bouts or fights. At night thousands of campfires winked along the creek. A haze of campfire smoke hung low among the oak and cottonwood trees. Wagons of every size and description continued arriving throughout the days and nights. Before long, at least ten thousand persons were drawing mail at Quinette's store.

***

Oliver had decided to attempt registration again tomorrow morning. He questioned Mr. Hawp for information about what was required during registration.

"Well, not much, really, Oliver. First, I had to swear out an affidavit,"

Affidavit? Papa repeated to himself, *Gee-hoss-a-fat!*

Hawp loved the attention. He counted the things off on his fingers, "Had to swear I was twenty-one or more, swear I was a citizen of the United States, swear I was the head of my household--good thing Myrtle wudn there or she'd'uv argied the point. Swore I didn't already own 160 acres of land. And, the last thing I hadta swear was that I hadn' homesteaded anywhere else. Then I signed that paper with a notary watchin' me."

"A notary?"

"Yeah, one of them men in there. After you sign it, he clamps his mark down on it."

"Another one of them men'll write down your weight, height, age, color of your eyes--he can see that--and the color of your hair, too. He'll ask you if you want to be in the drawing for the northern or the southern district. And, he'll ask the post office where you want the notice of your drawing number sent."

OLIVER WHISTLED a happy tune as he stood in line. He was in company #72. He'd solved the "company" problem. When his turn came, today, Oliver was ready. He held a folded piece of Minnie's note paper with everything written on it that he needed, and he could read the whole list. He was patting himself on the back now. That little impromptu reading lesson last night had proved successful and he had the words all written out, too. Why, he could copy them right off of this paper. Only thing was Oliver's writing was about as legible as that of any other beginner.

After talking with Mr. Hawp last night Papa hustled Minnie over to their wagon while everything was still fresh on his mind. Carrying one of the kerosene lanterns inside, they sat down on her pallet on the floor.

"Take a clean page out of your diary, Minnie-girl. You're gonna help me get registered."

Oliver counted off the things he needed to know. Birth date, height, weight, age, eye color, hair color and 'yes' and 'no'. He was halfway there.

"Ready when you are." Minnie said.

"Okay, now Minnie, I need you to show me how to write: my birthdate, my height, weight, age, yes and no, and green and black..."

"Green and black?" Minnie laughed, "What's that for?"

"Eyes and hair."

"Oh, of course," She was still grinning. She couldn't help it. It was funny seeing Papa all of a sudden desperately wanting to learn to read a few words.

"And there is one more thing...what was it?" Papa sat thinking for a moment. "Oh, yeah, they'll want to know where to send my notification."

"General Delivery–Fort Sill, O.T. then?"

"At'll do it, Minnie-girl."

Minnie wrote the address on the piece of note paper as Papa unfolded himself with a few accompanying grunts from where he sat on the wagon floor.

"You've been a big help," Papa said climbing out of the wagon to go to bed, "Thank you much, Minnie, I'll dance at your weddin'." He always said that.

<u>July 13</u>
Mrs. Elmore, Hawp, & I washed clothes before dinner and Jim & Sam after dinner. I also finished the book "Romance of Gilbert Holmes." Nearly all the men went to town this morning and (Co.52) Jim, Doctor & Sam registered before dinner & left Papa and came back to camp. Papa registered about 4 o'clock, Co.72. So the men went back to the Ft. for him in the evening.

Chapter 9
Lookin' Over the Land

Excitement within the Nebraska group grew in anticipation of one of their names coming up matched with an early number in the drawing. With registration out of the way they were eager to go out and see what it looked like. They wanted to investigate the possibilities.

There were other reasons for pulling camp, too. It made a lot of sense not to use the creek water for anything, if they could help it. There'd been talk that persons with typhoid and smallpox were mixed in with the crowds along the creek. It was possible. Very likely, there were those who carried the disease but were immune themselves bathing in the creek.

Many of the landseekers took their horses right out into the creek to water them and they didn't always make it out the other side before their bodily functions –functioned.

Oliver Johnson absentmindedly twisted the hairs at the end of his moustache. He had another reason for wanting to pull camp; aside from his usual one of wanting to be on the move.

July 14, Sunday
We spent the day reading, writing, fishing, etc. An
Apache squaw came to camp & got up a game of Monte,
and won 50 cents off Sam Joice. Of course, he got the
horse laugh.

Courtesy Archives & Manuscripts Division of the Oklahoma Historical Society

Note on photo: "Comanche Indians--one thousand camped north side of Lawton, O.T. Three miles south of Fort Sill –August 10, 1901"

continued--Sunday, July 14
Later in the evening we heard the cry, "Mad dog, shoot
him!" I was reading a story and, being very interested,
could not understand what was the matter but being told
to hurry and get in the wagon, I did so. The men also
were in the wagon and had their guns and were about to
shoot him when someone cried out, "Don't Shoot", so
we didn't touch him. He ran on down the road and
acted as if he was starved and lost, instead of mad.

Oliver had noticed that there weren't many women in the area and those there were, were looked upon as a curiosity and almost--Oliver feared--an enticement. Always in his mind was the promise he'd made Mary.

Pondering the situation now he figured that by getting away from the crowds of people there would be less chance of Minnie's being exposed to the tawdry activities that often times accompanied crowds of this kind.

Each person who'd registered for the drawing, was given a *Land Inspection Certificate*. With it, the bearer would be allowed to explore the Indian land without interference; provided he did not attempt to *"settle"*in any one place. Settlement on the Indian Lands was prohibited until after the 90 day period of filing claims.

At this point no matter what the drawing held in store for them individually, it would be to the advantage of all to assess the land. It was of such enormity it would take several days roaming to completely investigate and appreciate its extent and qualities.

Minnie was anxious to see the tent town they'd heard was mushrooming around the edges of the new townsite. She didn't dare say so, though, for fear of the hoorawing this bunch might give her. Leaving camp the wagons traveled southeast skirting the raunchy tent town whose name they'd learned would be "Lawton." It was growing around the perimeter of a surveyed, platted; but as yet–still empty–townsite.

They passed through the grounds of the Fort Sill Indian School, a boarding school for Comanche and Kiowa children. They were able to view more closely its dormitory and other buildings. Parents of young Kiowa and Comanche children were encouraged by Indian agencies to send their children to the school while they were still young. To all observers it was a heart-wrenching scene. The little, brown faces streaming with tears as their parents scolded them to comply with the white man's way. Once there, the children would be taught to read, write, speak English, wear uncomfortable shoes and uniforms and have their braids lopped off. Their parents could visit them once a month.

Traditionally the Comanche people only cut their hair as a gesture of mourning upon the death of a much-loved and respected member of their tribe. Thus, some Indians viewed the hair-cutting as symbolic and, in a subtle way, appropriate to mourn the passing of the old ways.

The wagons of the Nebraska bunch bounced along east of the new townsite. Already platted, no one was allowed to camp on its 320 acres. They encountered still more campers down along East Cache Creek, to the south. But these were not landseekers. These were businessmen, here to begin the business of the new town. Bankers, doctors, dentists, druggists, and storekeepers, they were the people who would be selling food, clothing, lumber, and supplies to the residents of the new town. They would be running butcher shops and newspapers, churches, dry goods stores, and providing other necessities.

In any group of people around a boomtown like this, one had to be wary. More than the average number of those who operate on the outer fringe of the law were sure to be found lurking: gamblers, prostitutes, swindlers, sure-thing fellows, and the alcoholics and laudanum addicts, who parasitically live off that segment of society. It was comforting to know that most wouldn't be around a year from now.

Within six months the town would have its own council, make its own ordinances, and could bar whatever activities were deemed immoral by the town citizens. The parasitic types would, for the most part, fold their tents, load their wagons, and rumble off looking for the next lawless loophole in which to operate.

> July 15
>
> This morning we left camp at 6:40 and came on down to Ft. Sill, got some provisions and came on south thru the Indian College and camped a mile or more this side, east, under some elm trees. Mr. Hawp was very sick last night and is yet to-day. Dinner at 12 noon. After dinner we drove to Dry Beaver and on to Beaver. In the evening, I took a bath in the creek and retired.

"MRS. HAWP, that you?" Minnie half-whispered.

"Yes, baby, it's me."

"Would you like some company?"

"Oh, I guess so. I didn't wake you up, did I?" Myrtle said wearily. It hadn't been a good night.

"Oh, no. I was so tired last evening that I went to bed soon after supper. I've just been catnapping for the last hour," Minnie assured her.

It was about 4:30 a.m. No one else in their camp was stirring. Minnie seated herself in one of the wooden ladderback chairs near Mrs. Hawp who stared at the red and black coals of last night's cook fire. "I haven't been able to sleep all night. I got out of bed so my tossin' and turnin' wouldn't keep Earnie from getting his rest. Bless his heart. He sure does need it. I'm so worried about him. He's been having stomach cramps and diarrhea. I mean bad diarrhea. We were having to stop the wagon every little whip stitch today for him to 'go' behind a tree. I'm glad Mr. Johnson noticed and held back for us to catch up."

"What do you think is wrong with him?" Minnie asked trying to avoid watching Myrtle fidget.

"Well, Minnie, what's worryin' me is, I distinctly heard the words *'typhoid fever'* mentioned back at Fort Sill by those people camped on the west side of us."

When Myrtle said the words "typhoid fever" her voice took on an ominous tone and she looked at Minnie sideways.

"I suppose it could be a lot of other things, too."

"What are you going to do?" Minnie asked. "Maybe you should take him back to Fort Sill? There is probably a doctor there."

"I just don't know, Minnie. That may be what I have to do. Guess I'll see what he feels like this morning."

<u>July 16</u>

Mr. Hawp no better however we moved camp about a mile to another large grove where we could use spring water. I spent the day reading and helped with the cooking. The men went out to look for section corners and other survey lines and returned in the afternoon.

July 17
Mrs. Hawp took Mr. Hawp back to Ft. Sill, (as soon as we found the horses--which was at 10 a.m.) as he was very little better. In the afternoon (3 p.m.) we hitched up and came on down the creek 8 mi. The men killed two Polecats while looking for a spring.

"HA-A-E-EY, JOHN-SON!"

"Ah--hoo-ah-ee, over here." Sam rounded his mouth and let the sound resonate through his nose to carry more distance.

The men on horseback had fanned out in several directions to gain different views for the party. Coming back together at intervals, they compared notes on their observations. Papa and Minnie from their vantage point on the wagon seat scanned the horizon in the direction from which the voice was coming. Finally they spotted Sam Joice, waving his arm in a wide arc--hat in hand--signaling. Papa waved his hat to signal back. All three wagons and the buggy turned and started up the slope toward the point at which they saw Sam.

Still at too great a distance to tell Papa couldn't wait to know what had been located. "Whatcha got?" he yelled ineffectively in Sam's direction. No answer came since, by now, others on horseback were arriving and dismounting much more quickly than the heavily laden wagons.

Minnie had to hide a grin as Papa, forgetting himself, cursed under his breath, squirmed on the seat, and used his whole body with the exception of his hands to urge the team forward. She knew he didn't dare force the horses into a run. No matter what Sam found it wasn't worth the risk of losing a wheel, a wagon tongue, or an injury to one of the horses.

It seemed to take an eternity to cross over the crest of the rise. Finally, they saw Sam, Jim, Mr. Elmore, and their horses, converging at a point just above a tree-lined draw. Jim was kneeling down inspecting something there on the ground.

They watched as Arnold, one of those on horseback, arrived at the point of interest. Papa watched him dismount and then squat down to scrutinize what the others seemed to be discussing. Something there on the ground.

"Arnold, what is it?" Papa hollered at his son knowing that Arnold clearly understood he'd better give his father some kind of an answer or pay for it later."

"Marker," was the brief reply. That much of a response was enough to satisfy Papa till he could get there and see for himself.

A small pile of rocks on a piece of alkali ground from which no grass was growing was the first "marker" of any kind they'd seen. A discussion was underway. The question at hand was whether or not this particular pile of rocks was left by the federal team of surveyors; and was therefore, an authentic land marker. The team who'd been here in March of this year and measured and marked the huge grid of section lines.

"Dig under it!" Arnold urged.

"What if something is buried there?" Sam said.

"...or someONE!" Jim added. Minnie, still seated on the wagon seat, shuddered.

Papa rubbed his chin, "I thought all the mile markers were supposed to have the number of the range, township, and section written on it, in white paint. Didn't I hear that somewhere?"

"Hey, look here." Arnold said from where he knelt on the ground a short distance away, "An arrowhead!"

The men gathered around and agreed that it was, indeed, an arrowhead and a pretty good specimen at that.

"I'd hold on to that for good luck, kid." Jim said. "There probably won't be too many more of those 'manufactured."

"We hope." Sam emphasized with a laugh.

"Let's just go on the assumption that the pile of rocks is not a mile marker and leave it alone. What d'ya say?" Mr. Elmore finally voiced the consensus of the group.

Mounting their horses the men fanned out again looking for a mile marker. After they found the first one, they could begin sketching in section squares and identifying areas they might be interested in homesteading. It wasn't long before they found another pile of rocks; larger and "fresher" in appearance than the other pile had been. On its top was a rock about the size of a gallon bucket with the distinctive white markings of the survey crew.

The point at which they found this pile of rocks represented the common corner of four square sections.

It read: *NW S 9; NE S 8; SW S 5; SE S 4 of T 1N, R 10W.*

After quite a bit of discussion, the men concluded that

it was to be translated as: northwest corner of Section 9; northeast corner of Section 8; southeast corner of Section 5;and the southwest corner of section 4 of Township 1 north, Range 10 west.

It could be confusing until a person saw it laid out on a map, Minnie decided.

From this known point the group could figure any place on the township. If they could establish due north they could locate other markers by traveling one mile in any of the four directions. Later people learned to tie a handkerchief or bandana to a spoke of a wagon wheel and count its revolutions. Then through multiplicationthey could figure the exact distance to the next section corner. A homestead was a quarter of a mile on all four sides.

Did they want creeks, springs, groves of pecan or oak trees, dark rich bottom land, or wide open prairie? Whatever quarter section of land a person selected could be located on the huge area map that would soon hang in the new U.S. Land Office in Lawton.

Minnie made a note of the Section, Township, and Range so that when Papa asked later she could tell him. She was also attempting a sketch of the area as it might appear on a map; trying to mark in section corners, creeks etc.

<u>July 18</u>
The next morning we moved about a mile to a good spring, where Mrs. Elmore & Jim Reid washed clothes while Papa & Sam went out to look at the land. At 3 p.m. we came down the creek seven or 8 miles. We camped on the bank of a bayou. Oh, what lovely land in and along this creek! The grass, knee deep, is fed on by thousands of Texas and Mexican steers and bayous in every bend of the creek. Trees in abundance such as Walnut, Pecan, Mesquite, Elm, Ash, Box Elder, Willow, Oak, and so many pretty wild vines which cover all the trunks of the trees in places and all dry limbs. Quite a few grape vines, also. The oak grows mostly on the hills. The other timber can be found along the streams in these parts.

This was the same fenceless expanse of grass that, up until a year ago, the Comanche tribe leased to the Texas ranchers. All of the longhorn were supposed to have been rounded-up and moved out but the group often encountered a few head that had been missed.

"Bet some folks are using these longhorns as a handy source of beef," Oliver observed, quietly evaluating the idea of doing just that himself.

> <u>July 19</u>
> Friday. Sam & Mrs. Elmore drove one wagon and Shirley and I, our wagon, on down the creek a couple miles, while the rest of the men went out to look for section corners. Mrs. Elmore, Arnold & I picked some grapes and we made pie while the beans boiled. At 1:15 p.m. we broke up camp again. Reids & Elmores started back to Ft. Sill and intended to go to Anadarko from there. We came on down the Beaver and camped for the night at 3 p.m. Papa took one of the blacks and went out horseback. Arnold & I are left in camp and are contemplating a coon hunt. There are also possum, wild turkeys, squirrels and so forth, but we have seen none yet as we haven't looked for them. It looks some like rain, thundering all about us.

The Reids, Elmores, and Sam Joice were interested in seeing what the land up around Anadarko was like. Until now it had been the site of an Indian Agency but would be established as one of the new county seats during the opening. The two groups wanted to look the land over there to compare with what they'd already seen down around Fort Sill.

> <u>July 20</u>
> Left camp 7:30 and came back up the creek through three or four sections of land all covered with oak and camped for dinner on the south side of a long bayou and fished till noon. We caught 5 bass and 7 bullheads and fried them all for dinner. Several different outfits stopped on the other side and called to us, "Is there any fish here?" etc.

After dinner we came on up the creek through the timber and camped upon a hill by a lot of fine springs. Before we reached camp, Papa shot a squirrel. I rode horseback this afternoon. While I cleaned the squirrel, the men went in search of a bayou where they might fish, but in vain, they found naught. I had supper ready when they returned, but the squirrel we cooked for breakfast, as it wasn't done.

<u>July 21, Sunday</u>
The squirrel was fine; better than chicken. Started about seven, and on our way to the creek, we talked with some campers about the road and came on across the creek and went west across Whiskey Creek and to Cash Creek for dinner 12:20. After dinner Arnold and Papa fished. They caught one Bullhead over a foot long and the rest were smaller. Had fish for supper. Thundering and looks much like rain.

Chapter 10
Killin' Time

July seventeenth. It had been seven days since the beginning of registration. Otto Elling hated to leave his brother-in-law with all the chores to do while he went to El Reno to register. But time was getting away.

"You go on and get registered. Opportunity like this isn't gonna come along again," Lee insisted.

When his sister Anna said she needed some things from town, he saddled up Nubbins, walked back to the house, got the list of items from her, and headed down the lane toward the gate.

"Just keep on headin' southwest, till you hit the good road. It'll take you right on in to El Reno," Lee said again as he walked along beside Otto and Nubbins down the lane as far as the gate.

It sure did. Along with a line of wagons stretched out for a couple miles along it.

Once there, Otto felt sure he had only to ask around to

find where the registration was taking place. The problem became finding someone who actually lived there and knew the town. Much easier said than done.

The planners of the lottery thought they'd made it clear in a statement issued along with the proclamation--*There will be no advantage in hurrying. The last to register will have equal opportunity with the first.* Nevertheless every road and railway was filled with land-hungry men and women. El Reno, a town of 7,500 residents, grew to 60,000 within twenty-four hours of the proclamation's coming out. It was phenomenal. Every hotel and boarding house was filled to capacity and beyond. There were folks camped wherever they could find a little patch of ground in town and out. Mostly good fellows, well-behaved, optimistic, andthey had money and expected to pay for what they got–food, lodging or drink. If El Reno could stand the pressure, the little town could benefit quite nicely– economically.

Otto found the main street of El Reno. There was no mistaking it; filled boardwalk to boardwalk with tents and food stands offering food and drinks to those here for the lottery. They were set up and wedged together in an attempt to get as many as possible in to accommodate the massive needs of the crowds. As he walked along the street leading Nubbins, Otto tried to identify a local to ask directions. Spying a gent in a straight back chair leaned back up against the front of a store Otto approached the man and asked about where he might find a registration site.

"Wull, it's a list uvm rat tere on nat paper in the winduh and on nerly ever storefront in town!" the old codger answered disdainfully.

"Thank you, sir," Otto said, tipping his hat. You're *much* too kind." His verbal jab was lost on the lame brain.

Stepping over in front of the sign Otto began reading the list in the store window. It appeared he had several choices of places. As he focused in on the addresses, he felt someone's presence behind him and turned to find the "codger" standing close enough to smell his sweat.

"Kin you read dat?" the man asked leaving his mouth in the shape of a perfect "o."

"Yes, sir, thank you, I can," Otto said puzzled by the man's behavior.

"Wull, why dontcha read it out loud den?"

Ah, the old geezer couldn't read. He probably doesn't know where the registration sites are. Otto would read it to him; maybe the next person who asks'll get a more civilized answer.

"Okay, let's see here," Otto said. "Says a person can register at the following places: the sample room at the Kerfoot Hotel, the colored school building, the school building on South Rock Island, the probate court room, the Buse-Sackett building, and the west room of Mrs. Fulton's House."

"Yup, at's right. Ah'll be durned, you **kin** read," the man snorted loudly in genuine surprise when Otto actually accomplished the feat. Stifling a laugh Otto decided there must be *one* in every town.

"Say, could you tell me where to find the Buse-Sackett building?" he asked the man.

"Oh, yeah! Sure can! It's on down 'bout four blocks," he was pointing south and had one eye closed and the other one cocked up and to the right, figuring which way to go, "an nen turn back right on–what's the name of tha–Barker Street!" he almost shouted when he thought of it.

There was a line at the Buse-Sackett building, but not too terribly long–compared to what some people had endured. Otto stood out in the sun forty-five minutes before setting foot through the door. In talking with others in line he found some who'd tried a week ago but had dropped out of line when faced with standing up to eight hours.

Having filled out the required papers, Otto stood before a clerk who wrote down his description. When asked, Otto designated the southern district as the area in which he wished his name to be entered; figuring that perhaps there might not be quite so much competition for the area with no train access. He signed everywhere and swore to everything they asked him to. The last item gave him a certificate authorizing him to examine the lands to be settled. After asking a couple more questions he found that the drawing would begin on July 29, here in El Reno and would continue as many days as it took to draw all the names out of the boxes.

"Say, sir."

Otto kept on walking, sure the man wasn't speaking to him.

"Sir. uh...Mr. Elling."

Upon hearing his name, Otto turned and found the clerk who'd registered him walking hurriedly in his direction.

"Mr. Elling," the clerk said in a much lower voice having caught up with Otto, "I notice that you have a quite legible hand. A very nice hand." The gentleman had a very clerkish way about him–tight, precise movements and a pair of pince-nez glasses. He was short, thin and balding.

"Yes, thank you?" It wasn't the first time his handwriting had been complimented. Otto was all ears.

"Yes, well, we've been asked to watch for persons whose handwriting is legible and yet write rapidly enough to be efficient. You see, during the drawing we are going to need of several men who can generate legible lists of the names as we draw them in the drawing booth. As you can imagine, we are going to be needing several copies of these lists; what with practically everyone in Washington needing copies."

"Oh, yes. I see. Several lists would indeed be needed." Otto replied. *Was there any money associated with the job--* was what he was thinking.

"So, anyway, I wonder could you–do you suppose you'd be available to help out here during the drawing?"

"Let's see, that'll be the 29th through th...?"

"We don't know exactly how long it's going to last. Possibly five or six days."

"Well...m-m," Otto stalled while he thought.

The clerk cleared his throat.

"Would the fact that the job pays three dollars a day, help you make up your mind?"

"Say, it sure would! I'm pretty sure I can arrange

things so I can be here."

He found a food stand with his favorite kind of food and ordered corned beef and sauerkraut. A place on the front side of the boardwalk was the only place he could find to sit down. As he ate, he relaxed and let his thoughts unravel. Thinking over the job he'd just been offered–and taken–he figured how much time he would have left to work on the farm before returning here to El Reno. Twelve days, at most, he concluded.

He found a general store on his way out of town as he fought against the tide of human bodies. Purchasing the package of needles, spool of black thread and 5 pounds of sugar for his sister, he started back to the farm.

***

ARNOLD, MINNIE AND OLIVER were by themselves now; for the first time since they'd left Gordon, back in May. Minnie had total responsibility for the cooking and other domestic chores. This was a big job making everything on your own–from scratch. She would quickly learn to "make-do"; substituting one ingredient for another when they were out of the needed ingredient.

Papa decided they'd take their time and see as much of the country as they could before heading back to Fort Sill. He figured they wouldn't need to be back among the crowds for another week yet; with the drawing set to begin on the 29th. Reports of gold prospecting in the Wichitas had piqued his interest. They could check on that while they were killin time.

> <u>July 22</u>
> Started 7:20 and when we came to the creek where we wished to cross. Arnold and Papa cut trees down & dug the bank away so we got across, but a terrible steep one. We saw trees three feet in dia. here & such heavy timber. We came on west and camped on a slough for dinner. After dinner we crossed over to West Cash Creek and came on west up the creek through a portion of the Big Indian Pasture where we came past several Indian houses. A heavy cloud coming up in the west caused us to camp

before reaching the creek. It began raining as we were
pitching the tent but nothing got wet. We had a real
nice shower. A ranch not far away where the men
watered the horses and gained some important
information concerning the land.

Minnie sat on the bank, watching her father and
brother work, in exasperation. She couldn't understand
why Papa insisted on crossing the creek at this particular
place. It appeared her father was determined to spend the
day cutting down trees and digging away at the bank.
Such work it was causing them and there'd be a steep pull
on both sides for the horses! It seemed to Minnie with the
hours spent in this particular endeavor they could have
ridden along beside the creek for 6 or 8 miles found a
better crossing and been on their way.

Oh well, whatever Minnie's thoughts were on the
matter, it was NOT okay to question Papa. She shook her
head, sighed, and said softly, "Guess the good Lord didn't
mean for me to understand my Papa 'cause I sure can't see
his reasoning sometimes."

<u>July 23</u>
6:50 a.m. We drove N.W. a couple of miles and then
came out of the Big Indian pasture. After we came to the
reserve (fence) line we came on west, tracing the survey
lines and camped for dinner on a slough. We brought
good water with us from a well by a ranch back east.
This slough or bayou is very pretty. Its surface is nearly
covered with water lilies, some of the round leaves are two
feet in breadth. The lilies are cream colored. Arnold
caught too much; a large turtle, which he nearly made
hash of before he could get him off the hook. Several
large Pecan trees are scattered along the banks of this
slough, and a heavy timber is formed by them along the
creek. Just west of us, the same, named Pecan (or
Boulder). There is a large bunch of horses in this valley,
the first we've seen since we left the northern part of the
state. We can see Pecans, Oak, Cottonwood & Walnut
trees from all points when back on the divide; there are so

many little creeks all of which have more or less timber on them. *We can see a range of the Wichita Mts. N.W. of here more than 25 mi. away.* The country is so level between the creeks, we can see from one creek to the other. This is splendid soil for farming purposes, very black and covered with red grass (or sage), buffalo (grass) and mesquite.

3:40 p.m. We started and drove 2 mi. up the creek. Several campers both above and below us. Two Texas gentlemen camped right near got some fish hooks of us. After supper we all fished. I got tired and quit. Arnold caught four, a big mess for breakfast.

July 24

Wichita Falls, Tex.--This morning Joe Yates & K.N. Grant brought us a couple of squirrels which I put out to cook for dinner right away. Papa & those two men went out to look for lines while I washed clothes and Arnold fished. He caught 17; catfish, bullheads & sunfish. Late in the after-noon we hitched up and came on about six miles. N.W. toward Observatory Mt. and camped above the forks of this same creek, Boulder, where we went fishing and caught fish as fast as we could pull them out. The last thing before retiring was to salt fish...

July 25

...and the first thing this morning! Papa caught a bullfrog on his hook before breakfast which we afterward used for bait. I caught several fish; also, but camp duties prevented me from fishing as much as Arnold. I salted more than half a two gallon jar. Nearly all croppies and sunfish. While I was frying S.D. for dinner it began to rain. I put my mackintosh on and finished my job while Papa found refuge in the wagon and Arnold in his canary waterproof. *After dinner:* we are over two-and-one-half miles on from our dinner camp and have driven our team and wagon in shelter of some trees until this shower goes by. It is raining very hard but scarcely any wind. *As at noon*, we didn't notice any rain clouds until it was

beginning to sprinkle. We haven't experienced any wind
storms as yet and are about to think they don't have such
things here. We crossed the railroad survey, just below
our last night's camp, the one that is being built to
Anadarko through Lawton. Camped for the night on this
side of the townsite of Lawton.

***

GIVEN THE DAILY wranglings with his father on the
very touchy subject of the land lottery, Clarence Pool was
relieved to be hopping a train headed south this morning.

McKinley's proclamation verified the opening would
be by lottery and with the guidelines set forth in the
proclamation, Clarence was satisfied that it would be a
civilized affair. He decided to go and take his chances.

Today he rode the train. Tomorrow evening he should
be in El Reno, Oklahoma Territory. Amazing!

The train rumbled southward. It became increasingly
clear that thousands had also decided to take the train to El
Reno, as well. He'd somehow been lucky enough to secure
a seat in Des Moines. Now folks were seated in aisles,
leaning up against the back wall of the car and anywhere
else they could find a spot. He heard bits and pieces of
conversation saying there were men riding on the roofs of
cars, too.

Women were given first chance at seats–when possible–but for the rest it was going to be a long ride, stuffed
in as they were like cotton boles in the middle of a bale of
cotton.

Clarence's sister, Hellen, had shown interest in coming
down to the territory. But, this wasn't an experience he
would want to expose any lady to. Better to wait awhile.

The atmosphere and merriment grew lighter–and
louder–with each passing mile, as passengers became
acquainted, and started sharing stories and gossip, even
lunches.

<u>July 26</u>
We got up at daylight and put Arnold on the road to
Ft.Sill by sun up. Only four miles away, but we wanted

the mail, and to get it before the rush he had to go early. Papa went into Lawton and looked it over also bought a supply of provisions, while I did some patching and made a pair of black half-sleeves. They both returned early, and "Oh my heart! What a surprise!" Arnold brought me only eight letters and two home papers! Lots of good news from home and other points. Made us all feel better. Papa said he saw Mr. & Mrs. Hawp & that they were coming out to camp with us. Right after dinner they came and we drove back to Boulder Creek and camped near the dam. It rained on us all the way here and then some, but I don't care if it does I enjoy it. As our tent nor wagon sheet don't leak we are well protected.

Minnie was ecstatic. Nothing else could describe it. *Just let it rain,* she'd said. She was so happy.

The eight letters were as welcome as if they had been eight big, beautifully wrapped Christmas presents. She forced herself to take her time about opening them. It was such pure joy to receive one letter, but eight! She was beside herself--could hardly wait to read them all. One of the letters--the one about which she was most excited--was from John Perdoux!

They rode along in the afternoon, moving their camp to Boulder Creek. She'd opened the letters from home and shared them with Papa and Arnold. She would wait until she was alone to read John's letter.

After supper, she could wait no longer. She crawled into the wagon, lay down on her pallet. She pulled out the letter from John.

> *Dear Minnie,*
>
> *Hope this letter finds you and your family doing well. I also hope you have not been scalped, yet--or robbed. ha ha. Bizness at the Soda Shop is going fine. Seems like every body wants to come in and try it out. I see your cousin and her frends two or 3 times a week. They are*

*lots of fun. I wisht that you lived in
Cambridge too, because then we could see
each other everday.
I sure did enjoyed meeting you. You are a
very nice girl. I hope sometimes that our
paths would cross again.*

*Sincerely,
John*

After reading and rereading the letter for the umpteenth time, Minnie folded it slowly, slipped it back into the envelope, and slid it under her pillow. Laying her head carefully down on top of it, she tried to figure out how she felt.

She'd waited so long for a letter from John. But, this wasn't how she'd imagined feeling. She finally realized that what she was feeling was a whole lot like disappointment--crestfallen, maybe.

At length she sat up and said "Well, one thing's for certain...a poet, he is not." Deciding not to ponder on the situation any further, at least for now, she went out to join the others.

<u>July 27</u>
*All went fishing after breakfast except myself. I washed a
few clothes and laid all our bed clothes out on the grass.
We are a mile from the dam and on the lower side of it
are two springs where we get our drinking water. Here I
saw a squirrel as I came down for water.*

<u>July 28, Sunday</u>
*The first thing on the program for me, was to salt fish.
Papa caught about 25. Before dinner Mrs. Hawp & I
fished. She caught 14 and I 17. After dinner we rested
and I wrote a letter. After supper the rest went fishing.
Arnold washed his Sunday-go-to-meetin' pants and I
wrote.*

Courtesy Archives & Manuscripts Division of Oklahoma Historical Society–Olivet Baptist Church Collection

Looking to the northwest the photographer takes us from a point at approximately 1st and G Avenue–past the Land Office and identifies mountains beyond. His numbers refer to: 1. Mt Scott 2. Land Office 3. City Nat'l Bank 4. Post Office 5. Court House 6. Mt Sheridan 7. Mt Signal–Lookout 8. Boses the Snakecatcher 9. Hotel de Lawton.

<u>July 29</u>

*After breakfast we loaded everything and pulled for
Lawton and got there by 11:30. After dinner I went to
Ft. Sill with Mr. & Mrs. Hawp and got the mail, also
went to the Ambrosia Springs to get good drinking water.
While they were filling the keg, I walked around the
spring house and saw a memorial stone. It was dedicated
to Ambrosia Elvira Taylor, the wife of Mr. Dr. Taylor;
Post Surgeon who died in 1884 while the spring house
was being erected. She was a nurse and an inscription to
this effect was on the lower part of the stone. "As these
waters o'er flow perennially: her heart flowed for her
people." This marble stone was on the corner of the stone
house that stood over the spring. The water ran out of
one corner and went trickling down to the clear watered
brook over many large stones. Either side of the creek
stood tall trees, proud of their beautiful surroundings. Ivy
clinging to the wall seemed there to reach for the cold
waters. Papa & Arnold unloaded the wagon this morning
& went to Ft. Sill on business and haven't returned at this
writing--4:00 p.m. I have performed household duties
about the tent all day. Two letters; Mother & Helen.*

Camp was set up southwest of the townsite along
Squaw Creek. They were far enough out, so they only had
folks on two sides, rather than being surrounded.

Minnie became concerned when Oliver and Arnold,
who'd left early to go to town, hadn't returned by four
o'clock. Upon their return, she learned they'd been
waiting for telegraph reports from El Reno–watching the
postings go up. It was the first day of the drawing.

Oliver H. Johnson's name wasn't on the list today.

Oh, well. There was lots of time.

Chapter 11
The Drawing

"S'cuse me, sir," the big, red-faced man in the poorly fitting brown suit said--again. After bumping Clarence with his suitcase, he'd backed into him and stepped on his foot. It was the same man who'd puffed his smelly cigar two seats up the aisle in front of Clarence all the way from Wichita.

"Heads up, coming through, coming through." Now, it was a porter, headed directly toward him, with a heavily loaded baggage wagon. Clarence skipped aside, sure the man would have knocked him down.

The El Reno Depot was a jumble of loud, discordant noises. Besides all the confusion here on the loading dock, Clarence had just been through the hairiest unloading of a train he could ever have imagined--people crawling out of windows, tempers inside the car rose in direct proportion to the temperature in the unmoving passenger car.

After being bumped and knocked around Clarence decided to hustle his skinny self to the shade of an elm tree near the depot and let the place clear out a little before trying again to collect his baggage. While he waited, he peered intently eastward toward the main part of town, wondering if he'd be lucky enough to find a room.

El Reno appeared to be a modern, bustling, currently overcrowded little town. Clarence could see by the electric and telephone poles that a bit of the civilized world had reached this far. He was surprised to see the town had a business of horse drawn coaches to transport passengers to and from the station to downtown. He decided he'd take one of them, after collecting his bag.

Nice enough little town, Clarence determined, stepping down from the dock, finally having found an opportunity to locate his valise. He handed his bag up to the assistant and bending his tall frame over, stepped up inside. The bus was equipped with two long bench seats built along either side under the windows. Sitting down he turned sideways on the seat so he could look out the window. Noting that the coach was pulled by three teams of horses--one team more than a plenty. Laying it on a little thick, they were. It was new and brightly painted and on its' top was a luggage rack for trunks and baggage.

After checking all the hotels up and down Bickford Street–including the Kerfoot–for vacancies he decided to give his hunger some attention. Concession stands and business tents had been set up along the center of main street to sell food, drink, and other necessities to the enormous crowd. Clarence lucked into a seat for one at a lunch counter--indoors. He sat down beneath a slowly turning ceiling fan and ordered a meal of blackeyed peas with ham, cornbread, sliced tomatoes and onion.

When the proprietor came by to fill his coffee cup, Clarence took the opportunity to ask if the gentleman knew of a place where he could find a bed for the night.

"By golly, you don't ask easy ones, do you?" the man said in the jovial manner of people who like waiting on customers. "Let me think. Now, they asked everyone to reevaluate their home situation and consider renting out any conceivable space for cots. Asked 'em to consider putting people up in their sheds and barns. Last I heard, the widow Gunderson was considering putting some out on her porch if they could get her some extras. You might try her place."

His meal arrived, looking delicious. It was. After eating he asked for directions to the Gunderson house.

A large, two story, frame home painted a light yellow with white gingerbread trim, Mrs. Gunderson's rooming house seemed attractive and inviting. A hastily made sign of brown cardboard was tacked to one of the posts of the wrap-around porch. It read:

COTS FOR RENT
50 cents per night
INQUIRE WITHIN

Clarence turned in at the gate and walked up the red brick walk. As he climbed the porch steps he could see the front door standing open. That was natural. So was every other front door in town–for ventilation. The hooked screen door marked the line behind which flies and people need wait for an invitation to enter. Preparing to knock on the door trim, Clarence noticed the silhouette of a person inside the house, walking toward the door. The sun, shining through the windows at the rear of the house, made it impossible to see features until the person came closer. He could tell by the rustling sounds that skirts were involved.

"Good afternoon." said the lady of the house, in a not so very "good afternoonish" tone. Her graying, dark hair was pulled back into a severely twisted bun at the nape of her neck.

Finally seeing the woman's face, he wondered what had happened in her life to make her so lacking of anything resembling warmth. Poor thing, bet she never once got the box of chocolates for being "fairest of the fair" at a pie supper.

When Mrs. Gunderson spoke, it was in a haughty tone. Standing behind the screen in a gray-and-white striped blouse with a brooch at the center of it's high, stand-up collar, she appeared to be a person who detested life and what she was doing–being forced to "let" rooms–to make ends meet. Of all the happy people in this town, Clarence had to draw this old heifer. Ah, well, it was a place to lay his head.

"If you're here about a room, I don't have one." she said through the locked screen door. "I have cots."

"Yes, Ma'am I saw your sign. I--"

"My rooms were spoken for a week ago," she went on as if she hadn't heard him, "I only have space for two ladies upstairs in the hall. Like the sign on the porch says, I have cots. I can have a cot put out on the porch for you, if you want to pay 50 cents a night in advance for it. Take it or leave it."

"Yes, ma'am, I'll take it," Clarence said reaching for his money. Again she went on, ignoring his words. "You may leave your bag and other belongings inside this closet under the stairway."

Finally she opened the screen to let him in. They stood in the entry foyer that extended all the way from the front door back to the kitchen, where wide, breezy windows allowed air to circulate. A stairway led to the second floor on the right side of this long center room. Clarence had his money out ready to pay her, but Mrs. Gunderson walked to the door of the closet beneath the stairs and gestured toward it with her limply outstretched hand. The tour was not finished yet; her speech would continue.

"Your things will be quite safe here in this closet. I keep the only key and I–personally–unlock the closet anytime anyone needs anything from it. I stand here while they get what they need. Then I lock it–securely–myself."

Clarence had no doubt about that.

Stopping just long enough to swallow, she turned stiffly to gesture toward the kitchen. "You may take your meals here, if you choose, but you must tell me twenty-four hours in advance of any meal you wish to take with us." The widow droned on with the memorized lines, she'd said far too many times in her life already. It was like a museum tour. Her mouth was permanently drawn into a dour, pinched expression.

"Excuse me, I would like the cot on the porch, Ma'am, and I *am* in a hurry, so...." Clarence's voice trailed off as she gave a nod to acknowledge his statement, but went right on with her oration as if she *must* finish it.

This woman is a little strange. Like a school girl who has a speech memorized, nothing–it seemed–would prevent her from saying the whole thing. She seemed so stiff–anger hovering just beneath the surface. It was as if she chose to concentrate her thoughts only on her speech, not really wishing to communicate with this lowly traveling person.

"You will use the visitor's privy. It is in the backyard to the south of ours," she went on. "You will be given a pitcher of water, a basin, a towel, and a clean wash rag daily. Are there any questions?"

"No, Ma'am," Clarence said quickly, "I think you've covered everything." He couldn't help but grin. "Please, allow me to pay you for two nights and let me go. I'm in a hurry. I have business to attend to and will be back later this evening." He handed her a dollar for two nights, and turned for the door.

"Sir?" she said, "I request that all my boarders sign-in. Please come and write your name and address on my registration tablet. It is in here on the sideboard." Her request halted his departure, once again as she ushered him into the parlor, a room on the right. It was dark and stuffy–badly in need of ventilation–probably never used.

"Do you wish to leave your bag here now?"

"Yes, Ma'am, I do. Thank you."

"And how late will you be returning?"

WHAT? Clarence could not believe his ears! THIS pathetic excuse for a boarding house hostess wanted to know what time he'd be in? What the hell did it matter? He was sleeping on the porch!

"I have no idea, Mrs. Gunderson," he said in exasperation, "I'm here to get registered for the Land Lottery–the town is overflowing with people just like me. I have absolutely no idea how long it will take." He turned and began walking toward the door, leaving his bag on the floor.

"Needn't be rude," Mrs. Gunderson said in an admonishing tone. Then noticing his bag was still there beside her--

"Y-your bag, Mr. –." She hurried to find his name on the tablet. "Mr. Pool. Oh, Mr. Pool."

On the front walk Clarence could hear the widow

Gunderson calling his name. Resisting the urge to just keep on going, he paused–checked his pocket watch–turned and looked back at her.

"In the hall closet will be fine. Thank You, Mrs. Gunderson," he said.

***

REUBEN E. POOL, Clarence's father, was a veteran of the Civil War. Wounded twice, he'd been with Company C of the 6th Regiment of Maryland Volunteers. Once, at the battle of Locust Grove, Virginia, he'd sustained a wound to the left side of his chest. Given up for dead, left lying on the battlefield, they found him there--still alive-- the next day when they returned to bury their dead.

In the presidential proclamation of July 4, 1901, there was the statement *"honorably discharged soldiers and sailors may make application for registration with due proof of their qualifications through an agent of their own selection, providing that person is representing one veteran only."* It appeared that Clarence might be able to act as his father's agent and register for him. The problem was he and his father hadn't had a chance to discuss it.

Just three days from today, at 9:00 a.m, on Monday, July 29. the drawing would begin. Once begun it would continue daily from 9 to 5 until all 160,000 envelopes had been drawn.[11]   All entry cards now enclosed in plain envelopes held the description of the entrant written down by a clerk at the time of registration. The numerical order in which a person's envelope was drawn from the shuffling bins represented the order in which that person would be allowed to file for the 160 acres of his choice. The earlier the number, the better the selection.

Lists of names in the order drawn would be posted in El Reno and at the Quinette Store at Fort Sill (until such time as the new land office building was available on the new Lawton townsite.) Postal cards were to be mailed to each registered individual at the address given when registering. Newspapers in the area promised to publish all 160,000 names.

Before the drawing on July 29, the population of El Reno would grow to 100,000 homeseekers.

***

AT PRECISELY 8:57 a.m. on Monday, July 29th, the officials, clerks, and the young designated "draw-ers" for the drawing took the stage. They quickly arranged themselves in predetermined places. The stage had been designed especially for this event. It was built so that onlookers could see everything that occurred on the platform. The sides between the floor and the cover of the booth were open to full view on all four sides. Covered with chicken wire fencing--presumably to block thrown tomatoes or the like--it stood like a lonely little island in the middle of a sea of people.

Along the front of the stage, placed end to end, were two, 10 foot long boxes, measuring 3 feet by 3 feet square. They had been constructed especially for this event and rested on sawhorses. Each bin had a crank attached to one end. When turned, they caused the box to turn, tumbling and shuffling the envelopes inside. Along one side of each box, there were 5 openings with covers that slid aside. One box held the cards for the northern district--one the southern.

Ten young men between the ages of 16 and 19 had been selected to assist in the drawing. They were stationed at each of the openings and would draw envelopes, one at a time, in rotation. All the young men were required to be under twenty-one years of age so they could have no financial interest in the matter. They would be paid three dollars a day for their services.

Behind the row of young men were lines of tables at which clerks were seated and ready to write lists in longhand and transfer information from cards to lists. One lucky gentleman had a new-fangled typewriters in front of him. He sat arms crossed waiting for information to be typed. The crowd was restless; anxious for the drawing to begin .

Commissioner of the General Land Office, W.A. Richards, former Governor of Wyoming, was in charge of a large group of land office employees sent from Washington, D. C., to conduct the lottery. Governor Richards, as he was still called, was known for his skills of oratory. Bellowing loudly, he made the sound resonate. The technique not dissimilar to hog calling, involved long, drawn out sounds. The governor's voice carried a long distance. As with other politicians of the day, the skill of speaking loudly and enunciating clearly had been a necessity in election campaigns.

Stepping to the front of the stand and grabbing the lapels of his suit he began.

"Ladiees and Gentlemen, wee are here today to con-soo-mate the most important portion of this Grrreaaat Laand Lottery. This being the drawing for the ceded lands of the noble Kiowa, Comanche, and Kiowa-Apache Tribes"

"This dr-aw-ing is n-ah-t for the land itself, but for the ORDER in which lands will be selected. We will now begin the drawing."

He pronounced Kiowa like most white men–"ki-waw" rather than "ki-o-wuh" as the people themselves said it.

The crowd went wild. They stopped him cold, with yells, whistles, and catcalls. Gathered on the north side of the Irving School building were at least five thousand people; some estimated higher.

"We would ask..."

Realizing he had uttered that last sentence a little prematurely the former governor picked up a megaphone placed on the stand in front of him for this reason.

"We would ask that each of you show courtesy to those standing near you by being as quiet as possible so that all can hear."

The crowd roared again.

Some man down front asked that the young men roll up their sleeves to be sure there were no cards hidden there. The boys obliged and the crowd settled down.[12] They wanted to get the show on the road. There was a long pause during which the first card was drawn. The speaker bellowed again:

"The number one caard in the El Reeeeno District is Mr. Joseph Holcourt." Cheers, hoots and applause stopped the show.

"The number one card in the Fort Sill area is Mr. James Woods of Weatherford, Oklahoma Territory."

Men working in the drawing booth, El Reno, July 29, 1901

The scene inside the drawing booth just after the first names had been drawn. Note the rolled up sleeve on the young man closest to the camera.

Side view of the drawing booth. June 29, 1901.

Archives & Manuscripts Division of the Oklahoma Historical Society
Shuffling boxes at El Reno--Shanafelt Collection

He gave the name of the number two draw in the El Reno District.

"The number two card for the Fort Sill District is--Miss Mattie Beal of Wichita, Kansas."

"Number three..."

"Number three in the Fort Sill District is Mr. Winfield S. Laws of Langston, Oklahoma Territory.

By noon the men on the stand were thanking the good Lord for the canvas canopy covering the stage. It gave them some relief from the relentless heat of the sun. The temperature would be in the high 90's today.

By afternoon of the third day the drawing and announcing had become routine –almost boring–unless it happened to be your own name being called. The crowd was restless, talking and joking in small groups.

Standing in the middle of the sweaty crowd late in the afternoon, his head above most everyone else's, Clarence held his coat in front of him, his arms folded around it. He wished he'd left it at the rooming house. Shifting his weight from one foot to the other, he was tired of standing and listening. Suddenly, during a moment in which he'd become preoccupied watching an adorable little girl playing in and around her mother's skirts, he heard what sounded like his name being announced.

Was that my name? He was dumbstruck! Looking at people on both sides of him to see if they held a clue, didn't help. They didn't know his name. For awhile he didn't even move from where he was standing. Not having been paying close enough attention and with all the noise it seemed it was impossible to know. His pulse quickened and a lump formed in his throat as he found his way to the edge of the crowd.

Walking first one way and then the other he tried to think. At first he didn't seem to be having much success at it. There must be some way to check this out.

Figuring they'd soon be closing down for today he waited and finally asked the right questions of the right person to find out where lists were being posted. He made his way quickly to the south door of the school building. It was here he found the lists. He ran his finger down page after page of names. It wasn't there.

Disappointed he began pacing trying to think. He could still hear the sound in his mind–the sounds he was sure had been his name.

At last darkness fell and Clarence found his way back to Gunderson's rooming house and his cot on the porch.

Mrs. Gunderson had been almost civilized when he'd paid for the extra days. She'd taken care of his bag, even offered a laundry service–for a price. His cot was on the north side of the house. Though it was dark and several cots were now on the porch he found his cot and lay down upon it. Laying awake for a long while watching the fireflies and listening to the *nyng-ing* of mosquitoes he finally resolved to go back and check the listings once more in the morning.

***

JUST ANOTHER WAGON in the line of white ribboning its way through the Wichitas, Mr. Jeagorsen kept the team in check. He'd decided only a week ago to pull up stakes in Dodge City and see what profit he might find in the new boomtown down south in Indian Territory.

"Any of you girls wanta come along 're welcome. You know I'll treatcha fair and square. I don't hold with nobody hitting ya and ya know I don't hit ya myself. You know that but you gotta be square with me."

Hannah Bell didn't care one way or the other (about much of anything.) But Doralee was excited about the possibilities and convinced her young friend it might be fun to see a new crowd–some new country for a change.

Only seventeen her next birthday–August 16 or 17–she was never quite sure which, Hannah's life had not been a bed of roses. Both parents were gone by the time she was five. Her mother died at home after lying around sick and coughing for what seemed like forever to little Hannah. Never having known her father she'd been taken on by an old spinster in Emporia at the insistence of the lady's preacher.

Doralee, Hannah, and three other working girls were now bouncing southward in the wagon. Having raised the sides of the wagon sheet to allow a breeze to blow through, some curled up and slept while others eyed the travelers and the scenery.

not quite dawn and as he'd taken a wrong turn on Wisteria Avenue he found himself at a greater distance from the school than when he started. He finally got his bearings and started in the right direction. Now he saw the three-story building rising a few blocks away. As he got closer he began to run a few steps, walk a few and run a few more. It was going to be there–he knew it! He felt it. Arriving at the place where the lists were posted he discovered that fresh clean, corrected lists had been posted overnight. There it was: Clarence O. Pool, Number 1,611.

<u>July 31</u>
Papa & Arnold spent most of the day in Lawton, again. I wrote letters nearly all day and Mr. Elharinons daughter visited a part of the time with me. Some of the Texas boys came up, very merry and announced that one of them drew a piece of land in 8 hundred something. James Wood of Weatherford, Okla. drew 1st prize and Mattie Beal of Wichita, Kansas, 2nd for Lawton District. Over 2,000 people witnessed the drawing that took place in El Reno and at the announcement of each gave tremendous cheers. Joseph Holcourt 1st prize in El Reno District Okla. and an I.T. (Indian Territory) man 2nd.

Courtesy Fort Sill Museum

Man proudly displays mail received at Fort Sill. Was it his notification card for the drawing?

Staying in camp day after day while the men went to town, the only news Minnie was able to receive was word of mouth–unless Papa happened to buy a newspaper. People would pass by the camp with bits and pieces of news about winners or who had drawn what number.

Each day the menfolk went to wait for new lists to be posted. Some were beginning to receive notifications of their lottery number in the mail.

Minnie was able to get a lot of reading done, swapping books with other ladies camped out along the creek.

***

CLARENCE, eyes fixed on the list, was satisfied for now just to drink in the wonderful feeling of being a "winner,"--not allowing any of the "shoulds," "ought-tos," nor "what if's" he would soon need to consider.

He purchased a morning paper at a news stand and found a place on the boardwalk to sit. The paper would be something tangible to hold onto, carry along with him, to prove to himself in times of doubt that it was real. He relaxed. Finally he opened the paper and found his name with number 1611 beside it. It startled him to think how quickly this had all happened. He'd best be making arrangements to get to Lawton. What date was the opening set for?

At the ticket stand Clarence learned that the train track wasn't yet finished as far south as Lawton. It would be necessary that he go to Marlow. Though it was 30 miles east of Lawton, the ticket master assured him there would be wagons, buggies, and hacks lined up to transport people to Lawton. Men were making a living this summer providing rides to Lawton, he was told. They were there waiting every time a train came in to the Marlow station. The ride would take the better part of a day and would cost about $7.00, unless one shared the ride.

On the train, Clarence met a couple other fellows who agreed to share a ride to Lawton. Somehow, by the time they got the thing decided and their luggage gathered up, the only conveyance left was a light buckboard with no covering, an old driver, and a team of worn-out-looking mules. Better than having to walk–but not much.

Somewhere around noon the driver stopped in a shade and brought out a lunch–for himself. It didn't appear that he had any for his passengers. At length one of the fellows said, "I'll give you a dime for that sandwich." All of a sudden the old fellow discovered that his wife had packed plenty of sandwiches; fifteen cents apiece! Nice sandwich. Outlandish price, but what was a fellow to do?

About sundown, the wagon and team of mules were getting close enough for the weary travelers to see the flickering campfires of settlers and campers close to Lawton. The old driver stopped and asked for his pay before crossing East Cache creek, a mile east of the town. He said last week he'd had a gent jump out of the wagon and run off without paying.

"Once burned, twice shy." he said, "Don't aim to let it happen again."

Clarence and the others finally arrived in "rag" town twenty minutes later. They were dropped off on "Goo Goo Avenue" at ten o'clock at night. All around the huge, bare, 320 acre rectangle designated as the site for Lawton was a massive gathering of people, wagons, tents, and activity.

The tent town was growing dustier, hotter, noisier, more shameless, bodacious, and lacking in refinement by the day. Especially along the area called Goo Goo Avenue.

"Yee-hah."

Photo courtesy of Fort Sill Museum, Fort Sill, Oklahoma

Make-shift post office in Trader's Store, 1901

Chapter 12
Minnie Sees Rag Town

The name *Oliver H. Johnson* hadn't yet appeared on any of the lists outside the land office, nor had he received a card informing him that his name had been drawn.

Oliver was having trouble with this waiting business. He couldn't get away from the crowds and roam around the countryside. There was a need to learn the results of the drawing, and to do that he had to stick around close to where they were being posted. Along with thousands of others, he'd shown up every morning for the last four days and stayed a good portion of each day.

Today was the first day of August, a Thursday. Next Tuesday, the sixth, would be opening day.

Papa Oliver returned to camp for the noon meal. Now, squatting in the shade, cleaning his fingernails with his pocketknife, an idea was hatching in his mind.

Fresh lists were put up outside the new land office twice a day but he couldn't take standing around with the crowds any more. If he could get Minnie to go along this afternoon, it would make mail call a snap.

Couldn't hurt.

He got up and strolled over to where the ladies were cleaning up after the noon meal.

"Say, Minnie, I sure could use your help this afternoon when you finish those dishes," he said in his most sincere voice.

THE JOB OF POSTMASTER at Fort Sill had become the most consuming one in the country. Within the past thirty days Mr. W. H. Quinette, Post Trader, Indian Trader, and U.S. Postmaster, had experienced the most overwhelming change in routines since coming to the area in 1876.

His postal duties had multiplied by the thousands and the new residents had completely cleaned out his store. There was no time to restock or clean up--only to sort mail and hand it out to the eternal line of settlers at the window. Quinette telegraphed Washington for permission to hire temporary help but was told that first an agent would need to be sent out to observe the problem. Within an hour of the agent's arrival permission had been given for five temporary assistants.

In addition to the mail for the army personnel on post Quinette received and distributed mail for all the folks now filling up tent town, and the thousands of homeseekers and settlers camped around the vicinity. This would continue until a new post office in Lawton was opened. Now, with six clerks handling 3,000 pieces of mail per day, Quinette felt he was getting the job done satisfactorily--considering.

He had a system in which men calling for mail stood double file in one of three lines, depending upon the first letter of their last name. Ladies could walk straight up to the window at anytime and call for their mail. This is where Minnie's assistance would help Papa immensely.

The view on Goo Goo, August 8, 1901. Note the watermelon rinds, on the ground and on the stand to the right. Looking far down into the center you begin to get an idea of the masses of people, tents, wagons and mules/horses in the vicinity.

Archives & Manuscript Division of the Oklahoma Historical Society

I read & wrote before dinner and then had early dinner as Papa was going to Fort Sill. After dinner I took a notion to go. So, I donned my hat & went--just as I was dressed. We passed the long file of tents on Goo Goo Ave., Lawton, and watched with interest the busy people. Among the next features, an opera house where so many people...

(page missing from Minnie's diary)

...No. 1 and those between H. & N at No.2: O to Z at No.3. The men form in double file & await their turn to call for mail. Ladies are given room at the window and never wait over two minutes to get to call as there are so few ladies. We did not stay there very long. I called for the mail & we returned. It was nearly sundown when we arrived at our headquarters. I had a very enjoyable afternoon. Everything is new to me as often as I go over the road. Of course, there is always something new to see.

So far Papa had maneuvered events so that Minnie hadn't yet seen "rag town," the area around and to the south of Goo Goo Avenue. The promise he'd made his wife kept ringing in his ears. The route he took on the way today, however, went right through tent town and down the one mile strip of Goo Goo Avenue.

Not one building stood on the site yet--with the exception of the almost finished land office. Like the dust and grit stirred up by the wagons and horses; anticipation and excitement filled the air. People bustled around-- in a hurry to get things done--to make things happen.

As the Johnsons' wagon rolled past the tents on Goo Goo Avenue, Minnie could see beyond to more and more rows of tents. She couldn't keep from staring at some of the sights.

Lawton was already an enterprising settlement--it's disorderly appearance notwithstanding. The tents weren't laid out in neat and orderly lines like the ones of military tent towns. They'd been put up hurriedly, and looked as if they'd been flung out like a handful of sunflower seeds.

Business endeavors of all types marketed their wares or conduct business of other sorts out of tents and wagons.

A few brush arbor shades had been erected, looking very similar to the ones the Comanche people had in their encampment near. It was astounding to see what some of the tents held--hard to believe business could be done this way.

There were places where one could purchase fresh meat and baked goods. Vendors sold dry goods, lumber and hardware--several establishments were serving meals. Two or three pharmacists had arrived and were selling their medicines and cures. A barber had hung a sign on the back of his wagon and as soon as he could get out the wooden crate for his customer to sit upon, he was in business.

There were tent saloons and gambling joints. Several people just had a card table and a couple of chairs, and were conducting crap games. Doctors, dentists, lawyers, sign-makers, newspaper editors, preachers, prostitutes and peddlers were all finding a way to do business.

"That's the land office over there," Papa volunteered, indicating with his chin an almost finished building on the otherwise bare townsite. It was a 24'X 48' "box house," the kind that was quick and easy to make. Two men could put up a small one in a day.

"They'll be finishing it pretty soon," he added, "at least they better be; the opening's Tuesday."

"Is all that empty space around it going to be town, then?" Minnie asked, gesturing toward the huge vacant area.

"That's the way it's planned," Papa said, seeming happy for once to explain something.

"That's 320 acres, a half-section of land. I don't know if you can tell, but it's a rectangle, and we are going east on one of its long sides--it is a whole mile long. The east and west sides are just a half mile each."

"They have soldiers on guard around it day and night, making sure no one tries to set up a tent or do business on it till after the opening."

"This area over here," Papa indicated to the area on the other side "is going to make somebody rich. There are two 160 acre homesteads side by side. On opening day they'll most likely be selected by the persons who got the numbers '1' and '2' in the southern district. That land should become quite valuable as the town grows, adjoining the townsite as it does."

"I see," Minnie said,puzzled to find Papa in such a talkative mood, today. "That explains all the flap about Mr. Woods and Miss--uhm--oh, what's the lady's name-- the telephone operator from Kansas?"

"Beal." Papa supplied the name.

"Yes, that's the one. Mattie Beal--*Miss* Mattie Beal," she corrected herself.

"So, you say, they'll probably claim this land right over here--not so much because of any farm value it might have, but in speculation of its future worth."

"That's right, Minnie-girl."

"So when will they be allowed to sell any of the property or rent it out?"

"Not until they've gone through the whole 'proving up' process. They'll have to be careful. They must carry out the whole homesteader's agreement, stick to all the same rules."

"What do you mean?"

"Fourteen months of building fences, breaking land, planting trees, building something to live in and stay right here on the land the whole time. After they've "proved" to Uncle Sam that they are a serious homesteader, they can pay $1.25 an acre and own the land outright."

"Ah-h," Minnie's voice sang, "and then would appear the happy dollar signs?"

"That's right, girl!"

"Haven't some folks figured on it taking five years to 'prove up?'"

"Well, yes. The original kind of homesteading allowed a person, who doesn't mind waiting five years for a clear title, to live on his farm for five years and get a clear title without having to pay a dime for it; that is, other than the fourteen dollar filing fee he's already paid."

Minnie nodded her head and turned again to gaze at the assortment of tents and people as their wagon rolled past. She was still amused at Papa's talkative frame of mind.

There were men of all types--wealthy to dirt poor, ugly to "Don Juan" handsome, ruffians in dusty canvas work clothes, dandified gambler types in fancy suits with stiff, white collars, businessmen with white shirts, ties, and vests ordinary men like Minnie's brother, in light cotton shirts and those canvas pants, made by Levi & Strauss. Everyone wore long-sleeved shirts to protect their skin from sunburn.

Papa had a natural aversion to the fancy dude types. Minnie had heard him on several occasions comment, "Now how can you trust a man who walks around in this kind of heat with a stiff collar, buttoned up under his sweaty chin, wearing a suit, and acting like it don't bother him. And you know blame well, it does! He's just showing his self to be a fake and a shyster with his phony actions." It was one of Oliver's pet peeves. Minnie hoped he didn't get going on it today; she was enjoying the outing.

They approached the sign for the Opera House Minnie had heard about:

OPERA HOUSE
featuring
"The Flying Lady"

The Opera House (tent) had a stage show with a variety of acts in the evening. Some were comical, some dramatic, some musical. Vaudeville was all the rage. A traveling show that played in El Reno two weeks earlier; it originated out of St. Louis. From the railroad station in Marlow, it had been brought in wagons to Lawton. During the evening shows, a woman with a beautiful voice called the "Flying Lady" sang a song named, "Just Because You Made Those Goo Goo Eyes." It was from this song that Goo Goo Avenue--later Goo Goo Alley--got its name.

Entertainment for the more conservative among the settlers was almost nonexistent, except what might be obtained from an occasional fiddle, accordion, or harmonica serenade. But the melodious voice of the "flying lady" could be heard clearly throughout the tent town every ninety minutes during the evening. It broke the monotony of the twilight hours.

Minnie craned her neck in every direction, trying to see

everything. Some sights were so outrageous they commanded her attention. She wished Papa would stop the wagon for a little while and just watch the people, but she knew he wouldn't do it.

A water wagon approached from the opposite direction. Minnie watched in amazement as people scurried around grabbing their buckets and other containers for the opportunity to pay twenty-five cents to fill up their buckets with water. Twenty-five cents! Unbelievable! One could purchase a real nice roast for twenty-five cents. Either they didn't have a wagon to go out and find a spring or a creek that was clean, or they didn't have the time.

No sanitary conveniences (toilets) existed yet on the grounds. The government men in charge would have a few privies with burlap siding put up by opening day.

People routinely shared water dippers and used untreated drinking water. The practice of boiling water before drinking was not common at this time. Those who'd heard about the research of the French chemist, Louis Pasteur, concerning germs, sterilization, and the passing of diseases from one person to another usually drank only coffee or tea, to be sure their water had been boiled.

> *"The sanitary conditions were extremely bad, and as a result there were many, many cases of typhoid fever. When the Comanche County Medical Society formed in October, we had seventy physicians as members."* [13]

Minnie observed that there were those who'd made a small business selling drinking water at five cents a dipper. They were located all around tent town. Their business capital consisted of a box or crate, a bucket of water, and a dipper. In this heat, they usually had a line of customers waiting. When one customer finished, the dipper was passed on to the next one in line.

As Minnie's "tour" down Goo Goo Avenue progressed, she became increasingly aware of an odor that occasionally wafted through the air. The odor was decisively horse (and likely, human) manure heated by the hot August sun. Though numerous dogs and tumble bugs kept some of it cleaned up, a person still had to watch his step. There not being much breeze today, it was especially noticeable. Added to this, the intermittent stench of a newly oiled tarpaulin, baking under that same hot sun, brought on a pretty strong assault to Minnie's nostrils. She grimaced, reached for a hanky and held it to her nose.

Seeing this, Papa shook his head and chuckled, "That's what we human beings get for cramming too many of us animals into too small a space. It ain't natural, and the results are never much good."

Minnie counted twenty-three saloons, so far, but that was just the ones lining the "street" and didn't include the gambling joints and social clubs where they were three and four deep.[14] Most reports said there were many more than that. They had intriguing names, some borrowed from other boomtowns: The Wigwam, The Golden Horseshoe, Two-Johns Saloon, Fort Sill Saloon, The Palace Club & Saloon, The Silver Dollar, Dick Russell's Saloon. The gambling tents were doing a rip-roaring business as well. It was said that cheating was unrestrained and complaints about the gambling joints were widespread. There never seemed to be a shortage of customers. Strange.

"Oh, my goodness, the flies! Just look at them swarm!" As they passed a watermelon stand, Minnie noticed the rinds had been tossed out onto the ground. It looked like they no sooner hit the ground, than they were covered with flies!

"A church?" Minnie said incredulously as the wagon continued to roll along. "Papa, that was a Methodist *church* tent in between the Huffine Cafe and..." her voice trailed off as the next sight caught her attention.

Three tents down, a man and woman were having a vicious, screaming argument! A big bovine of a woman was cussing a man–probably her husband–forty ways to Sunday. Behind them, wedged in between two larger tents, was a smaller one with a sign out saying, "Gerta's Stew--Best Yet." It had three tables with some currently empty chairs out in front. A crowd was gathering, not to eat, but to watch the sideshow. The situation looked nasty, as if it might come to blows. Minnie was unnerved, to say the least.

The man, who could have done duty as a draft horse, boomed, "I knew I shouldn'a brung ya here! You're trouble, woman, and you know it! They's always gotta be trouble everwher you go." He looked as if he might have had a drink or two from the bottle he carried.

Having no other choice, Papa disgustedly allowed the horses to come to a stop, seeing that the wagons and teams in front of them were stopped as well. They couldn't move. The street was clogged with onlookers. Papa enjoyed an oddity as much as the next fellow, but he'd sincerely hoped not to expose Minnie to such low-class, boorish behavior.

The woman, red-faced and livid, screamed out of control. Veins popped out on her forehead and temples. She was saying something about how much meat she'd told him to buy. She picked up a large piece of meat with one hand. It was a hefty slice of round off a hindquarter of beef. The dark red meat sagged from the little round bone near its center. She got a good grip on it and swung it at him, bone-end smacking him on the left side of his face. Then she dragged it back, ready to strike again. He stepped closer to her and wrested the meat away from her, holding it up to examine it with one hand and holding her back with the other, yelling all at the same time.

"Dumb, w-woman, you's sposta make stew outta this. You think these people's gonna buy our stew now?"

Becoming more enraged, he staggered forward and backward, clenching and unclenching his fists, muttering obscenities. The crowd had grown larger by the moment, now was pressed tightly together.

People began jeering and egging it on. "Fight!" "Hit 'er!" "C'mon, whatcha waitin' for, Bub?" The man took another step forward. The woman, standing in front of a work table, put a hand behind her, feeling around on it for something. Soon she found what she'd been looking for. The crowd inhaled in unison. She'd wrapped her fingers around the handle of a butcher knife.

"Cover your pocketbooks, folks."

The slow, sing-songy voice coming from behind them startled the crowd. The incongruity of the wearily delivered words and the situation at hand was a jolt.

"Keep a tight grip on your money."

It was U.S. Deputy Marshal Heck Thomas. Tired from too many hours spent "keeping the peace" in this rag town, he leaned on his left arm which rested on the saddle horn. Attempting to maneuver his horse through the crowd, he was trying to get to the source of the disturbance. Meanwhile he was taking the opportunity to do a little good natured preaching.

"Ain't chall figgered out b'now, that the pickpockets just love it when you bunch up like this." Heck went on in his easy-going way. No one that knew him took offense. That was just Heck.

Dealing with domestic arguments wasn't Deputy Marshal Thomas's cup of tea. Judge Isaac C. Parker, the hanging judge of Ft. Smith, Arkansas, knew and respected Thomas for his genius in bringing in some of the most wanted outlaws, thieves, and murderous gangs in Indian Territory during the last ten years. Some he brought in dead, some alive and ready for hanging.

This assignment down here in this new town called Lawton, in Indian Territory, was getting on his nerves. It was turning out to be a hell of a lot more depressing. There was no freedom nor spontaneity to it. He had to try to "talk" people into doing the right thing, when most of the time he didn't feel like talking. He hadn't had a good night's sleep in weeks.

He groused about it, but the chance to work again with his old buddies, Bill Tilghman and Chris Madsen, made it worth the trouble. They were also U.S. Deputy Marshals, and the three of them had become known as "The Three Guardsmen." Their successes at bringing in outlaws were legendary.

"You're walking targets, folks. Y'never know whose gonna be standin' right next to you." The crowd became quiet. Many were checking their pockets. Deputy Marshal Thomas had quite a sense of humor, and he could be "pulling their leg" or he could be seriously warning them. Fact was, Heck thought the audience needed reminding that a thing like this could be staged, just to gather a crowd. Who's to say this one wasn't?

"S'cuse me, folks," Heck said, trying to wend his way through the crowd.

"Let me through here, please, sir."

"Thank you. Thank you."

He finally arrived in front of the crowd, near the "fuss." Minnie heard the long squeak of leather as Heck slowly stepped down from his horse. He took a few steps toward the couple, who by now were working hard at trying to cool down from blowing off steam, knowing if they didn't shake it off they'd probably both be under arrest or thrown out of town. They stood hot, sweaty, and silent now, ready for whatever fate awaited them. No doubt there would be a charge of disturbing the peace again.

Thomas, who as a young man in Atlanta had seriously considered the ministry, placed his foot on one of their chairs. Leaning over, resting a forearm on his knee, and allowing the reins to dangle from his hand; he began to speak quietly to the still smoldering couple. The lady stood, hands on hips, chest heaving, sweat pouring down her face and dripping onto her sizable bosom, head turned indignantly away from her husband. The husband, who'd evidently decided to take the friendly approach, wore a grin that was much too wide as he reached out to shake the Deputy Marshal's hand.

"Naw, now Billy, don't be trying to get so friendly with me. Y'all were about to get pretty deadly here. Haven't I talked with you folks before about this?"

Finally they heard words like "no next time" and "better clamp a lid on those tempers" and "into custody" filtered from Heck's mouth and out through the mass of people. The crowd began to disperse.

The show was over. Oliver Johnson flicked the reins once and clicked his tongue against his cheek in the universal language that means "giddy-up."

August 2
Nothing of interest until in the evening. Papa, Arnold.
We also saw Mr. C. A. Schrandt and Papa had quite a
talk with him.

ON AUGUST 4TH the murder of an eleven-year-old boy sent shock waves through the rough and ragged town. Joseph P. Beanblossum had been shot and killed during a hold-up on the road between Fort Sill and Rush Springs. The victim's father, a physician, was on his way to set up a practice in the new town. On their way to the opening, the Beanblossums had joined a group transporting several loads of freight to Lawton.

A man named George Moran had been identified by witnesses as the murderer and was now wanted in connection with the hold-up and shooting. So far, nothing suspicious had been reported since the robbers rode off to the northeast. Officers in cities and towns in that direction were telegraphed and asked to notify the U.S. Marshal in Lawton if they saw or heard anything in connection with the shooting. So far, no clues had turned up. People who were already leery of the new town and its wild goings-on, now had even more reason to be cautious, raise cain, or leave.

August 5
This afternoon Papa, Arnold & Schrandt went to Sill for the mail and met John Reid and Sam Joice whom they brought back to camp with them. Schrandt made his headquarters with them. A great deal of robbing and killing has taken place in the last three or four days, and is likely to for the next few days to come.

"Tomorrow's the big day! August 6th!"
Most everyone seemed enthusiastic in anticipation of the big opening. Tomorrow the empty townsite would be covered with people. The ground would become pulverized into dust, as the new town mushroomed into being.

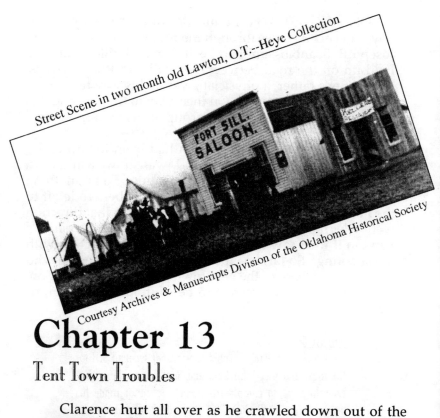

Chapter 13

Tent Town Troubles

Clarence hurt all over as he crawled down out of the wagon. Their chauffeur had provided nothing in the way of seats, cushioning or shade for the comfort of his passengers. Their ride had been a seven hour marathon of jolting, bouncing and pitching in the bare, open bed of a buckboard.

"I have never had such a miserable experience in my entire life," Clarence hollered at the driver. "By rights, you don't deserve a fare." He and the other two travelers watched as their driver and his pitiful old mules pull off into the darkness.

"I ought to file suit for bodily injury and assault with a deadly wagon!" All three men were stiff and sore, but had to laugh.

Clarence had endured some real pain. Not having much in the way of natural cushioning anymore, the thin layer of skin and tendon over his hip bones had sustained quite a but of bruising. He'd folded up his jacket and sat on it for awhile, then he sat on his valise. He'd even tried laying down first on one side and then the other. Nothing helped for very long.

Saying farewells, the group went their separate ways. The other two were to join up with business acquaintances. Clarence turned slowly in a full circle assessing his new surroundings. So this is Lawton--the new country--the land of opportunity--the promised land. It had been described in all these terms in the newspapers during recent weeks.

Not exactly sure what he'd expected, Clarence knew this wasn't it. It was a rag town, for sure. Tents--hundreds of the--of all sizes and descriptions filled the prairie in every direction.

By the light of an almost full moon and a couple of gas lights, he could see the biggest conglomeration of tents and wagons, livestock, dogs and people he'd ever witnessed. It was like a county fair, only bigger, more intense. This was serious business. Noise, the likes of which he'd never heard came from what appeared to be a line of saloon tents, and gambling concerns. Goo Goo Avenue they called it. People shouted to be heard above the din--yee-hahing, squealing, and laughter poured out onto the dusty thoroughfare. Blaring player pianos, all playing different tunes in different keys. And smells? My Aunt Sadie!

Finally moving out of the way of the always-in-a-hurry crowds, Clarence stepped over beside a darkened tent. The occupants had either gone to bed or were out. He sat down on a nail keg beside the tent, to absorb the moment.

He fished around for a pencil to make some notes. He was going to write this down, by George, so he could remember every detail of this "momentous" occasion.

Licking the lead end of his pencil, he opened a small black calendar booklet taken from his vest pocket and reflected over the situation. Here he was--a good enough person--young, fairly decent head on his shoulders--best he could tell, not too terribly out of kilter with the rest of the world. But SOMEHOW, he'd managed--at a price paid in physical pain--to get himself into this this mess! Smack in the middle of a wild assortment of tomfoolery called Goo Goo Avenue, tent town, Lawton, Indian Territory.

and him with an eternal case of dysentery that kept his body drained of all strength--to boot. How utterly ridiculous and horribly absurd.

It was late, but Clarence found an eating establishment--Big John's Saddle Rock Cafe--the hastily painted sign propped against a wagon wheel read. It had a canvas canopy attached to the wagon and stretched out to a couple of tent poles. Under it were a few tables and chairs, a couple of men eating, and a big man in a grimy, white apron

"Yeah, we can serve you," Big John answered, "if you can settle for dumplins."

"What kind?"

"Meat."

"Chicken 'n' dumplings or beef or--?"

"Started out bein' chicken two days ago. Since then I've added a couple rabbits and a squirrel. I keep adding meat--Maggie keeps adding dumplins, and we both keep the fire goin'."

"I'll have a dish of it, sir. I'm sure it'll do," Clarence said. "I'm pretty hungry."

They gave him a dish of rice pudding for dessert and he downed four glasses of water.

With his hunger pangs subsiding, Clarence asked Big John where a man might find a decent place to spend the night.

"Wull, they's a Rev. Carpenter got a big tent 'bout six or seven tents west. He keeps a gent with a side arm on guard duty through the night."

Clarence thanked the man and started walking west studying the fact that a guard seemed to be a necessity for a good night's sleep.

Soon after procuring a cot in the Reverend A. B. Carpenter's[15] Christian lodging tent for men, he laid his weary body down. First thing tomorrow, he would analyze this endeavor. It was definitely time for another sit-down-and-think-it-through session. If he was going to do this thing, he needed to do some figuring. What was it going to take to "prove-up" on 160 acres? He really hadn't thought past getting a number in the lottery.

""Tomorrow...tomorrow," he said in resignation, his awareness dwindling. The night noises faded to occasional voices of men calling back and forth across the townsite.

A gun shot pierced the night air.

Followed by two more, the shots seemed to have come from somewhere to the east. He and a few others on cots around him roused up in concern and curiosity. Sitting halfway up, he could hear people outside rushing in the direction from where the shots had come.

A drowsy voice from the other side of the tent said, "Go on back to sleep, gentlemen. Happens all the time. Best thing to do is stay in bed and buy a newspaper tomorrow."

The advice sounded good to Clarence. He laid back down and was soon asleep.

***

Clarence was awakened soon after sunrise. Busy activity had already begun out on Goo Goo Avenue. He didn't really feel like getting up yet. He would love to just lay there awhile longer enjoying the coolness of the morning, and getting a little more of his fifty cents worth out of the cot. But, with all the racket going on, his laying there probably wasn't doing him much good.

"Might as well get up," said a voice two cots over.

Clarence raised up and peered sleepily over at the young man--now struggling to get his boots on--who seemed to be speaking to him.

"No point in layin' there--it just gets worse."

Still not ready to reply, Clarence sat up, stretched long and took inventory of his aches and pains It appeared he'd live, durn it.

"Name's Locke, Buford Locke." said the man thrusting a hand toward Clarence.

"Clarence Pool. Nice to met you." Clarence lied.

"Like to come along with me--find some breakfast?"

"Well, sure, if you don't mind waitin'. I'm not up to full speed, yet."

Dressed and leaving his valise at the Christian tent, Clarence stepped out into the sunshine with Buford.

Finding a food tent offering breakfast food, they sat down and had a steaming cup of coffee in front of each of them in no time. The side flaps of the tent were rolled up allowing a breeze to flow through.

While they ate pancakes and bacon, Clarence removed his calendar booklet from his vest pocket. On a piece of blank note paper in the back of it, he began a list as he would think of something he needed; essential items. Things that he could also use later on while homesteading.

"Whatcha writin', Clarence?"

"I like to keep myself organized and last night it occurred to me that I hadn't thought much past getting a lottery number."

"Makin' a list of whatcha need?"

Clarence nodded. "Yes. Thought I'd go shopping, and look the town over."

"Whatcha got on it so far?"

"So far, I've written: small tent, cot, bucket or some container for water, a coffee pot, some coffee, and a cup-- maybe two cups. Who knows? I might accidentally want to offer you a cup of coffee sometime, Buford."

"How 'bout a bed roll?"

"Well, I will keep my eye out for one, but I don't think it's a necessity."

***

Before noon Clarence happened onto a great deal. He acquired a second-hand tent, a cot and a bed roll for three dollars and fifty cents. A worn and weary looking man had approached him on the street saying he'd lost all his cash in one of the gambling tents and needed some money to get started back home. After a few minutes conversation, they'd struck a deal.

Now Clarence wouldn't have to pay fifty cents a night to sleep on someone else's cot. Nor; however, would he have the added protection of an armed guard. He wondered if his new friend, Buford, would want to share his tent--for safety's sake.

At Simpson's Dry Goods wagon he found a small camping kit that included: two tin plates, two tin cups, and two of every eating utensil. At a food wagon, he bought half a pound of coffee, and some sugar.

"Man shot last night. Got the story here in the Democrat." a paper boy called out.

Clarence paid two cents for a newspaper, and found out what all the shooting was about the night before. Two men, sharing a tent, were held up at gun point . When ordered to put up their hands, one of them took his time about it and said, "I don't know whether I will or not," and was promptly shot. He died later in the day. But, not before he was able to give a statement to the newly appointed District Attorney, Mr. W. C. Stevens.

In the afternoon, Clarence pitched his tent east of the farthest east end of Goo Goo Avenue. He met up with a group who'd just arrived from Texas. They heard about the murder of the Beanblossum boy, as well as the other robberies, murders, and shootings. They'd struck upon an idea to form a tight circle with their wagons and tents. Then they could all chip in together and pay a man to stand guard through the night, or take turn about at it.

Still looking for a coffee pot, Clarence happened to run into Buford .

"Didja find everything on your list ?"

"Everything but the coffee pot. Did you hear about the killing last night?"

"Sure did. Ain't tat awful!"

"Unbelievable in this day and time. This place has turned out to be a whole lot wilder than I ever expected." Clarence continued, "The man I bought my tent from had just lost his last cent in one of the gambling tents. Said he just needed some cash to get started home. He'd sold his wagon and one of his horses. He was going to ride the other one."

"Now that's a cryin' dam shame. But the fool shouldn'a been in a joint like that in the first place."

"You're right, of course, but some folks don't under-stand that. Say, I was wondering if you'd be interested in sharing my tent with me for the time being?"

"Could be. Where'd you set up?"

"I'm going there now. Come along with me, and see."

Buford agreed to pay their tent's portion of the

watchman's pay, and buy a coffee pot in lieu of his "rent" for half of Clarence's tent. He had his own bedroll and could sleep on the ground.

Robberies, shootings, and schemes of all kinds were being perpetrated at all hours. A person could just as easily be relieved of his funds in the day as at night.

Some robbers used guns. Others used trickery and meanness. There were several ruses for getting a trusting man to show his money. In a soon to be familiar scenario one man would approach another; ask if he had change for a five or a ten. When the helpful person went for his money, the thief snatched billfold–money and all–and disappear-ed into the middle of the crowd.

Thankfully, most people with whom Clarence came in contact were decent people. The kind you'd like to sit down to supper with–get to know better–when things settled down.

✳✳✳

THE SUNDAY MORNING before the opening, Clarence happened to be walking down Goo Goo Avenue. Hearing the sound of hymn singing reminded him that his Mother would be wishing he was in church. Locating the source of the music, he found a few souls gathered having church. He decided to go in. He'd nothing better to do, at the moment. He took a seat at the back of the tent, on one of the benches made of 2"X 12's" held up by kegs placed strategically under it.

The church service was being held in a tent that just a few hours before, during evening and night time hours, had been used as a saloon. This was fine with Clarence. Everybody here was learning to make-do with what was available. Why not a church, as well. No doubt the new town would need plenty of churches.

The preacher stood on a wooden platform raised up about six inches off the dirt floor. Three sides of the tent were down, with the one in the back left open as an entrance.

"And now, for those of you who have your Bibles with you this morning, our scripture comes from Psalms 105, verses 8 through 11." The preacher paused a moment while the lady in the congregation with a Bible, found the scripture.

It was in the midst of the scripture reading that a slight bumping and shifting of the flexible tarp wall behind him began to distract the congregation. A shuffling sound made it seem as if someone or something was behind the tent.

The scripture having been read, the minister launched into a dramatic delivery of today's sermon.

At first there were the barely audible groans–just a few. These caused a matronly woman with a permanently pinched brow to clear her throat, adjust her position and focus her attention once again on the preacher.

At length, it became evident that some poor soul who'd partaken of the "old demon alcohol" in this tent last night, had either passed out between the two tents; or passed out in this tent and rolled out under the tent wall. At any rate, it seemed that somehow now, during the minister's sermon he'd started returning to life.

It appeared that the person behind the tent was attempting to stand up. First struggling to his knees, and after pausing there for a few moments, slowly pushed himself up until he stood–wobbling. Failing to remain erect, his body fell back against the side of the tent and slid to the ground, making an impression on the interior wall of the tent. Giving an audible curse, he slid slowly down into a heap, where he remained silent, unmoving–seeming to return to sleep.

Just when the congregation had forgotten him and was listening to the good pastor again, there came the first small pitiful sounds of a wretched soul whose stomach is refusing to contain it's "morning after" contents. There were two small, fairly discreet dry heaves–ones that *could* have been overlooked–had not the third one been the *mother* of all retches. It started slowly, down deep in his gut, growling as it wrenched upward through his vital organs. The sound that accompanied this deeply moving experience was that involuntary wavering low note that seems to lock in and go on and on and on, until the person turns white from the strain.

The tumultuous sound rebounded off the tents,

through the mesquite tree, under the wagons, all over that end of tent town. It lasted so long between the initial heave and the inhale that the congregation, forgetting the sermon, remained fixed for an eternity of seconds, waiting for the next breath to be taken.

Horses curiously pricked-up their ears, dogs–accustomed to finding "leftovers" after noises of this kind–came running and sniffing, as if the dinner bell had rung. One, especially large, yella-brown hound, took a short cut down the center isle and crawled out under the side of the tent.

When the dog fight erupted behind the preacher, he quit. He saw absolutely no use in trying to continue–this morning.

IN THE AFTERNOON OF that same Sunday, Clarence and Buford happened to be near the center of tent town when they heard excited talk about doing something about the gamblers. They watched in curiosity as a large group of men formed around a man who was speaking.

A tall, thick-chested man with a confident air was up on a whiskey barrel addressing the crowd.

"This town is goin' to hell-in-a-handbasket if we--you and I--don't do something to stop it. It's bad here folks! Don't try to kid yourselves. It is serious. These gamblers and saloons have got a racket going. They're like a bed of rattlesnakes right here amongst a flock of sheep. And I'll tell you somethin' else, men, I'm not too sure but what the marshals aren't in cahoots with 'em."

He paused for a dramatic silence. "

"Is this what we want our new town to be like?"

A few scattered "no s." answered him.

"How many of you have been robbed, or know of someone else who has been, by these gambling establishments?"

There were several nods and murmurings of agreement.

"How many of you have had money taken right out of your hand? Last night, a sixty-five year old gentleman of my acquaintance, had his entire bank roll snatched from him. Now, this man, who would have made a fine neighbor, must turn around and go back home. He has no money left to begin working a homestead. Is this the kind of place we want to raise our children?"

"No-o." Many answered in unison. He had 'em now.

"I tell you, men, WE must stop them! WE owe it to this town–our town–to stop them. If there is still a God-fearin bone in your body, follow me. Follow me, NOW, and let's put them out of business; put them OUT of our town."

They were on their way!

Clarence and Buford remained in viewing distance but there was no way Clarence would join a mob.

Whipped into a righteous frenzy by the speaker, they were picking up steam and numbers along the way. The group started with the biggest tent, a round affair with a tall center pole, made on the style of a one-ring circus tent. The numbers of the group increased as they began cutting the ropes, causing the tent to collapse. They broke up the equipment with axes, sledge hammers, and fists, chopping at the roulette wheels, breaking everything they found. When the tent fell, it trapped one of the dealers–the one on whom the leader's anger was centered. The one–it was said--who took the old man's money". The leader of the mob and others jumped him.

Intent upon sending a strong message that cheating and stealing were not going to be tolerated in "our" town, they became caught up in the leader's anger.

"We're going to **hang** the son-uv-a-b-----!"

That's where they made their big mistake. Murder was a capital offense, and there was a United States Marshal and six deputy marshals placed here on the grounds by order of the President of the United States to enforce federal law.

Marshal Fossett had been alerted to the problem and rode into the mob. Drawing his gun, he took the gambler into custody.

Walking the man straight to the courthouse square--a distance of about three city blocks--he hurriedly told Heck Thomas and Bill Tilghman to make arrangements for the prisoner to be taken out to Fort Sill and put in the guardhouse.

"See if you can slip him into Johnny Blumenthal's wagon. And ask Johnny to drive him out there. But, you men get all the other deputies rounded up. None of you leave the grounds. This thing isn't over, I'm pretty sure about that. I'll be needing you and the rest of the men with me here. Alert all deputies to the situation. Get 'em mounted and ready here on the square.

Lawton was in law limbo at this point. Until this mass of tents and people became a town--officially--there could be no civil law established, except as was authorized by U.S. statutes. The task of keeping the peace in the interim had been placed in the hands of the U.S. Marshal and his deputies.

There being no federal law against gambling, the marshals couldn't arrest on that charge. Under these circumstances, the accumulation of a crowd of this size was a paradise for gamblers, card-sharks, pickpockets and confidence men. Most of them knew it was only a matter of time till the town elected a mayor, city councilmen who could enact city ordinances. The saloons, gambling joints, pleasure palaces, charlatans, scam artists, were getting by with all the underhanded techniques and scams they could--working fast while Lawton was still in an unorganized state.

Some citizens had taken the matter to the commanding officer at Fort Sill. The C.O. told them that he had no authority over the marshals; in fact the army was at their disposal, assisting them in maintaining order.

A group of preachers felt compelled to lodge a complaint against the gamblers directly with Marshal Fossett. He told them, quite honestly--

"Gentlemen, I am sworn to the faithful discharge of my duty and cannot arrest anyone unless they violate federal law. There is no federal law against gambling. So, as I see it, I need evidence of violation of a federal law before I can make an arrest.

Clarence and Buford watched from the west as the six deputy marshals, mounted and pulled up in a semi-circle, watching the mob from the courthouse square.

Just as Marshal Fossett had predicted, the mob formed again. On Goo Goo Avenue, south of the courthouse square, three or four hundred men milled around. The zealot leader was preaching again.

"They'd better not mess with the likes of Heck Thomas," Buford whispered. "Over in eastern Oklahoma , where I come from and these marshals are well known over there. They're cool-headed in a crisis. If forced into it, they shoot to kill."

"It's not right! We can not allow these atrocities to continue!" the dark-haired man told the crowd. "I say we storm the marshals and hang that scoundrel that's hid out behind Marshal Fossett's skirts! It looks like our faint-hearted law men can not or WILL NOT do anything to stop them from robbing us blind."

The mob seemed to be growing angrier by the minute. Perhaps the marshals were on the take; now that they thought about it.

At a signal from Fossett the deputies slowly cleared the way to their side arms and rifles. Hands poised, they were ready. Marshal Fossett walked three steps toward the mob of men and drew a line on the ground. He faced the mob.

"Gentlemen," Fossett began in a stern but composed voice, "we do not want any trouble with you. We have a job we are sworn to do and we are going to do it. We are here by special order of the President of the United States to keep the peace here. We are sworn to uphold federal law. What YOU," he pointed first to the leader then indicated the rest of the men, "are proposing to do, is AGAINST that law. I am giving you fair warning that ANY man..." he paused "ANY man crossing this line will be shot."

He'd stated his case clearly and in simple terms.

The hot-tempered leader began walking closer to face down the marshal. He stopped and turned. The men were no longer behind him.

"I'll tell you what," he said to his straggling men, "I'm from Texas. Just you men from Texas, come on. We'll show these pantywaists how we clean up a town down there. Follow me. Follow me, now, men. We've got a job to do. You know we can do it. There's just seven of 'em."

But, the men–even the Texans–didn't move.

Someone back in the crowd put his finger on the problem when he said, "Then what?"

That started some mumblings of agreement, as the men began to think for themselves again. Indeed, what would they do, then? Hang the marshals, too?

The mob began to dissolve. Fossett stepped out to have a word with the leader.

"What is the matter with you, sir? What were you thinking of?" he asked in disbelief. "Why would you want to force a showdown?"

"You'd have forced us to empty our guns into that crowd and you would have been the first one shot. My men are experienced with trouble. They've shot it out with the craziest of outlaws and they would not have hesitated--they don't know HOW to hesitate in a situation like this.

"One man's life isn't worth *that*." the man spat out, snapping his fingers in a gesture as if snuffing out a candle. Marshal Fossett stared at him uncomprehending, repulsed by the man's arrogance.

Seeing the insolent look on the man's face, Fossett finally seemed to understand the man's motives.

"Glory and limelight. That's the deal, isn't it?"

"Am I free to go or am I under arrest?" the man asked.

Fossett stared unblinkingly at the man for a long moment. He'd give anything to have 'just cause' for arresting this piece of horse manure.

"Yeah, go! Get out of my sight." Fossett answered, controlling the urge to pistol whip the of the misbegotten man right then and there.

Chapter 14
August 6, 1901

At 9:00 a.m. the town would be declared officially open. The auctioning of town lots, both business and residential, would begin at the same time the new U. S. Land Office open its doors for homestead filings.

During the last moments before the fiery ball of sun peeked over the horizon, silence lingered over the grounds. Not even the hum of a single mosquito marred the quiet. In the relative coolness that remained all was peaceful around the townsite.

The calm before the storm.

It started with the twittering of birds announcing "gettin-up-time." The rising of the sun brought with it the noisy activity of last minute preparations for the big day. Hammering, sawing, creaking wagons rolling past, men communicating in hurried sentences and occasional shouts began the noises for the day.

"Take your boys over and add another line of two b'fours to that top section of bleachers. Way it is now somebody could fall."

"Where we gonna get the two b'fours?"

"They delivered 200 of 'em over there yesterday afternoon, James!"

"Wull, they gone now. Pilfered I reckon..."

"Aw, sh..... Wull, I'll get some more delivered. You an your boys be ready. The two b'fours'll be there in 15 minutes."

Smells of bacon and coffee began to fill the air.

Those who'd arrived late the evening before or during the night and slept in their wagons, hacks, or buggy seats began rousing, too. Those who'd spent the night in lodging tents went through their daily wake-up ritual--stretch, scratch, check pockets, shake out boots. Never knew what little prairie critter might find comfort in your boots. Rattlesnakes were having a real good season this year.

Men who would work in the newly opened land office rushed to find places selling breakfast food and coffee. They ate hurriedly. Though the decrees, declarations, and business weren't to begin until nine, much needed doing before then. They were a good-natured, capable group of men who could easily handle the 125 homesteaders who would file their homestead entries, as well as those who came in to file and pay for a town lot.

Copies of the "town planners' map" appeared here and there. Some business types were privileged to have their own copy. Others would need to refer to the large one tacked to the outside of the land office. It would be used to assist in designation and location of town lots. The streets had been given temporary names by those who'd laid out the map. To simplify matters, they numbered the streets going north and south, and assigned alphabet letters to "avenues" going east and west. According to the map, the auctioneer's stand was located at the intersection of 4th and B, the land office at 3rd and D, the courthouse square took in a mostly empty city block between C and D and 5th and 6th. Naughty Goo Goo Avenue wasn't recognized as such. It had been given the very ordinary *nom de plume*, of "F" Avenue. Six months ago the planners hadn't any way of knowing how notorious that one mile stretch between 1st and 11th Street would become.

Until this morning people had only been allowed to cross over the townsite to get to the other side. They couldn't stop or linger in any one place too long before one of the blue-clad soldiers from Fort Sill would be on his way over to ask the offender to move along. Today anyone who could stand the heat would be allowed to congregate on there.

The stand for the auctioneer was the seven-foot-tall structure with a canvas shade on top. The stand was draped with red, white, and blue bunting and would be accessed by a short ladder on its north side. Hastily constructed bleachers in front of the stand would hold only about 500 people.

The new land office stood alone the only building on the site. Nothing but dust and prairie around it. It was ready for business.. Register H. D. McKnight and Receiver James. D. Maguire had arrived on Monday. The chief clerk was J. R. Wallace. Other clerks were busy sorting out the stacks and stacks of forms and organizing the building into what they believed would be the most efficient arrangement.

The square for the courthouse had been designated two weeks prior. The marshals had used it as a center for their peace-keeping business. A full square block near the center of the townsite it was bordered by C & D avenues on the north and south, and by 5th & 6th streets on the east and west.

This morning the courthouse square held only a tent and a wagon. The wagon was on the southeast corner of the square to be used as a jail by the marshals and the sheriff. As arrests were made during the day the suspects would be chained to the wheels of the wagon until a hearing could take place.

The tent was set up to serve as a temporary courthouse for the new county of Comanche. It held the offices of temporary judge, Warren H. Brown, a court clerk, W. G. Gorman, County Sheriff Painter, County Attorney, W. C. Stevens, a Justice-of-the-Peace, and some county commissioners. These officials had been appointed by the territorial governor until such time as ones could be elected by the citizens.

Many folks arrived early, hoping to secure good seats within hearing distance of the auctioneer's stand. The wise had figured out how they were going to quench their thirst through the scorching heat of the day. If a person didn't want to pay a nickel each time he wanted a drink of water he needed to have an alternate plan. Canteens had been on sale at Simpson's Bargain wagon earlier in the week. They were sold out now. Mr. Simpson's brother in law--the man who claimed to have visited personally with President McKinley and given advance information on the specific date of the opening–had sent for more but they hadn't arrived.

An encampment of Comanche people was located mid way between Fort Sill and Lawton and to the west. Drums and singing could be heard in the evenings. They liked to gamble as well. A little later in the morning a few Comanche women and children ventured onto the townsite from that camp. They milled around the open townsite while it was still cool. Some spread out blankets to sit on. They'd heard this would be a big celebration. They weren't quite sure what to expect, but they knew it would be ridiculous. Whatever these white folks did usually was. Trying to be serious about it, they told each other things like:

"Might be goodt. Huuh!

"These white men couldt probly start a town goodt."

A pause, and then, "She-e-e-eh."

Then, they would laugh and laugh.

The sun climbed a little higher in the sky. Activity as well as the temperature picked up. The auctioneer, a Colonel Oben, arrived on the grounds. He was a hefty sort but he climbed the ladder to his perch on the stand with surprising ease. A crowd gathered around the stand. Not nearly everyone who wanted to was able to get within hearing distance. The day quickly became warmer the crowd tighter.

At nine o'clock the town was declared open and the

auctioneer introduced. The sweat already beading up and running down his face foretold the kind of day it would be. Removing his hat he wiped his balding head with a handkerchief. He stepped to the front of the stand and greeted the crowd in a big, booming voice.

"Greetings, citizens of Lawton. Welcome to your town. Those of you who do not intend to buy town lots please stand back. Let the bidders and the buyers move in closer. We want the men with the money down here in front. If you are interested in buying and have not yet registered as a bidder here at the stand, please do so now. You will be given a red bidder's ribbon and we will do all we can to assist you in obtaining a position closer to this stand."

Silent for a few moments he allowed the crowd time to do some shuffling and make adjustments, allowing those with bright red BIDDER ribbons pinned to their lapel to move closer. The auctioneer began his spiel. Bidding started right on time with the first lot up for sale.

Curious onlookers, not interested in buying or bidding yammered on while designated bidders–many of whom had been assigned by their employer to purchase a particular lot–strained to hear every word. Their faces grimaced in agitation. At twenty minutes after nine the first lot sold for $450. Business lots today would go for as little as $75 and as much as $4,555 That price was for the lot across from the new land office which was located on the northwest corner lot at 3rd and D.

The moment the auctioneer's gavel slammed down and the word "SOLD" echoed across the site, a buyer was escorted quickly through the crowd by soldiers to the land office where he was required to put down a $25 deposit. From this point he had thirty minutes to bring in the rest of the money, in cash. If more than that amount of time elapsed the deposit was forfeited and the lot went back on the list as one still to be sold.

Thirty minutes was just barely enough time to make a quick loan at one of the five tent banks that now sat on the sidelines around the perimeter of the town, or to run to the place where one's cash was hidden. Many people chose not to carry much of their cash on their person in view of the recent rash of robberies. They'd hidden their cash money away. The hem of a wife's dress, the lining of a man's suit coat, a hole drilled in the underside of a collar on a horse's harness, a false bottom of a trunk or chest, or a discreet cash box affixed somewhere in, on, or under a wagon were all places that money had been known to be stashed.

A new shift of soldiers arrived in wagons from Fort Sill ready for duty. Many more would follow. They would be in charge of making sure the land office was secure against robberies. With all business being transacted in cash money only, there would be a fair amount of cash accumulate. The soldiers would also be assisting with other problems that might arise in the crowds.

Security was tight. U.S. Marshal Fossett and Deputy Marshals Thomas, Tilghman, Madsen, and three others were mounted, armed and visible. They rode in and out among the crowds with side arms strapped to their leg. Much cash would change hands today. Checks were not acceptable currency for the sale. Armed soldiers on foot stood guard around the land office. Mounted soldiers formed a perimeter around them. Inside the land office there was one soldier in each corner with a rifle laying across his lap. Before the day was over, the unpretentious little building would have $42,000 cash come through it's door. No foolish business would be tolerated in Lawton today.

Plans had been made and a detail assigned for a guard of nine soldiers and an officer from Fort Sill to accompany the federal official from the Department of the Interior, whose duty it was to get the money deposited in a place of safety at the close of business on August 6. As soon as the money was counted and verified the troup of armed soldiers would be on their way to Rush Springs. They would return carrying the monthly pay of the Fort Sill soldiers.

During the day incidents arose in which persons mistakenly put up a tent and started business on the wrong lot. The marshals handled problems like this with ease. The offender would have to stop business, take down his tent, and get some help moving his freight and other things. The marshals helped find the correct lot and solicited people to help in the moving.

At the new land office homesteaders who held the precious numbers 1 through 125 would be allowed to file claims for their 160 acres, today. If anyone was not present when their number was called, they would have one more chance at the end of the day. Missing that chance, they were out of the running. The next day lottery number holders 126 through 250 would be permitted to file.

On an inside wall of the land office was a huge map of the whole, three county, Fort Sill/Lawton district. It showed all tracts of land available for homesteading. "X's" already covered the quarter sections of land that had been spoken for by the Indians, as well as those that were set aside for schools, school land, churches or missions that were already in existence. As quarter sections were filed upon, an "X" would be placed on the square representing their claim.

August 6

Today the land was declared open to filing announced at 9 a.m. I went up town with Mr. & Mrs. Hawp in the buggy and heard the first few lots auctioned off. First, for $425, business lot. The least was $75. for to-day. We didn't stay long as it was so warm and such an enormous crowd was gathered about the auctioneers stand that we couldn't get in hearing distance.

***

"We are ready for the number one draw, Mr. James N. Woods." the head clerk, J. R. Wallace, announced from the east door of the land office building.

"Here." Mr. Woods's hand shot into the air holding his notification card aloft.

Registration of Mr. Woods of Weatherford, O. T. began. Mattie Beal and her brother Frank waited patiently. She would be second and Mr. Winfield S. Laws of Langston, O. T. who waited patiently among the crowd would be third. Their names had been the first three drawn from the box for the Fort Sill-Lawton District in El Reno last week.

All three had been ready and waiting along with the rest of the jovial crowd at the land office door when it opened.

After a couple of minutes Miss Beal was invited to come in and then Mr. Laws. There were enough clerks to work with all three at the same time but the order of the numbers was to be respected in the entry process.

As Mattie and Frank stepped through the door they heard one of the clerk's voices raised in irritation.

"No, sir, Mr. Woods, I am sorry but you cannot do that," the head clerk said more loudly than he'd said it the first couple of times.

Mattie had thought this would be an enjoyable process. With the newspapers waiting to talk to her at every turn, the whole adventure had become such a lark. What could possibly be going awry? Eyes turned in the direction of the raised voices.

Becoming slightly perturbed, the dignified looking Mr. Woods repeated his claim.

"And I repeat, sir, that I can. May I speak with the superior official in charge?"

Silence and hurried huddles were engaged in by the officials and the clerks behind the counter.

Frank had already told their clerk that they would take one of the quarter sections adjoining the south side of the townsite. It all depended on Mr. Woods's selection. Whichever one he took Mattie would take the other one. It was only fair, Mr. Woods was number one, she was number two.

Mr. Woods was becoming more and more frustrated with the seeming lack of decisiveness and hesitation in registering his claim. Several bankers were waiting to talk to him. He had things to do, plans to make. He stepped away from the counter and made his statement again--more loudly. Everyone in the room and a few outside could hear.

"For the last time, could someone here make a decision, please? I wish to make my rightful claim of 160 acres in four tracts of forty acres each. These would be the ones lined up along here," he stepped over to the map on the wall and outlined the area with his finger, "directly south of F Avenue. And, yes it does give me the full one mile frontage on the south side of Goo Goo or 'F' Avenue--whatever one you want to call it." He looked in Mattie's direction. "Miss Beal, I mean no malice toward you, I am simply making what I believe to be the smartest monetary decision. I would expect no less from anyone else in my position."

"What's that?"

"What's he saying?"

The crowd at the door pressed forward to hear.

"Mr. Woods is demanding his 160 acres in a strip instead of a square. He wants the whole mile south of Goo Goo." The word was passed back through the immense crowd, and on out through the grounds. It went from one buzz session to the next. It would become the talk of the day, and for several days after.

"Don't believe that's allowed," the clerk helping Mattie stated confidentially leaning slightly toward Mattie and her brother.

"Yes, it is! It can be done," Mr. Woods heard and announced his reply emphatically. "I believe you will find that I am correct if you would choose to read your rules and regulations that govern this lottery."

Woods seemed absolutely certain of his right to claim his property in a strip. The possibility had not occurred to most folks. Everyone turned toward Mr. McKnight, who was helping Mr. Laws.

Mr. McKnight looked at Mr. Maguire, the register.

They both reached for their own copy of the rules and regulations, laid them out on the counter and began scanning through the complex set of directives. After a silence of at least five minutes, Mr. Maguire having found the pertinent sentence said, "Okay, I believe this is it."

To the clerks and Mr. McKnight, he said, "Gentlemen, if you will be so kind as to listen I'll read it to you– –"

"...an entrant shall be allowed to select up to four contiguous quarter quarters.."

"But isn't that in reference to farm and homestead land? Not land, I believe, that will most likely be used for commercial and business use? I can't believe that the planning committee meant for one man to make a king's ransom here." McKnight took issue with Maguire's finding.

"Based on my interpretation of this sentence, I must find in favor of Mr. Wood's claim–his being 'an entrant'. Now we can send a wire to Washington for clarification..." Maguire offered amicably.

"No, not the first rattle out of the box. We don't want them thinking we can't decide the first thing for ourselves. We'll go with your interpretation."

Upon hearing this, Mattie and Frank looked at each other and their hearts sank.

"Now, what do we do?" Mattie whispered.

***

AS THE DAY PROGRESSED, the grounds began to hint at the shape of things to come. A couple of dry goods stores moved tents in, wagons selling hardware were rolled into their newly purchased business lots, a small bank building already sitting on wheels was rolled into place. A couple of eating establishments sprang up and before too long, the vacant townsite that had been a mere piece of prairie seemed to disappear into what would be streets and avenues and buildings. The perimeter of the town site became a little less packed with tent and wagon businesses.

A Mr. English of the City National Bank had placed an order a couple of weeks ago for the construction of what was being called at the time, a box-house. In addition it should have a facade front and be placed on a base of wheels. His plan was to immediately roll their business onto it's lot just as soon as the purchase was made on August 6. The clerks and loan officers should have very little interruption in their conducting of business. They'd built a counter across the middle of the building using new, unfinished boards. Chicken wire nailed to a two by four frame served as the grate separating the customers and tellers.

It was Mr. English who at the same time asked for a small house to be constructed–ready to be to be moved onto the residential lot when it was purchased for his family.

SMALL, IMPROMPTU businesses sprouted into existence on the grounds in response to the needs of the day and the ingenuity of the people.

Fried chicken was being peddled by one man and his son. The man had set his wife and mother to frying all the chicken they could locate during the morning hours. He and his son cleaned out a couple of water buckets and lined them with their nicest tea towels. They went in among the crowds of people selling fried chicken--two pieces for a nickel.

Drinking water stands consisting of a crate, a bucket of water and a dipper were everywhere. The heat, bearing down from the savage sun, created an equally savage thirst.

Jeb Metheisson who'd arrived in the morning of the day before noticed that by noon he'd already spent a quarter on water--at a nickel a dipper--and the water was warm. If this kept up, he would have spent two dollars and fifty cents on water within the next five days! An embryo of an idea formed in his mind. When he saw a four-mule team stop in front of a tent grocery he watched as the driver pulled the tarp down off his cargo in the boarded wagon. Ice!

How nice! Now Jeb's idea became a mission.

Today, he was in business, offering people a welcome product--Ice Cold Lemonade. All a person could drink for ten cents! It was a superb idea. People were anxious for anything wet and cool. He'd netted twenty-one dollars by noon.

Late in the day however Jeb grew bored standing in the same place. Restless and less attentive to his business he allowed himself to become engrossed in a conversation, and turned his back on his lemonade tub.

After awhile, he became aware of people walking past, kinda staring at him and his lemonade tub behind him. Some were grinning. Then it occurred to him that none of these people were buying his lemonade. In fact, he hadn't had any customers in fifteen--twenty minutes.

A man approached him holding out a dime and saying, "I'd like to pay for the drink he just got." Jeb whirled around to find someone's wayward mule leisurely sucking up the lemonade from his tub. It was nearly all gone. What wasn't gone had mule slobber in it.

That was the end of Jeb's Lemonade stand.

He simply dissolved his business on the spot. Sold his entire real investment: one wash tub, two tin dippers, one small table, and three yards of used red, white, and blue bunting for five dollars. All together he'd made the tidy little sum of twenty-six dollars. After counting his profit, Jeb Methiesson pocketed his money and strolled over to the lot sale, whistling all the way.[16.]

The business of "locating" had been spurred by the needs of people who came by rail. And thousands, like Clarence Pool and Otto Elling would be doing that. If these people had a lottery number, they more than likely wanted to examine the land so as to make a more informed choice. To do that, the person needed some form of transportation. Locators provided that service. Some of them knew the land and could give valuable advice. Others merely drove lottery number holders around the country assisting them in locating the piles of marked rocks left by land surveyors. Locators were more than happy to offer advice in the selection of land but most knew less than their customers about what constituted good farm land. What they did have was a general knowledge of north, south, east, and west, a team, a rig, and time–the time to spend driving people around–for profit.

MINNIE JOHNSON AND THE Hawps returned to their camp on Squaw Creek. They'd watched the beginning of the auction and stayed a couple of hours, but the sun was having no mercy today. It wasn't worth the discomfort caused by the heat and the oppressive squeeze of the crowd, just to witness any more of this auspicious occasion. Since Mr. Hawp had not received notification informing him of his lottery number, it was more than the Hawps cared to put themselves through, as well. In fact, the Hawps had been making statements that sounded to Minnie like they were reconsidering trying to live down here, especially with the heat the way it had been over the last few weeks. It had been a big climate change for them!

Minnie felt the same about staying to witness the event. Even if she'd had the opportunity to stay on at the townsite and watch it all, she didn't think she would have enjoyed it. The searing heat made her feel sick, and there were no trees or other shade to be found. A couple of trashy, old mesquite trees, maybe.

Mr. and Mrs. Hawp lay on their cots under a cottonwood tree helping Minnie "hold down camp" while most of the others were scattered all over Lawton and Fort Sill. The place they'd found to camp was at the west edge of tent town, a pretty good place along the creek. They'd gone ahead and put up their tents since they expected to be around for a few more days.

***

MATTIE BEAL AND her brother Frank, still at the land office, stood staring in bewilderment at the surprising turn of events.

"Who'd've thought anybody would pull a shenanigan like that?" Minnie said.

"Well, the Mr. Maguire has ruled it legal–so it's legal. Nothin' to be gained by pouring over it. What's your second choice?" Frank asked leaping over their first hurdle and setting his sights on the next.

"Well, I've no idea. Let's take another look at the map." They crossed the room together, clerks though interested, cleared a path for them. The land immediately to the west, north and east of the townsite was not available for reasons decided by the planning committee.

After a few minutes, Mattie said with a start--she'd just had a thought-- "Why don't we take a strip, too? The four quarter-quarters, south of the ones Mr. Woods is taking? What do you think?"

"Looks okay to me," Frank said slowly, after a little thought. "Should still be valuable land."

Their clerk leaned over the counter and said, "You folks still may have the better deal. Some say that strip Mr. Woods took has some very low ground. It may be prone to flooding–if it ever rains."

Mr. Laws, third place, was now able to proceed with his selection. He would select the quarter section to the northwest of the townsite. It's southeast corner would touch the northwest corner of the residential section.

A clerk stepped to the door and called for those with numbers four, five and six to come forward.

A Four Township Grid

One Township=Twelve Square Miles

[<<< 1/4 mile >>>]

A "typical" 160 acre claim 1/4 mile square SW Quarter of Section 29 T2n, R12w

North Half of Section 31 T2n, R11w

Lawton Town Site

Claim #1 James "Hog" Woods 40 acres each quarter of a quarter section 160 Acres

Mattie Beal's Claim Claim #2 160 Acres

aahgraphics

[<<< ——— one mile ·········· >>>]

Elling Family Photo

Chapter 15
SUPPLY and DEMAND

<u>August 7</u>
The men, part of them have gone to Ft. Sill, the rest up town.
After dinner we all partook of watermelon with Schrandt and
saved the seeds for Jim to plant on his farm. He drew No. 632,
a valuable number.

Jim had great news! He'd been notified of his lottery
number. Jim Reid and Sam Joice returned from Anadarko
a couple of days ago. Along with the Elmores they were
looking at the land near the Washita River, but the two
men returned for opening day here at Lawton. His day for
filing would be Monday, August 12--less than a week
away. The Nebraska group was together again.

Arnold went to the edge of their camp and scraped the
remains of his breakfast out of the bowl onto the dry,
sunburnt weeds. He'd eaten most of his serving of rice
with sugar, butter, and raisins.

"Arnold, you going with me this morning, son?" It was Papa asking. He liked to have his day outlined in advance.

"Where you going?"

"Thought I'd go check for our mail at Fort Sill. You know your sister is expecting a letter."

Minnie's face flushed. Why did Papa always have to make light of her business for everyone else's entertainment? Well, two could play this game.

"Now, Papa, don't forget, you're still looking for that little post card from El Reno, too. Remember, the one that's 'lost' in the mail?"

Everyone had a good chuckle, enjoying the "cut" Oliver had sustained in his currently most vulnerable spot.

Minnie was stunned by her own words. Oh, for Heaven's sake. Had that come out of her mouth? She'd *thought* smart-alecky retorts to Papa before, but this was the first one that'd actually escaped her mouth. The heat must be getting to her. She covered her open mouth with her hand and her eyes--open wide--met her father's.

Oliver had sometimes made two trips a day to the post office in anticipation of that wayward postcard from El Reno. The one that would--he had no doubt--inform him that he was in the lottery line-up. Jim Reid's success was making the fact that Papa had received no notification harder to swallow. Minnie could tell it was hurting him. He deserved a number, by jove!

After a few minutes Minnie went over to Papa, seated at their small, fold-up table–the one he'd fashioned from pine wood, hinges, and some screws.

"Touche', Papa?"she said apologetically putting her hand on his shoulder.

"Unh-unh, Minnie-girl, don't come over here trying to make up with me. You hurt my feelings!" He winked at her though--letting her know she was forgiven.

"Are you going uptown this morning?" Arnold asked Jim. "I'd like to see some more of the auction."

"Don't you mean ACTION? As in–down along Goo Goo Avenue," Jim teased. Everyone got a kick out of teasing Arnold about the "shows" on Goo Goo.

It was Arnold's turn to be embarrassed now. He took it all with a grin. He knew it was all in fun.

"Yes, sir that's where I'm headed, Arnold. You comin' with me?" Jim reached over and placed an arm around Arnold's neck in a fatherly sort of head-lock–that grip that men not being prone to hugging had of showing affection for each other.

"Well, aren't we all in a merry mood this morning," Mrs. Hawp said sarcastically as she emerged from the tent. She wasn't in a good mood.

"You people would wake the dead. Didn't the mosquitoes keep anyone else awake last night? Dratted little hummers! I'll probably catch malaria or something." These were her second, third and fourth complaints of the day. In the span of two minutes Myrtle's whining and complaining effectively put a damper on any joviality that may have made the mistake of remaining in the camp.

"All aboard that's goin' with me," Jim Reid said heading over to his wagon and team--Sam already having got them up and harnessed. The campers evacuated the camp for their various destinations leaving the Hawps and Minnie alone in the camp.

Back in El Reno, after the tenth day of drawing, it became apparent that all the land that was worth anything, by now, had probably been selected. Interest in the drawing had waned. The town could now be able to return to it's normal routines. The tents and booths came down and soon there remained in the town only a few stragglers of what had been a half million homeseekers. They would have a big mess to clean up, but most of the residents had benefited in some way financially.[18]

***

THE CAMPERS returned to their camp on Squaw Creek for their noon meal. Minnie could tell without asking Papa that he'd once again been disappointed.

"Don't you worry, Arnold," she heard him say to her brother. "Your old man might have an ace up his sleeve yet." Minnie searched her father's face for a clue to what that meant but found none.

Mr. Schrandt, who'd gone with Papa, went around to

Street Scene, Lawton, Oklahoma Territory, August 10, 1901; Bank and in the tent to the far left the First National Bank.

Courtesy of Archives & Manuscripts Division of Oklahoma Historical Society

Four days after the opening. Note : U. S. Land Office, City National
Also note, young boys sitting on crates selling water and another one
leaning on a water barrel probably doing the same thing.

the back of the wagon and brought out a large, green striped watermelon.

"I brought dessert," he called out carefully placing it beside the trunk of the tree that shaded their camp. His announcement was met with an assortment of pleasant remarks. This would be a rare treat.

"Minnie, we better hurry and serve up the beans and cornbread so these gents can get on to eatin' their watermelon," Mrs. Hawp said, as if she had no interest whatsoever in it. Her humor had improved--slightly.

"Come on over, gentlemen, and get started," Minnie announced, shooing away the flies from the food. "The cornbread is here under the checkered dish towel, the beans are in the pot. There is onion in this bowl here and here's the bowls and spoons. Buffet style today."

After having invited the men she moved quickly out of the way. Men were served first in group meals of this sort. Children were next, and finally the ladies fixed their plates.

Mr. Schrandt cut the watermelon after they'd finished their meal. It was exquisite! Its sweet juice flooded their tastebuds. Minnie had eaten some years ago, but had forgotten how sweet and delicious it was. The juice ran down their chins and dripped on the ground. They spewed the slippery seeds at each other. Earnie even made a couple of "points" landing some seeds on Myrtle. His belly bounced in silent mirth and he wiped away the grin with his sleep when she fanned away what she thought were flies. Schrandt said they had to eat it all, once cut, because there was no place to keep it from spoiling. Everyone ate till they were so full they were uncomfortable. Most of them lay down for a quick siesta to allow their stomachs time to do something with all that watermelon.

***

DEPUTY MARSHAL Heck Thomas strolled up to the tent on the courthouse square to confer with Marshal Fossett and Deputy Marshal Chris Madsen. There had been a strange occurrence being reported around town. This was the third day in a row Heck had heard about it. It seemed to be happening all over town--not confined to any one particular area. "

"Another fellah came in this morning, Tilghman said, "reported the same type of deal."

"What do you make of it, Fossett?" Heck asked in a too serious tone.

"Hell, I don't know. Kinda puzzlin, ain't it?" Fossett replied, wanting to slap that look of sincerity off his face. He knew just as well as he was standing there that he was fixing to have to listen to the razzing of Heck, Chris and Bill about this "laundry phantom." They would manage to work it into a big deal--for laughs. They'd say how the U.S. Marshal's office really ought to be out doing a little more serious detective work on the problem. The kind that would make the likes of the Pinkertons proud.

"Guess all we can do is keep our eyes peeled 'till we catch the culprit," Fossett added.

"We've come a long way together, men," Chris Madsen said in mock sentiment; as if delivering lines from a stage. "It does my heart proud to know that together we can rid this town of the dastardly scum-sucking thief who's perpetrating this crime."

"Good grief, Madsen," Fossett said. "You, too? Tilghman, tell me you're not going to be pestering over this."

The Three Guardsmen,[17] they'd been called: Bill Tilghman, Chris Madsen and Heck Thomas. The three of them worked well together, had looked into the face of death together on numerous occasions. They'd been appointed to work as a team on cases for Judge Parker, the hanging judge of Ft. Smith, Arkansas. Outlaws hung out in Outlaw territory--the unsettled Indian Lands. He knew they had the tenacity to bringin the most difficult ones. One of their most famous quarry had been Bill Doolin and the infamous Doolin Gang.

Whether it was chasing outlaws, bringing in escaped murderers or rapists, or just having supper together, the guardsmen maintained a friendly rapport. They usually kept up joking banter or a running joke of some sort. It helped shake off the pressure. Fossett had great respect for the three of them, but they could sure get on his last nerve, at times.

"Heck, are you ready to eat?" Fossett asked.

"Always."

"Well, how 'bout you and me takin' early dinner?"

"Sounds good to me."

"We'll stay here and take reports on *'el bandito muy mal.'* It'll be a feather in our cap if we catch that scurvy dog. *'The Three Guardsmen'* just like old times." Madsen said, in a greatly overdramatized form.

Fossett and Thomas headed toward the east edge of the townsite, to a place that served up a pretty good smorgasbord and looked fairly clean most of the time.

The joke between *"The Three Guardsmen"* currently had to do with how ludicrously tame their lives had become. The mysterious occurrence to which they were referring today was laundry thievery. An honest-looking young man would appear at the door of a tent in the early morning, about the time men were dressing for the day. He'd ask if anyone had articles of clothing to be laundered. "I can take them now and will deliver them back here this afternoon, about five o'clock." Laundry is then gathered up and given to him, after which neither the young man nor their laundry is seen again.

Not near as many tents as a couple of days ago, Heck noticed as the two walked along together. The little piece of prairie was looking more like a town. The sign on a new business that had just arrived on the grounds this morning caught his eye.

"Looks like that new fella's services'll be needed here." Heck said.

The sign read:

Dunn & Dunn
Furniture Store
and
UNDERTAKING

"Let's stop in and introduce ourselves. I always like to get in good with proprietors whose services I might be needing," Fossett said. He could have a sense of humor too.

***

HANNAH BELL FELT the glow of the early morning light on her face even before she opened her eyes. She lay there, hoping to go back to sleep. Finally, one eye opened and scoped out the grounds around her. She stretched long and gloriously till she could hear her spine popping, still lying beneath the sheet. She sat up on her cot, which was located in the middle of three small post oak trees along the east bend of Squaw Creek, not too far south of the Wigwam Saloon. Her bed roll and the trunk beneath it represented the extent of her worldly possessions.

Hannah's only protection from wandering eyes was two sheets and a quilt clothes-pinned to a wire strung tightly in a triangle between the trees. It could be lowered, but late in the darkness of hot nights she preferred to throw the "curtains" back up over the wires so that she could feel whatever stirring of a breeze there might be. At sunrise however, it was necessary to lower them.

After lowering her curtains, Hannah Bell lay down again upon her cot, belly down, her upper body resting on her elbows. After listening to see if she could hear anyone in the vicinity, she reached inside her pillow slip and pulled out a soiled, white, draw-string pouch.

Hannah pulled several wadded up bills from the bodice of her camisole which doubled as nightwear. She carefully rubbed her fingernails over the wrinkled bills attempting to smooth them back into their original shape. She looked them all over carefully and placed all the ones that looked alike together. She knew that the ones that had two figures in the circle in the corners were worth more than the ones with one. The more she inspected them, the more she learned about them. Now she put them all with the other flattened bills back in the pouch.

Did she have enough yet? Hannah had scarcely any schooling, which explained her inability to read, write, or calculate numbers very well.

Her mother and father had both disappeared by the time she was five years old. An old maid in Emporia had taken the her in, at the suggestion of the pastor of her church. After the new wore off, the child began to get on her nerves. She began beating the girl–for infractions that never made sense to Hannah since they were explained while the woman was either screaming or hitting.

Hannah ran away as soon as she was able to figure out a plan to do so. She had been all of thirteen then.

She carefully stowed the pouch again in the pillow

and, through a parting between her "curtains," looked out at the people. This was her favorite pastime– studying people.

As ladies rode past in wagons or buggies, Hannah carefully analyzed their hats and clothing. She would picture herself in each hat or outfit. It was kind of like shopping through a mail-order catalog.

Studying the ladies' clothing, she found she was able to imagine how a particular style had been put together. Considering the lace-trimmed blouses with leg-o-mutton sleeves that puffed up so perkily, and the high-choker collars, she visualized how some of the effects might be used on her own dresses. Sometimes while sewing on buttons or repairing a seam she examined her own dresses, trying to determine the shapes of the pieces that had been put together in it's construction.

Hats of all shapes, decorated with ribbons, flowers and feathers, were inviting to her as well. Partial to the ones that dipped low over the eyes in front, she also liked simple, flat-brimmed ones made of woven straw. They usually had a ribbon around the crown, with a matching piece made into a bow, with its streamers hanging down the back.

Here comes a fabulous hat, now. Just a little "much" for Rag Town on a weekday, though. Hannah smiled at her own silent commentary. The surrey in which "the hat" was riding came closer, and she was able to see the occupants more clearly. A well-dressed, derby-hatted, banty rooster of a man awkwardly held the reins in his diminutive hands.

"Well, lookee here." Hannah said softly in astonishment. "Would you look at that." She said the words slowly in a monotone, for her own benefit. She recognized the lady with the HAT, and made mental notes of all the details of her clothes, her gentleman, the rig they were in, and the matched set of sorrels who pulled the rig slowly past.

"Hannah!" the voice shattered Hannah's reflection. "Han-nah Bell!"

It was Doralee, her well-meaning, self-appointed "big sister," who'd taken Hannah under her wing from the time of her arrival in Dodge City. A "working girl," she was teaching Hannah the tricks of the trade–how to have a good time, dance with the men, get 'em drunk enough so they "give" up their big bills.

Choosing not to answer the summons–she knew Doralee would be there soon enough–Hannah began pulling the combs and pins from her hair and brushing it down over her face. Doralee stuck her head in through an opening between the hanging sheets and said cheerfully,

"Hey, you ready for a shower? Don't wanta wait till the line's too long."

"Sure," Hannah said from underneath her hair.

A daily shower was a luxury here, but one they allowed themselves. Back in Dodge City, it had been long, warm, soothing baths. And soon–she hoped–there would be long, warm baths here too. For now, a shower and a shampoo was what she wanted more than anything else. Grabbing her towel, they walked down Goo Goo, toward Mr. Schomperrt's shower business.

"You'll never guess who I saw go past in a floozy little surrey this morning?" Hannah talked as they walked.

"Who?"

"Blanche."

"Blanche, who?"

"From Dodge."

"Ol' Bowlegged Blanche?"

"That's the one."

"Yes, Ma'am. None other than our old *friend* Bowlegged Blanche. I'd know that nose and that bleached stack of straw she calls hair, anywhere. The sawed off little shrew. And, don't you know–that nose was stuck straight up in the air like it always was. Squirrel-Tooth Annie always said if that girl ever got caught out in a good rain, without her umbrella, she'd drown!

The girls that worked in the same saloon with her in Dodge City said she went around like that 'cause she thought it made her look taller. She was stuck on herself–real sensitive about being so short. Fussed all the time about everything."

"I remember."

"Yep, Bowlegged Blanche, the plume of Dodge City."

Doralee was laughing, but still managed to ask, "Could you tell–Do you think she's working the town?"

"Nah, I don't think so. Remember? She left Dodge with that sawed-off little squirt. Seems like he worked in a bank or did something with money. He probably found a job here. Remember how she said he begged her? Promised her the moon if she'd marry him. They said she thought he was her last chance out of the "business." O'course, he had his good points--he *was* the only fella she ever danced with and didn't have to smell his belly button the whole time they were dancing. And he was low enough to the ground, he could actually whisper into her ear–instead of having to holler down to her."

Doralee was laughing so hard, she'd quit making any sound. Tears streamed down her cheeks.

They approached a tent which had a long piece of white material hanging up high on it saying: SHOWER BATHS. It marked the thriving business of a Mr. Clive Schomperrt, proprietor. He'd put in a shower business which afforded anyone with twenty-five cents the luxury of a cool shower. In this heat and dust; that was indeed a luxury.

Mr Schomperrt was making pretty good money. His dream was to make enough money to buy a town lot and put in a rooming house. He'd divided the tent into six shower cubicles with some tarp and 2X4 framing. Wooden barrels were poised above on shelves. There was a floor of pine boards with spaces between that allowed the water to run through and onto the ground below.

Stepping under the water spigot and turning it on allowed the water to pour down. By closing the valve while working up a lather Hannah was able to make five gallons of water last long enough for a wonderfully refreshing shower.

"Thank ya, ladies!" Mr. Schomperrt said cheerfully as they paid him, and he counted out their change. "Tell your friends about us."

They smiled and nodded, as if they intended to do just that.

Detail from 1901 photograph, looking northward
from Mattie Beal's hill--across Squaw Creek.

Chapter 16
Quinine Sulfate

<u>August 8</u>
*Nothing of great interest happening now-a-days for me to
write about except to-day, or this evening rather, Mr.
J.D. Elmore made us a visit. He arrived on the
"Transfer" from Richards, now the nearest railroad point,
15 mi. He reported the family well and left them at
Anadarko. His views on the location business is that
Anadarko will be a better town than Lawton.*

A tiny station house, at a place called Richards (Spur)[19]
about eleven miles north of Lawton, was now the furthest
southern point of the Rock Island Line. People arrived and
departed from there daily. They bought their tickets in
Lawton and were taken out to the station house in one of
the fancy new transfer buses pulled by two teams. New
arrivals were picked up there for the trip into Lawton.

I have had a dreadful cold in my head for a couple of days. Last night, I borrowed six doses of Quinine Sulphate of Mrs. Brown, & feel a little better this morning. The men are up town attending the "lot sale".
I have been reading, "The Man She Loved", by Effie Adelaide

"I'm going to miss you and Mr. Hawp," Minnie said, as she helped Myrtle pack the last of their dishes into a barrel. Minnie couldn't believe she heard herself saying these words. But it was true. They'd lived closely together for quite some time now. After you got to know her, Mrs. Hawp wasn't all that bad. Minnie had kinda become fond of the two of them. Myrtle didn't mean to be such a sourpuss.

"You helped me learn to make bread on a camp fire. I'm sure, when I try it on my own, it won't be quite as good as yours, but I'll keep working on it," she told Myrtle.

"That's kind of you to say, Minnie. I want to thank *you* for putting up with me. Lord knows, I can be difficult to get along with at times. I don't even know myself when I get in those moods. But you've always been patient with me, and I want to thank you for that." She reached out a hand and gave Minnie's arm a motherly squeeze.

"I hope Mr. Hawp gets to feeling better," Minnie said, as she tucked more towels in around the dishes they were packing for the Hawp's trip back home.

"Oh, I do, too, Minnie. I don't know what I'd do without that man. The doctor at Fort Sill said it might've been the heat. I think it was an ulcer, the way he was carrying on with his stomach he seemed to think drinking milk helped it. Anyway, we sure weren't cut out for this heat. Guess it wasn't meant to be. Sometimes things work out, sometimes they don't."

"But what an experience you've had."

"Oh, I know. Lordy me," Myrtle's voice went a few keys higher, " I s'pose I'll never get through telling people back in Gordon all the things we went through coming down here."

Minnie knew that was true and the thought of it made her smile.

***

<u>August 10</u>

Mr. Elmore took a "Transfer" and went back to Richards where he takes the train for Anadarko. I forgot to say Mr. Gus Reid took the train for Gordon, Neb. from Anadarko about August 3rd, just before Jim and Sam left there to meet us. Mr. & Mrs. Hawp intended to start home this morning also, but it looked so much like rain they put it off.

<u>August 11, Sunday</u>

Mr. & Mrs. Hawp started for Anadarko this morning with the intentions of staying there a week or so before leaving for home. After the "adieux" and their departure. Arnold & I prepared to go to church. Jim & Papa went out to pick his claim out as he files to-morrow. Sam & Mr. Schrandt joined us and we went up town together. Arnold & I left them up there and went to the M.E.S.S. & Church. Rev. Z.F. Hill of Ponca City preached. Arnold & I ate dinner by ourselves to-day. Jim & Papa returned about 5 p.m. and Mr. Schrandt & Sam a little later. After supper Jim, Schrandt, Arnold & I went up town. Arnold & I went again to the M.E. and they came for us near the close of the meeting. Today this church or tabernacle raised $370. toward buying a lot for sacred purposes and this forenoon they organized with about 25 members. Here is a list of Church people and other Lawtonites I have met:

    D.O. Wilson, Lower M.E.

    Dr. Maupin, Sec. M.E.

    Mrs. Munsey

    Mr. Waltham

    Deaconess Jacquess of Dallas M.E.

    Mr. & Mrs. Douglass

    Miss Weber, Texas

    Mrs. Geo. Smith

Mr. Reed, our S.S. Teacher
Rev. A. B. Carpenter, Christian
Mrs. Mc Knight, M. E. Reg.
Mr. & Mrs. Jones, Dem.
Mr. & Mrs. Ed Jones
Mrs. Brown, & Misses Bessie & Laura
Rob. L. McElhannon
Wm. McElhannon
Mrs. Mooreland
David T.S. Chabold
Mr. & Mrs. Patton, Woodward, O.T.
Mrs. Hubbard

***

The auction and the filing of homestead claims continued daily; though the excitement of opening day had paled.

Water problems were one of Lawton's most immediate worries. The lack of a dependable water supply, sufficient to fill the needs of the settlers and close enough in proximity to the town, was causing a lot of concern among those who wanted to make Lawton their home.

Profit from the lot sale was supposed to be returned to the town to be used in building streets and forming public utilities. But it would take weeks before city government could be formed and action taken to make that a reality. More water wagons were brought in. Water was being sold by the barrel now as well as by the bucket. Every business, home, and tent had a barrel or two for their water supply.

Laundering clothes satisfactorily was a problem. Those who had the time found places along East Cache Creek to do their washing. There were some legitimate laundry businesses operating. Where they were able to obtain enough water, no one knew.

The oppressive heat made it more than usually necessary that self-respecting people "wash off" at least once a week. Many walked to East Cache Creek and went swimming with a bar of soap.

Outhouses were desperately needed. Prior to the opening, there had been a few scattered around town. But the walls were made of burlap sacking material. At that time everyone was temporarily located. It didn't make sense to erect a permanent waste disposal unit until the masses of people were more settled. When the town's population had multiplied to gargantuan proportions before the lot sale and for awhile after, it became painfully apparent that this need could be ignored no longer.

At the time of the auction a Mr. B.J. Seddles, whose name unfortunately had not been drawn during the lottery, made an astute observation. The need for toilet facilities in the town of Lawton, like it's population, had mushroomed. He followed up with a right smart business decision and was soon off and running. He became a constructor of outdoor toilets.

Sitting at the small table outside the tent, while his wife washed the dinner dishes, B.J. did some figuring.

"Listen, Pearl," he said. He always tried out his ideas on her. It helped him to think out loud.

"Starting out, I'm guessing it'll take me two days to build one toilet—one day to dig the hole, and the next to build the shed. I can price a basic one-holer, four foot by four foot—exterior measurement, with a standard shed roof and metal hinges for fifteen dollars. No paint, no half moon carved in the door."

That afternoon B.J. approached the owner of a lumber yard with the proposition that he would build an outhouse for them—no charge—if they would provide the materials. They took him up on the deal.

"About here, then?" B.J. asked, stepping out to the place he thought the store owner was indicating.

"Yeah, just put'er as far back out t'ere as ya can." the lumber yard owner, Mr. Hollum, said.

If this worked out like B.J. planned, he'd have several inquiries from just this one privy going in. He could get his lumber on credit here at the lumber yard and pay it back when he was paid for the job.

After three days, business was going well. He was

taking orders–making a list. He realized that by refining his technique a bit–rounding off the corners of the hole in the ground, investing in a set of post hole diggers, and cutting his lumber by lantern light in the evenings after supper–he could build one privy a day.

After the first week, Mr. Seddles had to hire a helper to keep up with the demand. Two days later, he hired a 17 year–old kid just to dig the holes, while he and his carpenter assistant put up the lumber.

It wasn't too long before Mrs. Seddles got involved. At supper one evening she said, "Honey, I could carve out the hole in the seats if you could keep me supplied with boards."

Using a brace and bit to get it started, a key-hole saw to enlarge it, she rounded off the sharp edges with a rasp, and if she had time, she added a final touch of refinement. She sanded down the rough edges a bit, too.

"Makes it more comfortable. Not as many splinters." she said. "They's nothin' ruins your day more'n a splinter on that partic'lar part of your body." Pearl was able to make the holes, get supper, and watch the baby all at the same time. What a gal!

The finished product, all new and spiffy looking out behind a place of business, quite naturally caused passersby (would-be customers for B.J.) to inquire. A day did not pass during the month of August that at least one man didn't come up to B.J. and ask if he was the man to see about an outhouse.

By the end of the month, B.J. had built 41 regular out-houses at $15.00 each, and a two-holer out behind the "Opry House" for $35. His total bill for lumber, hinges, nails, post hole diggers, and an extra hammer for the hired man had been exactly $306.68. He was out $47. for labor. His business netted him the nice little sum of $296.32.

He took an afternoon off on August 10, to purchase a business lot for $80. He quickly moved his tent, wagon, and family onto it and went back to work.

"Gotta strike while the iron is hot!" he told Pearl.

By the time mid-September rolled around, he had a nice building on his lot, with a two-room living space for the family. Out in the front, beside a small American flag, a freshly lettered sign proclaimed:

B.J. Seddles, Builder, Don't "Seddle" for Less.

***

"HIRING A HACK," Otto Elling muttered to himself as he was being driven around the countryside looking for a likely piece of land. It sounded ludicrous here in Indian Territory. More like something out of a Charlotte Brontë novel. But this was the way people saw the land if they'd come by train and had no other transportation. Early this morning he'd hired a couple of locators.

He had to laugh when he thought about it.

Seated in the lap of luxury he was *not*. He did however, intend to see the land for which he would file. Word was that some homesteaders would simply look at the huge map on the wall of the Land Office and pick out one of the little squares. Otto just couldn't see doing things that way.

Today, August 16th, was the day designated for Otto to file on his quarter section at the land office in Lawton, and he intended to make the best decision possible by giving it careful consideration. That meant walking around on it, examining the grass, assessing the soil, the prospects for water and considering the location and its distance from town.

The hack rolled across the prairie behind the dark brown Morgan mare. Her driver, Shorty Crane, occasionally adjusted their course with a tug on the reins draped from his hands to the bit in her mouth.

Though it was awfully hot–they could see the heat waves undulating on the horizon–Otto was enjoying the beauty of the land. Especially for the last couple of miles he'd been particularly taken with the panorama here on the prairie. Now, he could see a distance of some fifteen, maybe twenty, miles in three directions. The Wichita Mountains looked magnificent from here. Several creeks and the trees that lined them were within view.

Shifting his weight forward, Otto waited for the horse to pull to the crest of a small hill, before asking the driver to stop. This was actually just a courtesy as the horse had already sensed the shifting weight and was stopping. Just one of those tricks, people in tune with animals knew about. Otto had a sixth sense with animals.

He hopped out and walked away from the vehicle. Moving through the grass, he took greater strides than he normally would have wanting to get a feel for the land. Out some 40 feet, he squatted down to examine the vegetation closer to the ground, the color and porosity of the soil. He knew what he was doing.

Just graduated from Kansas State Agricultural College in Manhattan, Kansas this past May, Otto had received a degree in agriculture. His curriculum had included the study of crops, soils and plant sciences.

"What was the number of this section again?" Otto called to the locator and driver.

"Fourteen. Are you watchin' your time?" Shorty asked.

Otto checked his pocket watch and started back toward the hack.

"Be a shame for ya ta miss gettin' to file."

"It sure would. Say, you men have ridden around alot over this area. Have you noticed any buffalo wallows around?" Otto asked.

The men looked at each other as if to say, "Did I hear him right?" It was a question they hadn't gotten before.

"Buffalo wallows? Hadn't been any buffaloes in a long time. They're all killed off." Shorty commented.

"I know that. These wallows were made years ago--there presence is supposed to mean good grass land. They're low places–about a foot–foot an a half deep, eight–ten foot across–where the buffalo ground out a shallow pit in the dirt by rolling around on their backs."

"You mean like a horse'll do sometimes?"

"Yeah, The heavy growth of woolly hair on their humps and forequarters through the winter–you've seen pictures of them, haven't you–caused "hot spots" where pieces of it got all matted up. They'd start itching in the warmer days of spring and through the summer and rubbed against low hanging branches of trees–anything else they could find–leaving wads of their dark brown wool, here and there. And they'd wallow out places here and there where there weren't any trees around to scratch on. Give themselves a good dusting."

"Uh-huh, now pull my other leg."

"No, no–it's the truth. Old timers say that where you

find some "wallows", the soil's supposed to be better. The idea was that where the herds stayed around grazing for more than a couple of days, they'd wallah out these low places."

"Wull, I'll be. Learn sumpthin everday, dontcha?"

Shorty Crane had earlier in the day given up attempting to help Mr. Elling. At first, he'd hopped in and out every time his customer did, and keep up a line of talk. After awhile the men decided this customer knew what he was looking for and stayed put unless he asked a question.

"Let's see," Otto said as he looked toward the mountains," this would be the south–east–" he hesitated, looked around again. "No, the south WEST quarter of section fourteen, one north, thirteen west?"

"Believe that's correct, sir," the locator said.

Checking the time on his pocket watch Otto took another look around, walked a few feet further, then turned and decisively strode back to his transportation, and climbed in.

"Back to Lawton, gentlemen; I've found my land."

During the twelve mile ride back to town, Otto leaned his head against the hood of the buggy, relaxing more than he'd allowed himself to in at least a month. His mind drifted; he built some "castles in the air" or in this case–sheds, chicken houses, barns, granaries, and, of course a nice house.

"I will settle on this land–and in ten years," he thought incredulously, "I'll have a wife and we will be raising a family. "

> <u>August 12</u>
> I baked bread for the second time today and had good luck
> with it. The men have planned a fishing trip to take
> place near the foot of the mountains tomorrow afternoon.
> This evening I made quite an extended call at Mrs.
> Brown's.

***

CLARENCE WALKED purposefully down busy 'D' Avenue, headed east. Between two long rows of half-filled business lots, he walked along the dusty thoroughfare that only a week ago had been prairie. There were thirteen buildings now on the townsite, and Lawton bore more than faint resemblance to a town. Many of the lots had some kind of a business set up on them. Though many were still housed in wagons and tents, they were now distributed along the more orderly platted lines of a town.

Clarence was out of quinine, a drug that relieved his symptoms. He needed to purchase more. He was looking for the new location of a druggist he'd used over on Goo Goo Avenue, before the opening.

He'd also made arrangements to meet a locator at noon to be taken out to look at land to the west and southwest. Already having been out twice, looking over the land, he'd gone east of town, and another time, north. It was getting harder, the locators told him to find unclaimed land.

He had to be ready to file on Tuesday, August the 20th. That was one week from tomorrow.

Finally he saw the sign: Green Tent Drug Store. He walked to the tent, bent his head down, and peered inside. After his eyes adjusted to the darkness of the interior, he was able to see the profile of a gentleman standing near the back.

"May I help you, sir?" a voice inquired.

"Yes, sir" Clarence replied, "I'm in need of some quinine."

"I'm not sure if I still have some," the man said tipping his head as if trying to remember. "Excuse me while I check."

He stepped out the back of the tent through a slice made in it's rear canvas wall–Clarence guessed to provide access to the wagon in the rear. The wagon had been backed up against the tent and there was a set of steps going up to its rear entrance. The man disappeared inside. It appeared the man had all his medications organized back there in the wagon. After a moment the druggist stepped back out carrying a small box.

A lady now stood beside Mr. Pool.

"Looks like you are the lucky one, sir. This is my last box."

Minnie recognized the familiar box of Quinine tablets.

"Oh, no. The last one, you say?" Minnie said

sounding disappointed. "That's exactly what I came for. Oh, well–" She turned to go. Arnold was waiting for her, outside the tent. The druggist raised his hand, pointing toward his left and said, "I believe there is another..."

"Oh, no, there's no need for you to go hunting, ma'am." Clarence interrupted.

Minnie turned.

"You will take this one."

"Oh, no, sir, I..."

"No, I insist. I had a mere headache. That is all. I'll go and find another druggist."

"How awfully kind of you, Mr..."

"Pool, ma'am, Clarence Pool." He tipped his hat.

"So glad to meet you, Mr. Pool. I'm Minnie. I thank you so much, but you needn't have." She gave the pharmacist a fifty cent piece; he began fishing around in his coin box for change.

"Miss Minnie. And where are you from?" Clarence liked her looks, her demeanor, her long slender hands, and rather hoped to find out more about her.

"Johnson, my last name is Johnson. We are most recently from Nebraska. And you?" she inquired politely, showing an interest that she didn't truly feel, while she counted the change being placed in her hand.

"Most recently from Iowa," he said using her phrase and smiling at her. Minnie nodded and smiled to the pharmacist as she placed the change in her coin purse and the box of capsules in her bag.

"Where else have you been?" she asked as they both stepped out into the bright sunshine. She was always curious about people.

"Well, I guess the most exotic place would be the Philippines. I joined the expeditionary forces there and promptly contracted malaria–or at least that's what they called it. The army politely discharged me and allowed me to purchase a ticket home on board a steamer."

"Malaria? Really! For goodness sake." she said. She'd never met anyone who'd been to the Philippines or who'd had Malaria either, for that matter. She loved hearing about faraway places and people's experiences, but she and Arnold must be getting back. Papa wanted to be leaving for the mountains soon.

"So you were in that fracas with Spain then, Mr. Pool?"

Clarence couldn't believe his ears. The lady has a brain as well. A woman who knew that the U.S. had fought the Spaniards in the Philippines! But a "fracas!" Surely she is joking with me. Even though it had lasted less than a year, it had been eventful enough for a war, in his mind.

"Mr. Pool, I'd like you to meet my brother, Arnold Johnson," Minnie was saying. Arnold stood up from where he squatted outside the tent flaps. Extending his hand they exchanged pleasantries.

"Thank you again, Mr. Pool," Minnie said extending her hand in a polite, sweet dismissal. "We really must be going. Perhaps our paths will cross again."

"Clarence, ma'am, please call me Clarence, and I hope they will."

August 13
I have been packing up all morning and then Arnold and I went up town and called for the mail. I also got some Quinine Capsules, so when I got ready to get dinner, I returned Mrs. Brown's Quinine and brought a fresh bucket of water.

Elling Family Photo

Mount Scott

Chapter 17
To The Mountains

<u>August 13--continued</u>

After dinner 12:15; we started, all very jubilant toward
Mt. Sheridan & Scott, but upon reaching the creek we
thought we would find fish in we followed it nearly to its
source which is beside Mt. Lookout. We camped within
4 mi. of this Mt. We could see the stone building on its
very top plainly now, and three or four men walking
around up there. This is the Mt. the large telescope used
to be kept on. Over fifty soldiers have been killed by
Indians in ambush on its sides behind rocks while on their
way to duty here, but none killed later than 1890. We
are camped on a beautiful mountain stream of cold clear
running water and very good. Of course, the men went
fishing and I likewise--ha ha. I caught one, and Mr.
Schrandt three little fellows. I put them in a pint cup and
later carried back to the creek. He moaned a great deal
over his poor luck in his jolly manner.

We loaded up and by 7 a.m. were on the road for Pecan Creek. Further west and south on our way we saw Jim's claim which this creek flows through.

Minnie took note that Jim's claim wasn't exactly "on the way" back toward Lawton. They had to travel seven miles south and three back west to "go by" it. But everyone seemed happy for the opportunity to see it. They could admire it and share in Jim's happiness and good fortune.

August 14--continued.
We reached our new camp by 10:30 and the men went fishing while Sam and I got dinner for both outfits together. The men soon caught a mess of fish which we also cooked for dinner making five different kinds of meat--plover, young rabbit, quail, bacon and fish. After dinner we all set out & fished. I fed the fish well but had poor luck catching them. Discouraged, I returned to camp and Sam & I gathered clam shells along the shore, and fished a few out of the water which were contemplated to cook for Mr. Schrandt, he being fond of them. However we cleaned the shells and Sam put them in his valise with the intention of taking them home with him to Gordon for the children. The balance of the day was spent in fishing and...

August 15
...this morning likewise until breakfast was ready. We salted a mess and carried back here to Lawton for Mr. McElhannons use. We had all the fish we could eat and had a very good time. Mr. Schrandt rode in our wagon on this trip as Jim's vehicle is so much smaller. We left our trunks with the McElhannons. We returned here just before dinner. It is now after dinner and the men are up town. I will close at present and doctor a bite which a small brown spider just caused.

Returning to the camp on Squaw Creek southwest of Lawton meant one thing to Minnie. Unpacking--again! It seemed to her she'd been packing and unpacking all summer long. A ritual, it seemed, that had no end. This setting up an outdoor kitchen in a different place every day, had been going on since late May. Now it was late August. She would be so relieved when they were finally located permanently and could leave their things in one place.

Minnie's felt an instant sadness at supper this evening when Jim Reid and Sam Joice said they would be leaving for home tomorrow. It was like having a rug pulled out from under her.

Why had the men decided to leave so suddenly it seemed! She'd certainly not been aware of any plans of this kind. In Sam's case, like Papa he hadn't gotten a number, so it was the likely thing for him to do-- eventually. But, Jim? It would appear rude of her to ask about it.

Minnie finally decided that he must have business to take care of back in Gordon and would return with his family later. She couldn't satisfy her curiousity by asking Papa, who probably knew all about it. If he knew the reason, he'd tell it only when it served his own needs to do so.

> *August 16*
> Papa is 45 years old to-day. He and Mr. Schrandt went up town about 7 a.m. and will return about 5 this evening. They are attending the lot sale. Jim & Sam left us this morning for Anadarko and will immediately go on home to Gordon, Neb. I have washed clothes and am now baking light bread.

***

Late in the day of August 16, Otto stood among a small group of men outside the land office waiting for their opportunity to file. Those whose number had been skipped earlier in the day waited also. This would be their last chance to file. Draw numbers from 1125 to 1250 were being filed today.

Finally Mr. Wallace came to the door and asked for the last group of men ready to file to enter. Otto along with several other men entered the building.

First they were asked to check the map on the wall to make sure that the quarter for which they were about to file had not been spoken for.

Quickly Otto located "his" square on the map. It wasn't marked with an X yet so he stepped over to the first available clerk who verified his lottery draw number as 1248 and asked for the fourteen dollar filing fee. A receipt was written out and several papers placed before him to be filled out. One, called the Homestead Affidavit, stated in part:

> "...this application is honestly and in good faith made, for the purpose of actual settlement and cultivation, and not for the benefit of any other person, persons or corporation and I will faithfully and honestly endeavor to comply with all requirements. I do not apply to enter the same (homestead agreement) for the purpose of speculation, but in good faith to obtain a home for myself and that I have not directly or indirectly made any agreement or contract in any way or manner with any person or persons, business, corporation or syndicate whatsoever by which the title which I might acquire from the Government of the United States should inure in whole or part to the benefit of any person except myself..."

It had to be sworn to, and signed, in front of the clerk who was a notary public.

Stepping out of the land office Otto gave a big sigh of relief. Now he had until midnight, October 4th to take up residence and begin "proving up".

August 17
The men are up town as usual. Arnold & I went up this forenoon and got the mail and took in the town. On our way back to camp, I called on Mrs. Brown and the girls, Laura & Bessie. They are lovely people.

The town looked dramatically different each time Minnie returned to it. There were twenty-three businesses that had a building of some sort on the townsite. The rest had merely pulled a wagon onto their business lot or put up a tent until such time as they could build.

Minnie enjoyed visiting with the Browns who were also camped along Squaw Creek. She'd met them at the M. E. church earlier in August. The father, Stephen Brown, was a partner in a grocery business. The two girls, Laura and Bessie, were near Minnie's age, one also had a teaching certificate. Mrs. Brown was a certified teacher as well, and had taught school before coming to Lawton. They were always friendly. It was always a rare treat for Minnie having been mostly with men for so long, to sit with these ladies and visit.

Some news that Minnie has missed out on, while on their trip to the mountains was that Mr. Laws, the man who had drawn and filed for claim #3, had apparently been beaten out of his claim in a poker game. It appeared that he would be forced to relinquish it. There would probably be a contest on it.

> August 18, Sunday
> Papa, Arnold, & Mr. Schrandt left camp for Richards where Mr. S. will take the train for Aurora, Neb. I did not care to go, so I stayed in camp. And about 9 o'clock got ready and went to M.E.S.S. and church. After dinner I called on Mrs. Hubbard and Mrs. Patton. I went to bed early, as I was alone.

It had been thirteen days since the noise and bustle of opening day. Some folks had already pulled up stakes and gone home. For whatever reason they hadn't found what they wanted here. The town seemed a little less raucous. Women began to feel safe enough to walk unaccompanied during daylight hours.

Minnie walked to the Methodist Episcopal church tent this warm Sunday morning. When evening came however she went straight to bed not wishing to call attention to the fact that she was alone.

August 19
After breakfast I walked up town and got the mail and returned at noon. Papa and Arnold came directly and brought Mr. T.S. Chabold, a Wis. man with them. After dinner they went up town and I wrote some letters.

The new post office in Lawton had been established in a large tent in the downtown business area at 303 C. The new postmaster, Joe T. White, came from Arkansas City, Kansas. It was a relief for the Johnsons not to have to drive the five miles out to Fort Sill and back to pick up their mail. Papa, though, would continue to check with the Quinette Store occasionally just in case a card or letter showed up there.

***

DURING THE LATER DAYS of the auction of business lots, Hannah Bell arose early each morning, dressed, and sauntered over to the auctioneer's stand. Today, however, she was on a mission. Though her stomach was all aflutter, the look in her eyes was one of determination. She was doing a pretty good job of acting merely curious, out for a stroll. Only someone who knew her well--and no one really did--could discern the anxiety that lay just below the surface.

The money that had been accumulating in the little pouch in her pillow was becoming quite a stash, and Hannah figured that it made a lot more sense to have something substantial to call her own than a pouch full of greenbacks. She wasn't a stupid lass, merely unschooled.

Hannah knew how to count to 100 she just didn't recognize all the numerals that represented them. She understood that 2 and 2 was 4, and that 5 and 5 made 10, but she hadn't figured out how to calculate more than that. She knew she had 27 one dollar bills, 7 tens, and 2 twenties. Though she couldn't decide exactly how much that was all together. To complicate matters she knew no one she trusted enough to ask to count it for her.

She was pretty sure it was enough.

Having visited the auction as an observer she'd

studied the bidders and how the bidding process went. She knew they wore red ribbons to distinguish themselves from mere onlookers. She was aware that all a person had to do was ask the man under the auctioneer's booth and he'd give you a ribbon. Yep, she was pretty sure she knew how to do it.

Sitting on the front row of bleachers with her bidder's ribbon pinned to her dress she felt her purse again to see if the pouch of money was still there. It was. She smiled to herself–thrilled that she was finally doing this–but filled with worrisome thoughts about how it would go. She had a sudden need for a drink of water. Her mouth was as dry as the dust beneath her feet.

The auctioneer climbed the ladder.

Hannah swallowed hard. It was going to happen. It was really going to happen. A description of the first lot to be sold was given but Hannah wasn't going to let that confuse her.

She was here to bid when the auctioneer began to sing.

"Good morning, Ladies and Gentlemen," his familiar voice echoed across the townsite.

"Are we all clear on the first lot up for bid today?" He took a moment again to look around and identify those who would be his bidders. Hannah felt him looking her way. She supposed it would be hard not to notice a young lady wearing a bidder's ribbon, seated on the front row. It was unusual but not unheard of.

Hannah's eyes locked on the auctioneer.

"Well-ahwho'lla gimme twenty? Twenty, ah saidah..."
Hannah waved her hand.
He nodded his head.
"Well-ah, ah got a twenty. Now whodah biddah thirty-thirty whodabiddahthata-thirty dollar bid?
Hannah waved her hand.
The auctioneer gestured down to Hannah--again, saying, "O-o-o-oh got me a thirty. Now, whodah biddah forty. Anybody got a forty?"
Hannah waved her hand.
There weren't many bidders out early this morning.

Behind her a couple of men were babbling. Something about someone giving the little lady some money to spend. Hannah had no time to try to figure those fools out. This was serious business.

"Oh, ah gotta forty--uh forty. Nowah who'llah..." Hannah on the verge of waving again stopped seeing that the auctioneer had been interrupted. A man had moved in behind the auctioneer and placed a hand on shoulder. The auctioneer turned around to speak with him, his back now to the audience. Pretty soon the auctioneer turned back toward the audience.

"Young lady."

Everyone began to look around to see who he was talking to.

"You, there in the first row."

Hannah gave him a "who me" look, and her heart began to pound. Above all she hadn't wished to call attention to herself.

"Yes, ma'am, you. Pretty little lady in the front row. We're gonna save you and me both some time and trouble. Would you give me fifty dollars for this lot?"

Hannah nodded her head. Her face was red and felt like a burning ember. She tried to swallow but her mouth and throat were too dry.

"Looks like the early bird gets the worm here this morning, folks. Ma'am, you have just bought yourself a lot." He struck the stand with his gavel.

"SOLD, fuh fit-ty dollahs."

NOW SEATED in the land office across the table from a clerk who was there to take her money, Hannah waited for him to initiate the exchange. She hadn't yet said a word.

"Let's see, looks like that'll be fifty dollars for the lot ma'am."

Hannah nodded and pulled the pouch out of her purse. Slowly she removed all her bills. She had them arranged with the twenties on top. She pulled off the first twenty watching the man's face closely, hoping there would be a clue when she'd laid out enough. She tugged at the second twenty dollar bill and placed it on top of the other one.

"Twenty, forty." the man counted.

The next bill, luckily, was a ten. Hannah pulled it out and placed it on top of the twenties.

"a-a-and fifty. We thank you ma'am," he said with finality--the clue Hannah was looking for.

She took a deep breath and let it all out relaxing as she did so. She tucked the rest of her bills back in the pouch and the pouch back in her purse.

"Now, if you'll give me your name I'll make out your receipt." Her heart did a double flip and landed in her throat! She'd forgotten about having to give her name.

This was another problem for Hannah that had never been resolved. She wasn't sure what her proper last name was. What if they wanted some kind of proof? What if he asked her how to spell it? Her cheeks were on fire again.

"H-Hannah. Hannah Bell," she hesitated for a few seconds. "M--murray," she said softly. She supposed that was her last name; it was the name of the old woman who'd taken her in.

"Anna Bell?"

"No, H-hannah--Hannah Bell Murray." The clerk nodded finished writing and turned it around for her approval. "Was that correct?" his expression asked.

"Yes, yes sir," she said glancing at it.

The clerk folded it in half and handed it to her. "Now if you'll move on down to the next chair that gentleman will help you with your deed."

In the next chair she was asked to sign some papers. That wasn't a problem. She'd watched people sign their names before. It was just a lot of squiggles and swirls. She'd worked on her's.

When finished at the land office Hannah walked carefully--as if on eggshells--all the way back to the tent that Mr. Jeagerson had finally purchased for her and Doralee. She wanted to run and leap and shout her happiness but she dared not.

She dared not even smile.

She wasn't telling ANYONE about this, until the time was right. In Hannah's world dreams had a way of disappearing.

August 20
I washed a few pieces and baked bread. To-morrow we
are going out to the mountains so I have to be prepared
for a weeks outing in the line of groceries. Mr. Chabold
is going with us.

August 21
It rained a little this morning, just enough to make us
hesitate in pulling camp. However we left at 9 a.m. and
camped in the foothills for dinner, which was rather late.
After dinner went on into the mountains. We camped
near a small lake surrounded by trees and rock cliffs about
40 ft. high. It is a beautiful place and the clear, placid
water no less. The men climbed a hill.

August 22
We went on to Mt. Scott and the men fished till noon
"and na bad four little fishes" too. It rained hard while
we ate dinner. I took refuge in the wagon with my plate
full and Arnold afterward. The men under the wagon.

When the others declared they were going to climb
Mount Scott, the tallest mountain in the Wichitas, Minnie
never once entertained the thought of staying behind. She
loved challenges. Though she wished that just this once
she could wear a pair of her brother's pants. But THAT
just wasn't done.

The rain passed, the sun peeked out and there stood
Mount Scott in all her glory beckoning to them. They'd
heard other campers say that it was a rough climb but it
was well worth it. From the top you could see the prairie
for miles around. "Spectacular view!" they'd said.
Curiosity and their sense of adventure got the better of
them, they decided they'd go ahead and give it a try.

Minnie led the rest carrying her parasol, wearing her
faded cotton dress that came down to her ankles and had
at least two petticoats underneath. Along with her father,
brother, and Mr. Chabold they ventured toward the trail
near the "river of boulders" at the bottom of Mount Scott.

August 22, continued:
After the shower and dinner we set out on foot to climb the Mt. Scott. I took my parasol and went bareheaded, it was so cool and cloudy. Well, we climbed and crawled and walked over rocks as big as loads of hay and smaller through oak timber, underbrush and cedar until we reached the top. We rested many times ;and found water in hollow places in the rocks for drinking. I was nearly worn out before reaching the top, but would not give up. After viewing the country for miles with a telescope for an hour, we started downward from the top. From the top we could see the plains that stretch southward to the Red River, a distance of fifty miles and if it had not been cloudy we could have seen the plains of Texas. It took us two hours to ascend & one and a half to descend--6:30 p.m.

August 23
We left camp about 7 and after going over the terrible rocky roads a few miles, we broke the wagon tongue square off so far back that it was difficult to mend. After nailing and splinting it we drove a few more miles, when it broke again, and so we dragged along until we found a good camping place for dinner. Here papa cut a hardwood pole: and replaced it. Arnold and I fished and waded and fished all afternoon and caught a nice mess for supper.

"Say again? The tongue is wh--," Minnie questioned as she leaned way over trying to hear Arnold who was speaking to her from underneath the wagon. She was pretty sure she knew what her brother was saying but hated to actually hear the truth.

"Broken?" Arnold was near Papa under the front of the wagon. Minnie was in the back--in the bed of the wagon.

"Is it so Papa can fix it?"

"Of course." was Arnold's cocksure reply.

Broken wagon tongues were not the kind of thing a wagon traveler liked to hear about much less have happen.

To wagons going west it usually meant a day or two layover and most likely being left behind by their fellow wagoneers. Some folks even kept a spare tongue in the wagon.

On their pleasant outing to the mountains they'd come up with a broken wagon tongue.

Minnie and Arnold wouldn't get too worried or upset. Always confident their Papa found a way to get them out of whatever predicament presented itself. He always did.

Giving credit where credit was due Minnie had to admit her father *did* know his way around a set of tools. But that wasn't unusual, a lot of men did. Oliver Johnson had an inventive mind and the belief that he could do anything he made up his mind to do. Fashioning a wagon tongue out of a post oak tree was a simple task for him. His children had come to take his natural gift for granted. He could "make do" in just about any situation.

Minnie had seen him create just the right tool, or come up with a remarkably "right" solution to a problem countless times.

There was that time, Minnie recalled, when the stack of wood for their stove had been decreasing at a much more rapid rate than it should have been. Seemed like he was having to cut wood twice as often. So, Papa, suspecting that the wood was being pilfered by the neighbors, took a piece of wood, bore a hole in it, poured in a little gun powder, sealed it over and placed the piece of wood back on the stack. A couple of days later they heard a "boom" next door. Nothing was ever said, but the wood quit disappearing.

Lawton, O.T.   September 1, 1901

Chapter 18
Jim's Claim

A shrill whistle pierced the moisture-thickened morning air startling Minnie in the midst of her breakfast clean-up routine. Quickly she realized it was Arnold. She'd heard him whistle for the horses hundreds of times but not when he was so close. The thick stand of brush oak--cross timbers--surrounding their camp made it nearly impossible to see any distance at all.

"Looks like we may have to help Arnold look for the horses." Papa commented.

Mr. Chabold got up from where he sat and headed in the direction they'd last heard Arnold.

<u>August 24</u>
This morning the men had difficulty in finding the horses. They were not far, but in the brushy oak timber, where we could not see them. There is so much heavy oak timber in large patches between the Mts. as well as on them, and only now and then a space of open ground.

> Lots of creeks and canons but water not very plentiful.
> All kinds of timber on creeks and the Mts. look like rock
> piles, rock very thick on the flats also hard to drive. We
> have seen lots of miners prospecting this forenoon and
> mining claims staked every little ways. We are now in
> the good mining country about the head of Sandy Creek
> for dinner. After dinner we drove to Park City, a
> townsite with a couple of buildings on it and quite a few
> campers. We got a supply of groceries and camped on the
> creek next to the town for the night.

Papa couldn't keep from starting a conversation with a
couple of miners they saw today. The newspapers in
Lawton occasionally stated a common belief that any day
now there would be a big strike. One editor even went so
far as to suggest that a person would do well to go ahead
and purchase a lot in Craterville, a small settlement on the
south edge of the mountains.

"Finding anything?" Papa called to an elderly looking
gent and his younger partner. Papa had stopped the
horses, got down from the wagon, and asked Arnold to see
that they were watered at the stream ahead of them. Said
he'd join them there.

"Not yet," the miner answered as Papa strolled up.

"We keep hearin' about someone findin' a nugget here
'n' there and around but we ain't actually laid eyes on any
of it," the other one replied.

"How does a man go about gettin a claim out here?"

"Get some stakes, mark off your corners, be ready to
defend it if anybody asks questions," was the misleading
reply.

> "Miners are in the Wichita mountains now by the
> hundreds. Hundreds more, captivated by the rumors
> of gold, copper and zinc in the mountains, and acting
> upon the hypothesis that there will be a dash declared
> by the interior department, are crowded close to the
> supposed mineral regions.[20]

Whether or not it had come to the attention of the
miners in the Wichitas, the fact was that on July 4, 1901,

the same day President McKinley signed the proclam-ation for the opening of the territory, he'd also issued one that received significantly less attention. This proclamation set aside the greater part of the Wichita Mountains as a *forest preserve* for the United States. When and if a gold--or any other mineral-- strike occurred, the national treasury would be the recipient of most of the income.

If a significant gold or mineral strike didn't happen, the mountains were still a nice little curiosity--arising as they do out of the middle of the prairie--that should be protected in it's native state. There had been talk of bringing back the buffalo from near extinction. The New York Zoological Society was looking for the right location to place the beginnings of a small herd.

August 25, Sunday
We left camp 7:30 and came on west through a very large prairie between the mountains. It was covered with Mesquite trees and Park City at the E. end. We camped on East branch of Otter creek for dinner and stayed there all afternoon. Three gentlemen called and made our acquaintance. One from Joplin, Mo. a city of 34,000 inhabitants.

August 26
The men caught a couple of messes of fish before dinner while I washed & baked bread. After dinner we drove on south through Mesquite prairie & camped for the night on Deep Red Run Creek.

August 27
Started at 6:30 a.m. We are now on our way to Lawton, 35 miles east & a little south. We soon got S. of the Mts. and then came on east at the foot of the foothills. We crossed about a doz. different streams all of a southerly course.

This morning as they left camp, Minnie made a brief entry in her diary as she usually did. The entry stated that they were headed for Lawton. Nothing had been said to the contrary--she presumed it. Consequently, it came as quite a surprise when after their noon stop near the Red Store, they once again headed south--Lawton was due east.

"Arnold." Minnie said in a coarse whisper, attempting to get her brother's attention. She stood behind the wagon; Arnold a few feet away. He didn't seem to have heard.

"Arnold, come here I want to ask you something." She gave a little more voice to her words this time.

"What?" Arnold asked, striding through the waist high grass to the place where she stood. They were near a stream. Oliver and Mr. Chabold had walked up the slope and now stood talking intently.

"Just where do you suppose we are going?" Minnie was finally able to ask in exasperation.

"What--What do you mean?" Arnold acted confused.

"Well, unless I've gone absolutely silly, Lawton is THAT way." Her arms folded in front of her, she jerked her bonneted head eastward.

"Oh, yeah. It is, idn it?" Arnold smiled sounding as if he'd not noticed the fact until now.

"Do you know something I don't know, brother dear?"

"No, Minnie. Truly, I do not," he said sincerely. "What are you thinking? That we're headed back by Jim's claim?"

"Well, it sure looks that way to me. I mean doesn't it appear to you that Papa is showing more than just a passing interest in Jim's claim?"

"Yep, sure does, but you needn't get all worked up about it." He chewed on a stem of prairie grass as a grin of pride--if only for his father's foibles--crossed his face. One eye closed in a squint against the sun he added, "You can bet whatever it is; Pa has it figured out."

This statement only served to infuriate Minnie more.

Arnold shot a look across the stream at his father and Mr. Chabold. "Shoot, how do we know; maybe Jim asked him to keep an eye on the place for him."

"Could be. But, it still bothers me."

"Why should you be bothered?"

"I just know Papa, that's all. Know him well enough to know that more than likely he's capable of bending the law, if not outright breaking it. "

"Oh, my yes," Arnold said in a fake feminine falsetto,

"and, my dear, what with Jim Reid, himself, on his way back to Nebraska." He rolled his eyes, and placed a hand on a stuck out hip doing pretty good imitation of Myrtle Hawp. "The plot does thicken now," he said, being just a little too much of a smarty pants.

"Oh, hush up." she hissed at him.

Miffed at her brother's failure to take seriously, a subject she considered important, and his lame attempt at humor, Minnie climbed up onto the wagon seat, put her feet on the foot rest, placed her hands in her lap, straightened her back, fixed her face with no expression and raised her chin. She was ready to go when Papa was. What other choice did a girl have?

Traveling still southward they passed the Deyo Baptist Indian Mission then turned slightly eastward removing all doubt in Minnie's mind where they were headed.

Minnie kept her mouth shut as Papa directed the team for the third time in three weeks onto Jim Reid's claim. She wanted to ask what the deal was, but that fought with her better judgement that told her she should just quietly allow it all to unfold. She didn't like this one bit.

"What are...?" she started.

"Going to spend the night here," Papa announced, climbing down from the wagon. "Won't set up the tent, though. Arnold you get a cook fire started. Minnie-girl, you get supper goin."

As simple as that, Minnie's distress over what they were doing was dismissed by her father's "tight-lipped" personality. She quickly looked over at Arnold. He looked back with a shrug of his shoulders and a look that said, "Don't ask me."

As they began the chores Papa had assigned, Minnie's brain--and stomach--churned. Didn't they call what they were doing "squatting"? If squatting was setting up camp on someone else's property; then they were squatting on Jim claim. And besides, people weren't supposed to "settle" out here on the reservation until the sixty-day-filing-period was up. Well, they didn't have their tent up. So, perhaps technically it probably wasn't squatting.

Camped for dinner a couple of miles east of a big store and after dinner came past the Baptist mission and camped for the night on Jim Reid's Claim.

When Papa announced at breakfast that he was taking Mr. Chabold to Lawton and would pick up supplies before returning, Minnie was furious. She thought he said last evening that they were "spending the night."

After a bit, though, she simply did the mental equivalent of shrugging her shoulders. It didn't do one speck of good to get angry about it. She'd puzzled enough on the subject. After all, what right had she to question Papa's decisions?

It couldn't be as bad as camping in town so close to other people. Sometimes it was embarrassing being pressed in among other camps. A person could hear almost every word in the camps nearby and with the water situation, the dust, and the crowds. Minnie once again she let it go–for now.

August 28
Papa and Mr. T. S. Chabold departed for Lawton early. Papa was going to get a supply of necessaries. Also a pick, shovel and washboard. While the former left us to go to his home at Monroe, Wisconsin. Arnold and I went down the creek exploring and viewed every object of interest. We two and no more had rice for dinner. After taking a nap, I patched some underwear. Papa returned 3:30 p.m. and brought me two letters, one from Hattie Craven & the other Cousin Annie. Also, a lot of newspapers & good news.

✳✳✳

CLARENCE KNOCKED on the front door of his home in Iowa. When his mother rounded the corner, leaving the kitchen and saw her son standing at the screen door she began to squeal and cry.

"Clarence. Oh, my soul! Are you alright? "

Reuben heard the commotion and came into the sitting

room. "Well, I'll be danged. Clarence, my boy. Did you get a piece of land?"

"Reuben! Is that the only thing you can think to say? Our son has been down in Indian Territory and has safely returned to us!" Lydia glared at her husband.

"Yes, Pop. Yes, I did." Clarence grinned at his father.

"Well, hallelujah, praise the Lord, and pass the ammunition!" Reuben said and stuck out his hand to his son for a congratulatory shake. "Momma get this boy something to eat. Sit down and tell me everything."

The twentieth of August had been Clarence's day to file. He'd been ready with the legal description of his selected quarter of land. It went well. It wasn't the most verdant piece of land in the world, but he believed there was a spring on it, and that was a definite plus. Hopefully, the spring was one that would provide for the needs of a farm.

Clarence knew he needed to let the folks know something. It had been almost a month he'd been gone. He knew his mother was worried about him. That was her main function in life. He hadn't written them once after arriving in the new "territory". So much had happened. He scarcely knew where to begin.

After the horrendous ride in the bed of that wagon it had taken a few days for the soreness to go away. He'd sworn he'd not go anywhere until the train tracks were finished and a train arrived in Lawton.

Every time he'd sat down to write his family he toyed with the idea of buying a ticket to go home. He could take one of the "transfer coaches–like he'd taken in El Reno earlier in the summer–out to Richards. Then he'd take a train north to Iowa and get out of this heat and dust and mess for awhile. It would be quite awhile yet until the filing process was finished and it would be necessary that he take up residence on his land.

Now, he'd done it! Come home to give his report. And good it was to be home; to make his father beam with pride and his mother a little relief from her worry.

Hellen came through the front door; home from a shopping excursion with a neighbor.

"Would you look what the cat dragged in!" She

crossed the room with her packages to give her brother a hug. "What--how are you doing? Everything all right?"

"Oh, yes. I got a piece of land."

"You did? Well now, that's something to celebrate." After she hugged him she stepped back at arms length looking him squarely in the eye and said sincerely, " I am so happy for you."

"I'm trying to talk Mom and Pop into coming back to Oklahoma with me. You ought to come, too? They are going to be needing a lot of teachers when everyone gets settled in. There will be a school in almost every township."

"Well, I'm committed here for the coming term. Already told them I'd be here." She turned to her parents seated at the dining table. "Is he serious? Are you really considering moving?"

"Well," Reuben said, "he just now brought it up. We haven't heard any details nor had time to think it over yet."

"What d'ya hear from Gart?" Clarence asked about his younger brother Garfield. "Maybe he'd be interested in coming to Oklahoma, as well. I'm sure gonna need some help 'provin-up' as they call it."

"He's keeping busy–working steady. Drops in on us now and then," Reuben reported.

"I want to see him while I'm here. I think I can stay a couple, maybe three, weeks which will give us–he gave a meaningfully glance to his mother and father–time to get prepared and go back down and homestead together. By the way, Pop, you would've qualified for the drawing. You still could buy someone's relinquishment or win one by contest."

***

<u>August 29</u>
Papa & Arnold went out to find the corner stones to Jim's claim as Pa has contested it. I washed 25 pieces and then cooked dinner. Afterwards baked bread. Papa went out again this afternoon, but rode Neg, as he took all the walking up before dinner.

"What? Say that again?" Minnie said.

"Papa has contested Jim's claim."

"What does that mean--*contested*? Sounds kind of..." she searched for a word, "ruthless, doesn't it?"

"I don't know." Arnold said with a shrug.

Minnie repeated the phrase several times to herself as she went about making bread. "Papa has contested Jim's claim." It had an ominous sound to it--a not very neighborly sound.

In the afternoon Minnie sat on her cot, under the shade of an elm near the creek. She had decided to write home to let the family know...*hmm...to let them know...what?*

Staring off into space she studied over how to phrase the letter feeling frustrated in her attempts to explain it. She hadn't sorted out her own thoughts and she really was having difficulty putting it into words for the family. She tapped her teeth absentmindedly with the end of her pencil. She couldn't say they were "squatting" on Jim Reid's claim--and, Oh, by the way, Jim's on his way back to Gordon. If she told them Papa had filed a contest--that might give them knowledge that would be uncomfortable for them to have, if they met Jim or his wife on the street.

Minnie was of an age that–had she been a man–she would have been considered an adult and been privy to Papa's intentions. Frankly, it was annoying her more than a little bit that she wasn't trusted with his plans. He was such a secretive man.   He always followed his own mind–did things his own way.

She recalled the time in South Dakota when Papa bought a flock of sheep and then grazed them right under the noses of the cowboys and cattlemen who passionately hated sheep. THEN, believing the men wouldn't bother little children, he'd sent Minnie, sister Helen and Arnold out to herd them.

Flying in the face of what was common, correct or easy–that was Papa. And a man's personality or character doesn't just change overnight. Nor, Minnie decided, does a young lady wake up one morning and demand that now she is "old enough" her father must tell her what was going on. Still she could not deny this feeling that she had a right to know if she was breaking the law. Her sense of obligation and responsibility had grown stronger as her body had. After all, she wouldn't always be "Daddy's girl," protected and controlled. Didn't she have a right to be in on decisions that affected her?

Looking up, Minnie saw Papa and Arnold returning to camp.

"Oh, fiddle!" Minnie said realizing she'd been sitting there for over an hour and had only written the date and "Dear Mother."

"I'll finish this tomorrow," she told herself getting up to stir the soup she was cooking for supper.

> <u>August 30</u>
> After breakfast I went with Papa and Arnold, to run the lines. About ten I started for camp as a heavy cloud was descending from the Mts. I had no more than reached here when it began to rain very hard and the rest were here in a few moments as they ran most of the way to keep out of the wet. It rained 4-1/2 hours and filled all the water holes and made the creek rise a little. After dinner I wrote a few letters and read.

Next day Minnie had time to dash off a letter to her family. It went easier this time.

August 30, 1901
Lawton, O.T.

Dear Mother and all,
   As I write to you today, we are sitting on what I think will be our claim. It is beautiful. It has been a long, round-about process, but I thought you should know that we are finally situated on a claim. Thank Goodness! No more packing and unpacking!
   The land is located on a creek--Pecan Creek. It runs through the 160 acres, which is very fortunate since getting good water has been a problem in the new town. It rained for four hours this morning so the creek is running a lot higher than it had been. It has been a good source for fish, so far. There are all sorts of trees along the creek. Pecan, of course, and elm, cottonwood, oak, locust, some cedar, and probably many others that I haven't recognized. It is simply a wonderful piece of land. The climate here

has been hot, hot, and more hot--so far. Perhaps the changing of the season will bring more temperate weather.

Papa and Arnold are doing well. They are out now looking for the four corners of this piece of property, so we will know where the boundaries are. We are all healthy.

The Hawps are on their way back home to Gordon, as are the Reids, and Sam Joice. You'll probably be seeing them around town any day now. Papa hasn't said anything yet about when he'll send for all of you.

You know Papa. He's not going to tell us anything, till he makes up his mind. He's been his more secretive self lately. Probably just wants to be sure we can make a go of it here.

I must get back to my tent chores. Hoping the days will not be long until we see each other. I miss all of you.

Affectionately,
Minnie

<u>August 31</u>
I have been reading all forenoon "Steeles Sciences". After dinner I and the men looked for a suitable place to build and they started to dig a well near the creek.

From a
Deyo
Mission
Publication
Edited by Harry
Wahhahdooah

Chapter 19
Deyo Mission

"You about ready in there, Minnie?" Papa called impatiently toward the tent.

"Almost," Minnie called out stretching the truth a bit. She was hurrying as fast as she could. Brushing, twisting and pinning her hair, lacing her shoes–she was becoming a little out of breath from rushing.

It never fails, Papa's always ready to go somewhere at the drop of a hat and expects everyone else do the same. Sure would've been nice to have had a little warning.

Next thing she knew, Minnie had started sweating, having worked herself into such a dither.

Its just like Oliver Johnson to suddenly toss out an idea to go to the Indian Mission today for church services, and expect her to be ready in two shakes of a lamb's tail.

This was their first Sunday since making camp out here on Jim's claim. They'd passed the neatly kept white frame church with its parsonage close by a few times while out looking at land. But it came as a complete surprise to her this morning when he volunteered to take her there for church.

Not knowing what time services began, Oliver, as usual was insisting on arriving plenty early. His reasons for going to church today were pretty simple. He wanted to meet the missionaries–people from back east–he'd heard. He wanted to satisfy his curiosity about his new neighbors. Right now they were the Johnsons' nearest neighbors. It being a mission for Comanche Indians he wanted to assure himself that Minnie would be welcome and safe there. Like her mother, she would always find a place to go to church. And, he wouldn't deny her that. He believed in keeping the sabbath.

Deyo Mission was only a mile and a half northwest from where they were camped.

September 1, Sunday
We got up late and after breakfast Papa and I got ready and went to the Baptist Mission to church, 2-1/2 miles by section corners. Arnold didn't want to go as he didn't feel well. We arrived at the church rather early so we went to the parsonage and made the acquaintance of Rev. Dayo and wife & child also his nephew, Mr. Dayo & wife. Before the last bell rang we went to the church where about 25 or 30 Indian men, women and children were gathered. The services were all in the American language, but the Rev. had an Indian interpreter who repeated the sermon in the Comanche language. At the close of the service, a young couple advanced to the altar and faced the congregation where the preacher united them in the holy bonds of matrimony.

When through, they were seated in the front row of seats and the benediction pronounced. Then the entire congregation went up and congratulated them. I also had that honor. They both talked good English. The bridegroom was dressed in black trousers and a black sateen shirt, short hair. The bride was dressed in a red silk dress, squaw fashioned, a white cashmere shawl fastened on like *an apron and a black one pulled up around her neck, both bordered with red roses, and she looked very sweet in her buckskin moccasins and deep fringes hanging around the calf of the leg. Arrived at camp 12:40 and had a cold dinner. After dinner we all indulged in a nap and later fished while Papa hunted a little. So, of course, had fresh meat for supper.*

In the afternoon, Minnie reclined on a blanket under the lattice-like shade of an elm tree. Its sun-scorched leaves made a good shelter from the sun on this mild September Sunday afternoon. The sky was a perfect blue and not a cloud. She'd been relaxing, reading, listening to the breeze rustling the grass and leaves and watching the diamond-like rays the sun made through the little spaces between the leaves. She allowed her mind to wander lazily, like a poplar leaf in a crystal clear stream.

Minnie was impressed with the Rev. and Mrs. Elton Deyo. They seemed genuinely hospitable and friendly. The Comanche people had become their family. They seemed to have a rare understanding of the Indians, seeing them not as wayward children, but as adults who had a different language, a different culture, and different standards. The Deyos loved their work.[21]

While visiting with the Deyos this morning before church, Minnie learned that the Deyos came to this territory from New York in 1893, soon after Mr. Deyo graduated from Colgate Theological Seminary. He'd heard an address by a speaker who appealed for missionaries to the Indians, and applied to be sent to the Comanche people. He asked for Anna for her approval and they were accepted.

After they were married, they traveled together from Rochester, New York to Comanche country. Arriving here in October, they found a partially built church. Later in their first year two women workers joined them: Miss Ida Schofield and Miss Lydia H. Birkhof. All four of them lived in the churchhouse until a parsonage could be built.

The church was organized in 1895 with Timbo, the first convert and the four missionaries as charter members. They named it the First Comanche Baptist Church. In 1896 there were eleven members. By 1897, two Comanche children from Fort Sill Indian School were baptized.[22]

The church had continued to grow and become part of the lives of the Comanche people.

In the spring of this year an outbreak of small pox had taken a heavy toll. One hundred and seventy-three Comanche people died in the epidemic.[23] Many more Kiowa and Cheyenne were also infected.

What a delightful surprise the unexpected wedding service was. She couldn't wait to include a description of the it in her letters back home. As Minnie thought about the wedding this morning her thoughts turned to the subject of marriage and the ever-perplexing riddle of love.

Naturally her thoughts wound up back in Cambridge, Nebraska with John Perdoux. That wonderful time had been ten weeks ago. Long ago and far away. Her heart no longer skipped a beat when she thought of him. If she tried she could still call to mind a picture of him the day he had taken her to church and they had gone riding. He had been so much fun–easy to be with. On the ride back home he'd put his arm around her and held the reins with one hand. He seemed to be a good man.

Since she read a lot, much of Minnie's impression about love came from novels. Her mother advised her daughters that it was greatly over-emphasized fiction. She said it was just a state of mind that sooner or later gave way to day-to-day reality. It wasn't until then–after all the illusions had fallen away–that so-called "lovers" discovered what kind of person the object of their affection really was. She said a person would be better off to pick a life partner that would match up well with them over the long haul.

John had promised to write to her and never forget her. Made her promise, too. The only letter she'd received from him left her feeling cold. His misspellings and crude wording could easily be excused, but his tone had been so impersonal. It had entirely changed the way she thought about him.

She'd written to him twice. First to let him know the name of the new town where she could receive letters. The other had been in answer to his letter. She decided to give him the benefit of the doubt–not everyone had the time nor the talent to create warm, interesting letters or to keep a relationship of any kind going at such a distance as there was between them. Guess John just wasn't a natural writer. Perhaps his interest in her was gone. Out of sight, out of mind, they say.

"What's the matter, Sis?" It was Arnold. He came up to where she was and seated himself on a mound of grass beside her.

"Nothing. Nothing is wrong. Why? She smiled as she answered.

"Your face had kind of sad look on it."

"It did? Really? Sad?"

"Well, maybe it wasn't sad. Don't believe I've seen that look on your face before. What were you thinking about?"

"None of your business," she said drawing a curtain on that part of her thoughts.

"Oh, him again," Arnold said knowingly with a teasing grin.

"Hey, want to go fishing?" He changed the subject, before Minnie had a chance to become annoyed. "I'm thinkin' about goin down to the creek and wettin' a hook."

Minnie smiled at him. "Always!" she said, thankful for the invitation and the interruption of her thoughts.

"Be with you in a minute. Going to change clothes."

"I'll wait."

***

THE DAY BEFORE Myrtle and Earnie were to leave for Gordon, they had been alone in camp. Minnie was visiting the Browns. The Hawps were getting things packed in preparation for leaving the next morning.

Myrtle was making her usual "suggestions" to Earnie. Today's lesson was on how to fold the tent. For the last half hour she'd been sitting in one of their chairs sipping coffee and squawking at him.

Earnie was painfully aware that the campers on either side of them were getting a kick out of her bossiness. It was embarrassing. Folding up a tent was not necessarily a two person job. One could do it. It was kind of like making a bed. If you had someone on the other side helping, you didn't have to traipse back and forth from one side to the other, keeping the two sides at an equal stage of completion. The job went more smoothly.

Earnie decided it was time to take action–or inaction–as the case may be.

"Hey, Myrtle," Earnie said, as if he'd just had the greatest idea.

"What?" she said glaring at him, wondering what in the world kind of crazy thing he was going to say now–here in the middle of his job.

"Come here."

Myrtle's eyes narrowed in suspicion and disgust. But she got up and walked over to Earnie.

"Here, hold these," his voice hushed; conspiratorial.

"Wh--?" She started, but decided to do what he was asking.

"Now, hold this in your other hand," he said picking up another corner.

Then lowering his voice he got up close to her face and said through his teeth, "Now when you get this thing folded let me know. I'll be at the lot sale."

He turned and walked away.

"Wuh!" Mrs. Hawp was speechless.

"Oh, Earnie, for Pete's sake!" she whined when he reached the edge of their camp. She stomped one foot like a horse with heel flies.

Seeing that he was not turning she used her loudest call. "Earrr--nie!" It had no effect on Earnie. He was still walking.

A baby started crying in the next camp. Myrtle suddenly became aware that the other campers around them were staring at her with narrowed eyes after that last screech--especially the mother of the baby! She didn't dare do that again.

Suddenly realizing how ridiculous she looked holding the tent corners and yelling she started fiddling around with it pretending she was doing the job herself. She dropped it once and started after Earnie but came back when she realized there would be no one left to watch camp. She sat down and fumed. She'd never felt so conspicuous.

***

MINNIE REFLECTED AS she looked around at the land from the top of a rise. She'd taken a stroll to see what was on the other side of Pecan Creek. She savored the pure blue of the sky, the lavender blues and purples of the Wichitas in the distance, the beauty of the tree-lined creek and the graceful tilt of the land as it ran down the slope to the creek's edge.

It WAS a beautiful piece of land--*Jim's land*.

She didn't know all the facts about claims, but she did read newspapers and listen to talk. She was reasonably sure a claim could not be won by contest unless there was evidence that the first claimant did not plan to "prove up" or was going to relinquish his claim. If this was going to be the basis for Papa's contest, what did he have as evidence that Jim was abandoning his claim?

Lots of men who'd secured a claim early on had returned home to sell their house, pack up belongings, gather the family. Most all of them planned to return to their claim before the deadline.

The proclamation stated and newspapers were still reporting that claimants should take up residence on their claims around October 4. Though there was beginning to be some evidence that an extension of six months might be granted if one could show sufficient cause.

<u>September 2</u>
I got up and dressed about 3 o'clock this morning as it was raining dreadfully hard and I was afraid something would get wet. After seeing everything was all right I laid down and slept till 7:30 when we all arose and got breakfast. The five hour rain raised this creek considerable. We were going to town but presumed Wolf Creek would be up so we couldn't cross. After dinner we went to town. Returned about dusk.

September 3
The men worked on the well, I sewed a little, read, and put in the day doing something.

September 4
It rained a little in the forenoon. We went to town about 11:00 and returned 6:30 p.m. Papa bought a plow and also a large box for well-curbing.

***

"I believe our Papa can find more excuses to go to town than any two other men." Minnie was thinking out loud; Arnold being the lucky recipient of her thoughts. He was a good brother.

"It just seems to me–and I have no objections mind you--" Minnie was kneading bread

"--as long as you get to go along?" Arnold finished her sentence for her. Minnie glared at him.

"--that every other day Papa is thinking of some reason to go to town."

"You know what I think?" Arnold rarely gave her his opinion on anything. She was all ears now. "I believe it has mostly to do with this quarter section of land--Jim's claim. This lottery *fol-de-rol* isn't nearly over; can't be until the contests are all decided. They can't even begin to look at the contests until the end of the filing period. I imagine he feels insecure about it--worryin' if someone else might come along and file a contest on this same quarter. I think that our being here ahead of time would be enough for someone to question Papa rights. He probably feels like he needs to keep up on new developments, announcements 'n' such. You know how restless he gets if he doesn't have every angle right under his thumb."

Minnie looked over at her sixteen-year-old brother with pride. When had he become such an insightful, intelligent person?

***

WHEN THE JOHNSONS were in town, yesterday Minnie was alone at noon. Looking around for a place to eat, she decided on the Saddle Rock. In its brand new frame building, it was advertising barbecue as their special for the day. She remembered how much she'd liked the taste of the barbecue beef her father bought in Cordell, on the 4th of July. She decided to go in.

Upon entering, she found no empty tables. There was one table however at which one lady was seated. Minnie looked at her with a question on her face. The young lady smiled pleasantly and nodded to the seat opposite her.

"Thank you," Minnie said, "I appreciate your letting me sit with you. Is the barbecue good?"

"Best I've had, lately." the girl answered, when she finished chewing. "But if you don't like your sauce hot, be sure to tell them."

"Thanks, I will. Oh, my name's Minnie, and your's?"

"Hannah."

"Pleased to meet you, Hannah."

Minnie ordered her dinner. It came quickly and the ladies ate their meal almost in silence, except for a few comments, here and there.

Hannah finished eating but seemed reluctant to go. She wasn't talking but she appeared to have something she wanted to say. It took her awhile to get up the nerve but she finally spat it out, "That's a nice blouse. Did you make it?"

"Why, yes. Yes I did," Minnie answered looking down first to see which one she was wearing. It was the light blue organdy.

"I've been wanting to try sewin' some of my clothes," Hannah said, "But I don't know where to begin. Could you give me some advice?"

Minnie sure could. She would love to help her out.

"A person usually starts with something pretty simple that doesn't require a lot of complicated skills."

"Like ...?"

"Like an apron or a night gown."

"I see," Hannah said. "Kinda like swimming? You don't just run and jump into deep water?"

"Exactly. At least, most people don't." They smiled.

"Would you--?"

Hannah paused for a long moment.

"I imagine I would. I owe you a favor for letting me sit with you. What do you have in mind?"

"There's a dry goods store three lots down, I was wonderin..."

"I'd love to," Minnie said, happy to feel like a "big sister" again.

At the Dry Goods store, Minnie and Hannah discussed options. Hannah decided to start with a night gown.

"That'll take two identical pieces, one for the front and one for the back." They selected a bolt of unbleached muslin and had enough cut for the simple garment. Minnie sketched a pattern on a large piece of brown wrapping paper they obtained at the counter. She explained all about laying the pattern on a fold of material.

"Now, cut two pieces in the same way–one for the front and one for the back. No sleeves yet."

"Yes, I see that."

"The places you'll need to sew I'm marking with a broken line. Sew with small straight stitches. Fold some ribbon in half to cover the edges of the neck opening and the armholes."

Minnie finally finished her instructions.

"As easy as that?" Hannah asked.

"As easy as that," Minnie confirmed.

"Oh, and always hide your stitches, best you can."

Hannah smiled happily in answer. She couldn't wait to get started.

As they walked out of the store and prepared to go their separate ways Hannah said.

"Minnie, you have no idea how much this means to me. Thank you for being so kind."

"Oh, now, you'll turn my head," Minnie said, waving off the gratitude. "It's been my pleasure, Hannah, I assure you. Hope to see you next time I'm in town."

"When'll that be?"

"Honey, with a father like mine, there is absolutely no way of telling," Minnie said good-naturedly. They both laughed as they walked in different directions.

Chapter 20
Days of September

September 5
I helped Papa and Arnold by draining sand and water off the well. Arnold and I blistered our hands and fingers which made the day memorable. Sunk the curbing just before we went to camp for dinner. As we were going to camp, a covered wagon came over the hill and camped for dinner near us, and cooked on our campfire. One man, Mr. F. J. Shebester (Orlena, Cooke Co. Texas) filed on the next claim east of us and has a family of seven children.

September 6
I baked bread and after dinner took a bath, did some patching and did a little tent cleaning.

We started for Lawton at 8:a.m. and arrived there 11:20. After unhitching the team, Papa and I applied for the following quarter sections of school land. Papa applied for:

1st choice-- NW 1/4 of Section 13, T 1 n, R 13, bid $59 with three year bonus $57. Appraised rental value $40.

2nd choice--NE 1/4 of same section. Appraised rental value $35. Bid $37.

My first choice--SW 1/4 of same Sec. Bid $65. Appraised rental value $40. Bonus $75.

Second choice--SE 1/4 of same Section (draft sent for $57 and $75), Bid $49. Appraised rental value $45.

I then went and got the mail and mailed the applications which Mr. Huff made out in Myers and Huff's Law Office. When I returned, we three and no more went to an eating house and had a good dinner. After dining we did our trading and retraced our wagon tracks to the Pecan Creek camp. Arrived here 5:40. We also learned of the sad news of President McKinley being shot twice-- once in the chest and one bullet through the abdomen.

While eating dinner at one of the restaurants in Lawton, the Johnsons heard talk that by coincidence Geronimo, the Apache "prisoner of war", was appearing at the same Pan American Exposition in Buffalo, New York, where President McKinley was speaking when he was shot by an assassin. Geronimo lived as a trustee at Fort Sill. He'd become a person of great notoriety and of interest to people across the nation. These days he willingly went along on public relations junkets around the country with a guard of army personnel.

September 8, Sunday
Papa hunted the black ponies which got away in the night but didn't go far. I wrote a letter and we all read mixed literature. After dinner we went down the creek and fished. Caught three messes.

*I was going to wash this morning but looked too much
like rain. Papa and Arnold started today to dig a cave
12x20 where we intend to build if at all. After dinner
Papa plowed.*

A cave? Not what Minnie would have prefered. She
supposed it would be better than freezing in the tent all
winter. Twelve by twenty was a good-sized room. Minnie
doubted that when the whole family of nine got together
they'd be comfortable for long.

The Johnsons first residence would be a "dug out", cut
from the side of a hill, so that only one wall and portions of
two sides would need to be constructed. A door and two
windows would be built into the front.

September 10
*I washed and baked. Papa and Arnold went to the Baptist
Mission and ground their ax.*

Minnie was becoming increasingly bored and restless.
She'd read all her books, several times and craved the
company of someone with whom she could have a
meaningful conversation. An honest exchange of thoughts
would be so nice--the kind of conversation a woman could
have with another woman. Intellectual stimulation, that
was it! With Papa being so uncommunicative lately, and
Arnold not inclined to discuss subjects in which she was
interested, Minnie felt as if her ability to be neighborly was
withering. At noon, Papa agreed to her riding Cole over to
the mission to visit Anna Deyo. She crossed the creek and
from there she headed toward the mission.

The mountains were spectacularly clear today. The
sky was a beautiful blue with a few puffy white clouds.
From the top of the rise she stopped for a bit to savor the
view. The Wichitas were in fine form today with pastel
hues of purple and blue touched with lavender they were
clearly visible seven miles away. She'd never seen them
look more beautiful. Their appearance changed constantly
with the movement of the sun.

Minnie noticed a horse and rider approaching from a

distance. The rider waved and she hesitantly waved back. She decided to move her horse along at a more rapid pace in the direction of the mission. She believed the person approaching from her left probably just wanted to pass the time of day. But, being a woman alone, it was best that she just continue on, not appearing eager to stop. Now the rider kicked into a lope and was more rapidly approaching her.

Curiosity got the better of her and she turned her head to see a man on horseback–gaining ground. It was apparent that the man wished to detain or speak with her. Not wanting to appear downright unneighborly she decided to pull up. At least she was in sight of the mission now.

What could he want? Minnie prayed she hadn't made a mistake in stopping. She would stay mounted. If this person so much as leaned too far in her direction she'd give him the boot and ride off–at a full run–toward the mission.

The man rode straight to her, threw a long right leg over his horse's back he stepped down and turned to greet her.

"Minnie? Minnie Johnson, isn't it?" he asked, removing his hat. She decided against kicking him just now racking her brain for where she had met him before.

"Oh, yes! The quinine sulfate--at the drug store. How could I forget such generosity. Forgive me, I've forgotten your name."

"Clarence. Clarence Pool."

"Nice to see you again, Mr. Pool. Your headache went away, I trust?"

"My wha-oh yes, the headache–it did–it cleared right up. I was able to find some quinine at another drug-- 'tent?" Clarence responded, adding, "It's hard to change your vocabulary for a tent town."

She laughed. "I agree, Mr. Pool, it most assuredly is."

"Please call me Clarence. Do you live around here? I haven't had time to meet any neighbors. Stayed in town mostly. Went back to Iowa for a while--returned yesterday. I've claimed the southeast quarter of this section southwest of us."

"Well, how about that–looks like we are neighbors." She dismounted then. They started walking, leading their horses and visiting.

"My father, brother, and I are located on the south-east quarter of Section 13, I believe it is?" She'd worded that sentence carefully. She would not intentionally mislead him into thinking it was their land until it actually was. "We have a family of nine. The rest are still up in Nebraska."

"Where are you going, now?" Seeing as how he was walking along with her, Clarence thought it'd be nice to know where he was going.

"I'm on my way to call on Mrs. Deyo at the Baptist Mission. Have you met the Deyos, yet?"

"No, Ma'am, I haven't had the opportunity. As I said, I've only stayed on my claim a couple of nights."

"Why don't you come along with me; I'll introduce you, and it will be two neighbors you've met this afternoon."

"Well, I was headed for Lawton but you make it sound as if I really ought to take the time," Clarence said. "Looks like you've talked me into it," he added with a smile.

"Rev. Deyo is thinking of starting a post office out here. He'd looking into the process, I understand. He's been so helpful--encourages the new settlers to use his home as a sort of 'clearing house' of information"

Since returning from the Philippines with dysentery, Clarence resisted meeting people. He felt self-conscious because of the extreme loss of weight. He'd been told he was a nice-looking man, but anymore he didn't feel that way. In fact, he avoided mirrors feeling repulsed by his skin and bones reflection. Those feelings were forgotten as he walked along beside Minnie, as if she didn't see his exterior.

"We went to church at the mission a week ago--my father and I." Minnie talked on cheerfully, thrilled to be in the company of someone other than her father and brother. "The service was delivered in English and translated into Comanche, but Rev. Deyo's message was still well done."

"Really?"

"We met some Comanche neighbors: Paddyaker's family, the Red Elks, Pekah and her family, Niyah and Topetchy, and I believe the other lady I met was the wife of Pacheka. Then, there was John Timbo, a sincere gentle man, who was the first one to allow himself to be baptized." Minnie was on a roll now. There was no stopping her.

"You see, it being a Baptist mission and most Baptists believe that a person should be baptized or--put underwater--to symbolize their conversion. I understand it took the Deyos a long time to convince just one of the group to allow Rev. Deyo to dip him under the water."

"Wouldn't you have loved to have been a fly on the wall the first time this very nice--but nevertheless *caucasion* preacher--brought up the subject of immersion? Can't you just see the interpreter having a questioning look come over his face and perhaps peering at him out of the corner of his eye. I'm sure he had to stop Rev. Deyo and ask him to repeat the sentence to be certain he'd heard him right. Oh, and the looks of bewilderment and curiousity, on the faces of the people. Can't you imagine--when they found they'd heard it right--and that he was serious?

"Or perhaps, they began to grin and chuckle thinking he was joking." Clarence put in. He was thoroughly enjoying Minnie's imagination and commentary as they listened and walked.

"Papa and I were present for the wedding of a young Comanche man and his maiden, the first Sunday of September. They had the ceremony directly following church." she added thinking how long it had been since she'd enjoyed such a nice chat.

"Really? My, you were lucky! Didn't the Indians seem to mind or frown upon your presence there?" Clarence asked.

"Hm-m, I don't think so," Minnie said giving the thought some consideration, "Oh, my I certainly hope not. Though it would be hard to tell, I suppose. The Comanche are extremely courteous and respectful. One of their customs is that if someone admires something that belongs to them, they are bound or..." Minnie searched for a word, "obligated' to give the admired object to that person?"

"Is that right?"

"Yes, isn't it a wonderfully selfless tenet? She says they've never known greed. It doesn't fit their system of beliefs."

"Sadly, we of European heritage will probably teach them." Clarence commented.

"Oh, I hope not. Anna, Mrs. Deyo, says that she has actually had to learn not to compliment or comment on a particularly nice blanket or shawl. Or soon it will be pressed upon her, till she feels she must take it or risk hurting the feelings of the one who is giving it."

"Minnie Johnson, you are going to enjoy being out here with the Comanche people."

"Oh, you're right, I am. I find them very interesting as people and as individuals, too. But there's more to it than that. You can call me a silly ole' sap for feeling this way, but..."

"Go ahead, whatever it is, you can say it. I'm not the judgmental type."

"Well, I feel kinda sorry for them--the way we are taking the land that was their's. I consider myself fortunate to have been able to meet and make acquaintences with them through the Deyos."

When Minnie had been sick with typhoid her mother had been so involved with nursing the new baby and trying to keep an eye on Papa's store while he was away that she needed help. It was a Sioux woman named Yukola who nursed Minnie back to health. Though the Sioux was another culture with different traditions, Minnie would always feel kindly toward Indians as a whole.

"Momma always says, 'Bloom where you're planted." So I'm taking advantage of this place where I am planted to learn new things. Also, it being the only church out here, it's an excuse to get away and see people other than my father and brother."

She looked over at Clarence for emphasis, "Now, don't get me wrong, they are both good men. It's just that after a whole summer of living so close...well...a little distance can be quite good sometimes."

"Perhaps there'll be enough interest out here to start a church for the settlers, if folks are so inclined," Clarence said.

"I'm sure there will be, in time. It is something to think about."

"When my father and mother join me down here; he's quite an organizer, and would, I'm sure, just love to get the ball rolling."

"Your parents may be joining you, then?"

"Yes, that's right. There's a quarter joining mine that Dad will qualify to homestead because of his status as a veteran of the Civil War. And, because of my health situation I'd like to have family near me."

"May I inquire about your health without being too nosy?" Minnie asked.

"Well, since you've asked so delicately," he smiled again. Clarence usually felt too self-conscious about this health thing but he felt different with Minnie. He felt he'd found a friend—a true friend.

"I picked up an intestinal 'bug' in the Philippines. The big name for it is, amoebic dysentery. The doctors told me it remains in a person's intestinal tract their whole life. Been treating it with Quinine—that's the reason I was at the drug store the day we met. It wasn't a headache."

He paused, looked up toward the mountains, then said, "That's the reason I'm so thin."

Minnie didn't look at his face yet. Let him speak his truth without her disturbing it.

"I've been looking into possible cures and treatments. I just won't accept that I must live the rest of my life like this."

"I've had typhoid myself but I just can't imagine going through what you've been through for,—how long now? A couple of years? Going on three? I can sympathize with you. I got awfully weak and thin, as well," Minnie said.

"Really?"

"You should have seen me when we started this trip. Or, no maybe it's best you didn't."

They were now approaching the Deyos' parsonage. They walked the last few yards in silence.

After the introductions Clarence made his apologies. If he wanted to return to his claim before dark he must be on his way. As he rode toward Lawton he felt more cheerful than he had in months. Yes, he had needed to meet the Deyos. Especially since Reverend Deyo might be taking on the postal assignment. And–that Minnie! My, she'd make anyone feel better!

> <u>September 11</u>
> The men plowed before dinner and I did as I always do when I have nothing else to do. Read. After dinner I rode Neg to the Mission and visited all afternoon with Mrs. Deyo. She lent me two books to read. One, "In His Steps: What Would Jesus Do? author, Rev. Chas. M. Sheldon. The other, "Tell it All: A Woman's Life in Polygamy", author Mrs. T.B.H. Stenthouse. After a pleasant afternoon I rode home to our house.

> <u>September 12</u>
> 7:45 a.m. We all went to town in the light wagon, and didn't return till 5 p.m.

Business District, Lawton, O.T.   October 1901

Courtesy of Oklahoma Historical Society: Heye Foundation Collection

Chapter 21

Trips to Town

<u>September 13</u>
Papa plowed and I cooked cabbage soup for dinner. We
had dinner early as Papa wanted to go to town early. He
left at 12:15 on Cole and intended to stay till to-morrow
night. Arnold and I scarcely did anything but read and
once in a while looked after the horses. Papa went with
the intentions of buying another team & wagon.

"Did you understand Papa to say he'd be spending the
night in town?" Arnold asked Minnie as they waved a last
good-bye to him and started back down the slope to their
camp.

"I was just wondering if I'd heard him right myself."

Brother and sister looked at each other searching the
other's face for a clue to the others thoughts. What did
Papa have up his sleeve now?

"Strange," Minnie said in a tone that implied nothing.

"Indeed," Arnold responded. Trying for an English accent like the Havershams back in Gordon. It was a silly little thing they did for laughs now and then.

"A bit curious I must say," Minnie played along.

"Quite so," Arnold responded with the closest thing he could come to an English expression on his face–one eyebrow raised.

"I shan't be atawl surprised if he does, then."

They both burst into giggles at their own silliness.

<u>September 14</u>
Saturday. Arnold & I were just through with dinner when he declared he saw Papa coming in a heavy lumber wagon, Cole tied beside a very pretty large bay team. He was right. We met him very welcomely as we always do when he returns from town as he nearly always brings a message from home. This time he also brought the sad expected news of the death of our President.

Stirring the meat and potatoes cooking on a low fire, Minnie watched as Papa unloaded the wagon. She glanced over as he dragged something made of something like binder twine out of the back of the wagon.

"Papa, is that what I think it is?" Minnie exclaimed, slamming the lid down on the Dutch oven harder than she'd intended and rushing to the wagon twenty feet away. Surely it can't be. But it was. Papa had purchased a hammock for Minnie.

She was not only overjoyed at having one again she was surprised he'd spent the money for it. She'd been making-do with that old broken-down bed so long.

Every now and then Papa did something like this that threw her off; forced her to admit that he appreciated her.

<u>September 15-Sunday</u>
After a few hours of leisure, Arnold & I prepared to ride the blacks to church at the Mission, which we did. We met Mrs. & Miss Hart and another young lady before the service. We returned to camp about 1 o'clock and dinner was ready as I had it prepared to boil before leaving.

> *Papa kept fire. O! yes, I must not forget to tell you Papa*
> *got me a nice hammock in town yesterday and the present*
> *was a complete surprise. Of course, I gave myself up to*
> *its pleasure this afternoon and read. An erasable memory*
> *of a year ago crept freshly into my mind, since it was the*
> *last time I enjoyed a hammock fully.*

> <u>September 16</u>
> *It is very damp and foggy this morning but the men are*
> *out plowing anyway. The last three or four nights have*
> *been much cooler. Heavy dews fall before dark and the*
> *mornings are serenely beautiful. I went to Mission.*

As Minnie rode across the prairie toward the mission, she began to wonder–again–about the number of things Papa had purchased lately. There was the plow, the heavy lumber wagon, the new team, the hammock. Wonder where the money for all this is coming from? Banks were advertising that they would loan money to people who had a claim, but.--

> <u>September 17</u>
> *I baked bread to-day but read most of the time. Papa*
> *plowed.*

Oliver Johnson wasn't letting any grass grow under his feet. He was breaking ground; digging a well and making plans to cut, rake, and stack the tall prairie grass on their leases a mile north. They would use the hay for their own animals and sell the excess to anyone who wanted to buy it.

The curious thing was that Papa was doing all this *before* the closing of the filing period. The proclamation stated that no one was to take up residence on the land until after that. Only after that date would the U. S. Land Office begin hearing contests and deciding who had rights to disputed claims.

The marshals and the sheriff had all the lawbreakers they could handle right there in Lawton. It was doubtful they were interested in going out into the countryside, looking for minor law breakers–unless there was a complaint.

To "prove up" on a claim, a person had to live on the land for 14 months. Whether they'd been lucky in the lottery, purchased a relinquishment, or acquired a claim by contest–all had to go through the proving up process. At the end of that time, they would list four neighbors, who must attest to the fact that the homesteader had made improvements. In this way, the homesteader "proved" he'd done his job; built fences, sheds, a shelter to live in, turned some soil. The neighbors signed affidavits stating how long the person had lived on the claim and listing each improvement made. After the statements were returned to the land office and a notice run in a local paper stating the homesteader's intent, he would be allowed to pay $1.25 an acre and be given clear title to the land.

Oliver Johnson was taking daringly large strides in view of the fact that it was impossible to be certain he'd be the owner of that land in the long run.

> September 18
> 6:45 we started to town. When nearly there, I got out and walked down to the (Squaw) creek where Stephen Browns were camped and found them still there. We had a good little visit, then Miss Bessie accompanied me up town and we did some trading. At noon she returned to camp and I sought a lunch room. Arrived at camp about 5 p.m.

Minnie wanted to visit the Browns again. She always enjoyed time spent with them. The long intervals of time without the friendship of another female out on the claim hung heavy and made her wish for the friendly chatter of other ladies--though she'd been happily surprised at how much she'd enjoyed the conversation with Clarence last week.

On the ride to Lawton she told Papa she'd like to pay the Browns a visit. When they reached the edge of the Squaw Creek encampment, he reigned in the team to let her off the wagon. She found the Browns still there and as welcoming as ever.

"Oh, my dear, yes!" Mrs. Irene Brown replied when Minnie asked if they were anxious to move onto their new residential lot.

"You see my husband, Stephen, hasn't been able to find a contractor who has an opening to begin our house. It seems all are booked for the next two months."

"Some folks are going ahead and moving their tents and wagons onto their lot where they plan to build," Laura commented. "But we've got everything arranged here, so it's fairly comfortable and we like being close to the creek."

"I know what you mean the water situation being the way it is," Minnie said.

"We plan to build a small, two-room, box house at first." Bessie put in. "Like everyone else in town." .

"Something to just get us out of the cold for the winter." Laura explained. "Next summer we can add rooms and a porch, maybe even finish out an attic room upstairs."

"Sounds good to me," Minnie said. "I've got my fingers crossed hoping Papa isn't going to still have us in the tent when the first blue norther comes through." They laughed with her. "He said the other day that he kinda likes the idea of trying to 'winter it out' in a tent. Can you imagine?"

"Patience, patience," said Bessie. "A few years from now we'll look back on this time and wonder how we made it. Existing in tents for so long."

We've been taking advantage of the time on our hands and are getting a lot of sewing done." her mother added. The girls showed their different sewing projects. A tablecloth–embroidered white on white–a project they'd all worked on. Each girl had finished a dress and a blouse. Mrs. Brown was currently working on a set of pillow cases and had crocheted several doilies.

When it was time for Minnie to leave she said she was inspired to take on a sewing project of her own.

"It always does me good to see what other folks are doing. I get all excited and resolve to start a new project of my own. A sewing project is just what I need. I know it would lift my spirits. The days are so long out there now. Most folks aren't going to be taking up residence until after the deadline. So we have very few neighbors."

"Well you just come on by and visit with us anytime," Mrs. Brown said cheerfully, "and get *inspired*." She said the word jokingly, like a preacher would use it in a sermon. Laura and Minnie left to walk uptown together.

They chatted about everything; teaching possibilities and when would there be school buildings finished and ready for classes? Both had teaching credentials for grades one through eight and expected to be employed as teachers in one of the many townships surrounding the town if not in Lawton.

"Father believes they'll be organizing schools in each townships soon after the 60 day filing period is over and that schools will be starting as soon as schoolhouses can be built."

"I hope so," Minnie replied. "I need to get back into a classroom. Teaching is something I really enjoy." After shopping and visiting Minnie and Laura said their good-byes and Minnie began looking for her father and brother.

***

Mr. Huff, Oliver Johnson's lawyer, spied him coming in his direction. Probably in town to pick up his mail and as usual drop by here.

"Mr. Johnson, come in," Mr. Huff hailed Oliver from the opening of his tent which had been moved to the back of his business lot to make room for his new office building. His tent now stood behind the raised walls of two-by-fours; the skeleton of his new office.

Oliver carefully picked his way past the carpenters sawing two-by-fours and the piles of scrap wood beside the structure. Arriving at the tent he extended his hand to his lawyer in greeting.

"Looks like you're gonna have a bonafide office here before you know it." he said as they shook hands.

"And, none too soon, I'll tell you that. I am ready to send for my wife and kids. I'm gettin' real tired of my own cookin'. How can I help you today, Oliver?"

"Oh, just wonderin' if there's anything new on that

contest we filed."

"No, sir, there's not. Like I told you they's not really anything we can expect to happen or that we can do 'till after the filin' time's up. Haveya heard anything from the registrant on that land? What was his name--Reid?"

"Yes, that's right, James–Jim Reid's his name. No, I haven't heard from him. I sent him the letter you helped me with, offering to buy his relinquishment, but haven't heard a thing."

The banging of hammers so close to them drowned out Mr. Huff's response. Oliver asked for a repeat.

"I said, that's actually good--for us--that is for our case, I believe." Mr. Huff had almost hollered that time."

"Oh, okay. I just wanted to check in with you while I was here in town."

"Glad ya did, Oliver. When those records are opened to us, after October 4, we'll be able to find out more 'bout what if anything transpired between your Mr. Reid and the land office."

"I understand."

"Say, you wouldn't happen to know if this Mr. Reid had a previous account with the U. S. Land Office would you? I mean had he ever had another homestead?"

Mr. Huff watched Oliver's eyes shift up and to the right.

"Don't recall him bringin' it up, if he did."

"Uh-huh."

"Say, I gotta be goin'." Oliver checked his pocket watch. "I left my son runnin' errands and am hopin' to meet my daughter over here pretty soon."

"Good seein' ya, Mr. Johnson." Mr. Huff said, thinking that his client was not coming across straight with him. Playing both ends against the middle more than likely. There is something he's not telling.

WALKING PAST Smith's Dry Goods, Minnie determined to go in and see what new things they might have in stock. She walked to the table with the bolts of fabric stacked high. Her eyes landed on one particular bolt of cotton print with a light blue background. Checking her pocketbook with her jealously guarded money she found she had enough to make the purchase. A sewing project to lift her spirits; that's what she needed. Sewing on a new dress would help her look forward to good times to come.

While she was having her yardage cut, she heard someone whispering her name.

"Minnie, over here." She followed the sound and discovered Hannah in the next isle looking at the display of ribbons and lace.

"Well, hello, Hannah, my it's good to see you! How's the sewing coming?"

"Oh, Minnie! What is it they say when someone hits upon what the work they really love doing? They find their...?"

"Their calling?"

"That's it. I've found my callin'."

"You have?" Minnie was both surprised by and happy for her young "student."

"Yes an' I never knew I could have so much fun in my life. I'm savin' up for a sewin' machine, now."

"Have you tried to set in sleeves yet?"

"Oh, dear me, yes. Had to take out the first ones a bunch of times; learnin' to get those gathers just right–but I kept workin' at it till I finally got the hang of it. It finally made sense to me. I'm workin' on my third dress!"

"Han-nah! You are putting me on!"

"No, I'm not. I sew every spare minute. I love it. I never get tired of it. I just love it." Happiness sparkled in her eyes.

"You are one amazing young lady." Minnie said. "I'd take my hat off to you, if it wasn't pinned on."

They both laughed.

"The reason I got you over here is I need some advice. What do you think a fair price to ask for a dress would be?"

"Oh? Someone asking you to make a dress for them? That's wonderful!"

"Let me see,"Minnie began to figure. "Let's say you pay between two and three dollars for the fabric, then your work ought to be worth that much, again--at least. I would think you could ask five or six dollars for a basic dress and not be out of line. I'd make it seven or eight if there's lots of fussy work like extra buttons, lace, ribbon or other complications on it."

Hannah smiled, excitement dancing in her eyes.

"That's what I was thinkin' too, but I thought I'd check with you and see if you agreed. I was worried that I might be way off base."

Hannah's math skills were improving too. She'd enrolled in the "school of life." Experience was indeed the best teacher. The worth of the different things she'd purchased and the value of a person's time spent working was beginning to make sense to her.

***

MINNIE WAS bothered over the fact that Papa had received no card to verify his registration. She recalled the morning in July, when Papa went to the Quinette store with the intention of registering and emerged late in the afternoon. Strange, wasn't it? Minnie recalled that Papa acted as though he was finally done with that task and was ready to go on out with the rest of the Nebraska folks, looking at the land. She'd assumed everything went fine. Had Papa been able to fill in the forms correctly? Had he gotten mad, left without registering? Perhaps his writing just hadn't been legible enough for them to deliver his post card.

According to the proclamation all who registered were supposed to be notified by postal card, no matter what their number was. Even if it was 8,399--*and there were only 6,500 claims available in each distric*t--they were still supposed to be notified of their number, to prove that their card had been in the lottery bin. To this day, no card had shown up for Papa that she knew of.

She suddenly recalled the day they ate Schrandt's watermelon. How they'd saved the seeds for Jim to plant on his farm. Looking back in her diary, she found the date--August 7. On that date, before Jim filed his claim, everyone--*including Jim*--assumed he would have a farm on which to plant those seeds. Now, he's back in Nebraska?

Chapter 22
Puttin' Up Hay

<u>September 20</u>
Papa and Arnold made a hay rack & grind-stone frame.
I baked and sewed.

Having been bitten by the "sewing bug" and purchasing five yards of the blue cotton print, Minnie was anxious to get started on her new dress. Without mother's sewing machine it would take a lot longer and challenge her stick-to-it-iveness. She'd been needing something to occupy her mind and exercise her creative side.

The pattern pieces for her favorite dress were stashed away in one of the trunks. She'd cut copies of them two years ago when she borrowed the pattern from a teacher friend.

Laying all the pattern pieces on the material Minnie cut out all the pieces before dinner laying them aside while they ate. In the afternoon she would get the bodice stitched together and gather the top of the full sleeves in readiness for attaching them. For her the initial part of dressmaking was always the most exciting.

> September 21
> Papa has gone to town. Arnold has been busy about camp. I have washed clothes this morning. Am now ready to do some mending. Papa returned at 8:30 p.m. with mower and rake.

As she lay in bed before falling asleep, Minnie again added together her estimates of prices for a mower and rake. Once again she wondered about their money situation. Maybe Papa has visited one of the banks in town.

She'd been able to get more sewing done on the dress as well as her other chores for the day. She'd finished the bodice except for buttons, button-holes, and putting down the neck facing. Buttonholes were Minnie's least favorite part of the process. She wondered if Hannah had learned to finish button holes yet. That girl was amazing. How quickly she'd picked up sewing. Guess sometimes people just have a knack for certain things.

> September 22, Sunday
> I being a little out of sorts we did not go to church, but spent the day in camp. Four men camped here for dinner, one of whom was Mr. Gem. The gentleman filed on the S.W. of Sec 11 (W.A. Emvikerson, Comanche, I.T. camped here about 10 days ago.)

> September 23
> Monday. Arnold & Papa mowed & raked all day. I baked.

There had been something on Papa's mind this evening. Minnie had no idea what it was but he'd only picked at his supper.

"Minnie," he said hesitantly after the dishes were washed and put away, "I was wonderin' if you'd mind--and if you'd feel up to--Arnold and I sure do need help bringing in the hay the next few days. I don't see how we're going to be able to get it all put up without some help. Y'see I've been counting on selling hay to folks as a way of making money to build a house big enough for the whole family. The cave will keep the three of us from freezing through this winter. But, we are going to need much more room when the rest of the family gets here."

There was no need to answer, other than to acknowledge that she'd heard. If Papa asked, you were signed on as a definite "yea".

Surpised and a little angered by her father's request for her help in the field, Minnie ambled down to the creek to walk it off. She'd never expected Papa to ask so much of her. He'd always been so firm about his daughters "acting like ladies." Now it would be hauling hay, cooking, washing dishes, mending, and washing clothes. As any woman knew those domestic chores constituted more than a full time job.

She'd been so excited about her sewing project, too! Spending time on the dress she was making was her way of giving a much-needed lift to her spirits. But she supposed it would be selfish to put her own wants before the family's needs. Minnie's thought trailed off as the next one shoved into the front of her mind. "H-m-m, there is something familiar about this–like a *deja-vu*.

Oh, yes! She remembered now. It was what her mother said to her before they left Gordon, when she was talking about marrying too soon. Mary Johnson had said to her daughter, "You deserve more than being the milkmaid or field hand for some two-bit farmer or no-account son of an immigrant down in the new territory."

"Well, Mom--guess what!" she said with a twist of irony.

Minnie's opinion of what should be the top priority was not the highest on Papa's list. The cave still lacked the front wall, roof, windows, and door and September was slipping away. Bringing in a crop of prairie hay and using it to sell through the winter was an ambitious undertaking--but weren't Papa's ideas always?

True, she was healthier now than when they left Gordon in May. There was no doubt about that. She wasn't as skinny and frail and her appetite was better. But was she really ready for long, hot days of field work? She wasn't at all sure about that.

She felt torn: she knew her father had been feeling tired and overwhelmed by all the things he was trying to get done. Though she didn't have any idea what was behind his efforts, she respected the fact that he was ambitious in his work.

Minnie turned around and started slowly back toward the camp. She straightened her posture which had been wilting and said to herself, "Okay, I'll wear a sunbonnet and use a pair of Papa's gloves to keep from turning dark. Don't need to LOOK like a field hand."

"Wonder which shoes a lady wears for tramping hay?" she considered, feeling better now and, attempting a humorous attitude to the thing.

> <u>September 24</u>
> *Arnold mowed and raked while Papa and I hauled. I*
> *drove and tramped the hay while he did all the pitching.*
> *Two loads.*

Minnie drove the team from place to place around the field. Papa threw pitchforks full of the dried prairie grass into the hay rack wagon. Then, Minnie, tramped it down by tromping and stomping all over it. This compressed the hay into a smaller space enabling them to put more hay in the rack and make fewer trips than if it were loosely packed.

> <u>September 25</u>
> *Today we continued yesterday's labor. Hauled five loads*
> *of hay.*

The field work did wear Minnie out! She came in terribly exhausted at the end of each day. Papa and Arnold had been doing the meal preparation and the dishes--thank goodness. But soon a laundry would need to be done.

> <u>September 26</u>
> *Arnold went to town for a stock of supplies. Papa and I*
> *hauled four loads to-day. Arnold returned at 2:30 pm*

and brought the light wagon back that we before had left
for fixing. I drove the range cattle out of the meadow
several times to-day. Bothered us more than usual.

"Guess what!" Arnold jumped down off the wagon.
"What?" Minnie dutifully asked
"The train has arrived in Lawton."
"Finally, at last!" Minnie said.
"Bout time," Papa said.

Arnold had gotten the scoop on the train this morning in town. Yesterday, the train actually pulled into the Rock Island station. The report went that the engineer, hearing the applause upon his arrival, said, "Careful, now, folks. Don't spook my horse."

Minnie was cheered by the news. Maybe it wouldn't seem so impossibly far-fetched for the rest of the family to join them. She felt relieved just knowing that train access was now available in Lawton. Perhaps now it wouldn't seem like they were quite so cut off from the civilized world.

<u>September 27</u>
Hauled two loads before dinner. This afternoon Papa is
fixing the hay rack and we have a sickle to grind. Then,
this evening we'll go after another load of hay. The hay
meadow is a half mile from here.

They waited until after the heat of the day to go back for another load. In the late afternoon Minnie measured out the ingredients for bread, Pa stirred it up and Arnold was timing it. While Minnie bathed off the itchy hay chaff at the creek, a man called at their camp. During the visit, the smell of bread cooking began to be more than he could take He asked Papa if he would sell him a loaf of the bread.

"Guess I'll leave that up to my daughter. She's the one that makes it and I've been imposing on her good nature to help us in the hayfield. We'll ask her if she wants to sell some when she returns from the creek," Papa answered.

Minnie could tell from her vantage point through the trees that there was a visitor in camp. She didn't feel like coming out into the open until the caller was gone. She was dog tired. The bath in the creek had helped a lot but there were times that a person just didn't feel like being sociable.

She waited and waited not knowing they were waiting on her.

Finally, Papa asked Arnold to go and ask Minnie if she wanted to sell a loaf of bread. Already perturbed at having to wait so long to return to camp, Minnie's answer was an emphatic, "No, I don't!"

She watched Arnold return to camp and speak to the visitor. It took him longer than she had taken to relay her answer to the visitor. Good brother. The visitor got into a buggy and rode away.

Walking back to camp she felt the clammy fingers of guilt began to knead at her soul. She should have been more neighborly. What if it turns out he lives close and I have to face him knowing I denied him a loaf of bread.

> September 28, Sunday
>
> Mr. Hyde and Papa went down the creek to look at some 80 acre claims. While Arnold & I rode the blacks to the mission. We came home just before 1 p.m. and prepared dinner. Mr. Hyde and Papa were just in time to eat with us. Before we were through, Mr. & Mrs. Deyo and Mr. Herndon, baby Clifford drove up and spent the afternoon with us. We were in turn invited to attend a prayer and singing service at their aunt's and uncle's parsonage this evening, which we accepted.

Minnie was overjoyed to see the Deyos coming over the hill. She couldn't believe her eyes. They were calling on the Johnson's--who didn't even have a house yet! When they told the purpose of their visit--the invitation--she was delighted.

"A social! Oh, my, I don't know if I can handle that much excitement," she joked, feeling a bit giddy as she made preparations to go. Wish I had my new dress finished. But it's not and this is just the thing to make me forget my "hay haulin' blues."

***

"COME IN, COME IN," Rev. Deyo greeted them at the door. You folks introduce yourselves to each other. I'll take your hats. Minnie, let me take your shawl."

Mr. Herndon stepped toward Oliver and extended his hand. They were soon exchanging notes on which quarter of which section the other lived on and who else they knew who lived or would be living in the vicinity.

While it wasn't the habit of some of these gentlemen to go to church regularly they were all equally happy to have been invited to the Deyo's "singing social." It was a wonderful opportunity to break the monotony of work and the feeling of separateness.

Minnie started playing with baby Clifford on the divan in the living-kitchen room. Pretty soon she was holding him. There was a good, comfortable feeling in this house. A feeling of welcome and gratitude for the opportunity to meet everyone else.

Smart of the Deyos to give this social. This way they get to meet their new neighbors and the neighbors meet each other. Everybody has probably been wondering who else was out there within riding distance.

Mrs. Deyo sat down at the piano and played a few chords. Then she played through a stanza of "Oh, Happy Day." Minnie sang along quietly.

"Come on over here, Minnie, and sing with me."

"Well, I love to sing but let me warn you all my voice is not the greatest. I'm no 'Flying Lady'!"

That broke the ice. Everyone who had been to Lawton in the past two months had heard about the "songbird" of Goo Goo Avenue. They all got a kick out of Minnie's comment. It was the joke of the evening.

Mrs. Deyo insisted that Minnie share the piano bench with her and suggested that the others gather around the piano. While they were singing "When They Ring Those Golden Bells", there was a knock at the door. The younger Mr. Deyo hustled over to open it. Everyone kept on singing until they'd finished the last line of the chorus.

Clarence Pool was welcomed in and joined the singing. When they'd finished, he said, "Goodness me, you folks are serious about this hymn singing! Makes me feel good all the way down to my toes!" He happened to be looking in Minnie's direction when he said it and her heart did a tiny flip.

"Well, it's not our custom to make hymns sound like a funeral is imminent," Mr. Deyo said in a preacherly tone.

"The Bible does say, 'make a *joyful* noise unto the Lord,' does it not?"

While Mr. Deyo had the floor, he said with a benevolent smile, "If you will allow me, I'd like to invite our Heavenly Father into our midst. I *am* a minister of the gospel, you know, and prayer is one of the requirements of the job."

Taking his humble request kindly everyone bowed their heads. Arnold, who'd been playing with little Clifford pulled the child onto his lap, making it easier to keep him quiet during the prayer. He'd helped with his little brothers and sisters in church enough to know the right things to do to keep a baby quiet for a few minutes.

The prayer was short and sweet and asked for "the harmonious blending of our good Comanche Indians and the settlers." It was followed by scattered "Amens."

"Do we have any requests?" Rev. Deyo segued effortlessly. After a silence during which everyone tried to think of a song, Clarence said, "How about the old Methodist Hymn, "Love Divine, All Love's Excelling."

"Ah, yes, that's one of my favorite Charles Wesley hymns," Anna Deyo said. Then looking around at Clarence with a twinkle in her eye, said "The man could write beautiful music–even though he was a Methodist."

More chuckles and laughter, and singing the song.

While eating sugar cookies and lemonade, each person was introduced to everyone else, and in turn they were each encouraged to tell a little about themselves. Some took the opportunity to tell about family members that would be joining them. Others told which piece of land they'd filed on and their hopes for the community.

When it was Clarence's turn he said, "I have a sister, brother, and my parents back in Iowa. My mother and father may move down here. He's a veteran of the War between the States and will probably be able to pick up a relinquishment. My sister, Hellen, is a school teacher-- probably about your age, Minnie," he added, nodding in her direction. "I studied law at the university in Ames, Iowa and went to the Philippines during the Spanish-American war.

When Minnie heard about Hellen Pool she was thankful. Thank goodness maybe another lady in the neighborhood. Someone to talk to and to perhaps make trips to town with.

When it was Minnie's turn she'd scarcely got ten a word out when Papa pushed in, telling them how well she played the piano. So, of course, they insisted that she play something.

"It's been so long since I played--three months, I guess." But she graciously went to the piano from where she'd been seated--eating cookies at the kitchen table--and played one of her favorites, Beethoven's "Fur Elise." Everyone applauded and asked for more so she played another piece that she had memorized.

Thoughts of her mother always entered her mind when she played the piano. This time she felt a sudden twinge of loneliness--a longing to see her and talk with her--to reassure her that everything was all right.

The last thought made her forget where she was in the piece she was playing and she had to start over.

"Has anyone met Otto Elling yet? He's going to be one of our neighbors I understand," Clarence asked and then went on. "I met him in Lawton about the middle of August. I understood him to say he'd filed for the southwest quarter of Section 13 which would be a mile south of me and across the easement or--let's see--three miles south of here," Clarence said. No one indicated they had so Clarence added that he believed Mr. Elling was finishing some farm work for his brother-in-law in Cashion--up north of El Reno.

"Seemed to be a fine gentleman. Born in Kansas and plans to return here before the deadline to establish residence."

Mr. Herndon noted "That's coming up pretty soon? October fourth isn't it?"

"I heard some discussion just recently that they are going to give those needing it an extension of time," Clarence said.

Talk went on among the men for another hour or so.

"By the way," Oliver said, "I want to say, before we all get away from here, that I'll be glad to help anyone who gets in a bind and hope that the rest of you will do the same for me. We're all in the same boat together out here." Everyone was glad that he'd said it. They'd meant to say something similar before they parted ways. They were all enthusiastic in their agreement with his statement.

The evening was a big success. Everyone enjoyed themselves and having the opportunity to meet their new neighbors.

No one seemed to want the evening to end.

"Does anyone know where I can buy fresh-baked bread?" Clarence asked and Minnie's heart sank.

Papa cleared his throat "Well, folks ,it's kinda late for an old man to be out. I'm not real sure we can find our way back to camp in the dark."

Others made similar comments hoping they could find their way home in the dark along with other friendly remarks. It seemed a good time for everyone to say their goodbyes. They eased toward the door still chatting and sincerely thanking the Deyos for a wonderful evening.

Minnie tried to say something to Clarence about the bread but by the time she got the chance, she only had time to say, "Papa's waiting for me. Maybe we can talk another time?"

"I'll count on that." he said.

> September, 29 continued
> ...After supper , the men hitched to the light wagon and we all went, Mr. Hyde, too. We all enjoyed the evening so much. I enjoyed the singing especially. Miss Scofield, a Baptist Missionary and Mr. Herndon and Blount were present besides the families of the Deyos. We are always welcomed by Mr. & Mrs. Elton Deyo, missionaries, and feel a warm interest in our new neighbors. We started for our camp at 10 and retired an hour later.

After arriving back at camp Minnie decided this evening had been more entertainment than she'd had since they left Cambridge. She lay awake for an hour, poring over the enjoyment of the evening. She replayed every scene till she fell asleep--smiling.

> September 30

Papa has not felt very well for days so concluded to get a hired man. He did a little riding this forenoon, and a Mr. Anthony Carter was up looking for horses whom he hired. Mr. Carter said he would be here in the morning. Arnold mowed and raked as usual, but the hay wagon was idle. Mr. Herndon was here and promised to get the mail for us. He is going to Lawton and will be back tonight.

October 1
Papa and Mr. Carter hauled five loads of hay and we got our mail. After some coaxing and promising, Mr. Herndon gave me my letter.

Minnie got a reprieve from hay hauling and was able to get more sewing done on her dress. Having hired help Papa still worked right along with Carter making sure he got his money's worth out of him. Mr. Carter was good help and Papa seemed to take on renewed strength.

Mr. Herndon rode straight home last night forgetting he'd picked up the Johnsons' mail. He felt duty-bound to bring it to them as soon as possible. He arrived at their camp with their mail, just before dinner. Folks felt there was something sacred about a man's mail.

Seeing Minnie's eyes sparkle when she heard she had a letter, Mr. Herndon thought he'd have some fun with her. Minnie played along amiably, but she wished he'd just hand her the blame letter.

On the envelope:

Tina Johnson
Cambridge,
Nebraska

Miss Minnie Johnson
General Delivery
Lawton, Oklahoma
Territory

Chapter 23
Letter from Cambridge

Minnie stared at her long, ivory fingers shriveled from being in the water so long. They looked bad. She stared so long she got that eerie feeling that everything else ceased to be.

She wondered what Momma would think. Dry, toughened, cuts and scratches here and there. No callouses yet, but every time a blister healed and hardened over callouses were one step closer. The nails were uneven and marked with little white bruises–tell tale signs of manual labor.

Helping Papa with the hay had severely taxed their softness. She wished for a jar of hand cream and an emery board but hadn't asked Papa to make the purchase. She figured he'd probably think them a frivolous expense. Next time she was in town she would see if she could locate some herself.

Minnie's spirits were down--to put it mildly.

She'd been in the water at the creek for over an hour now. She didn't care. She wasn't in any hurry. Papa was in town again. Arnold, near the tent, was reading and keeping an eye on the horses. It was a warm day.

Hidden from view Minnie threw back her long, wet hair and sank slowly again into the waist-deep water. Settling backward until her ears were beneath the surface she allowed her arms to relax and float to the top on either side of her. Her body drifted in the cool water of the creek. The current pulled her slowly southward.

She'd received Tina's letter yesterday.

Looking up through the lattice work of tree limbs and leaves above her Minnie lost herself in the blueness of the sky. Not a cloud. It was another sunny autumn day-- Indian summer. Since the rains earlier in the month and the coming of slightly cooler days living outdoors hadn't seemed quite so horrible.

The letter. There it was again.

It kept crashing, uninvited into her reverie. It was the reason she'd come to the creek–hoping the water would wash away thoughts of it. Tina's cheery, chatty letter with her lovely news. She and Warren were to be married.

How nice. How wonderful, and perfectly lovely.

Minnie knew exactly how long she could float before her bottom would run aground on the sand bar at the far end of her "pool". There she would stand–her cotton camisole and knee-length bloomers sticking to her skin–and trudge slowly back through the waist deep water and repeat the process over again. The water felt good, and the tears didn't show. They just blended into the creek.

John Perdoux would be Warren's best man. Tina truly wished Minnie could be there to be her maid of honor. But she'd gone ahead and asked Addie Smalley. She sure hoped that was okay with Minnie. Addie and John had been with them the night Warren proposed.

Dammit, she thought . And it felt so good to think it, she thought she just might say it–out loud!

For how long must she stand by and watch other girls get their lives started while she was off down here in this "promised land" hauling hay for Papa? What's to become of me? When do I get my chance at a life she interrogated the trees and the creek banks?

She yelled out so long and hard she exhausted every last bit of air in her lungs.

Minnie hadn't become this disheartened overnight. It had taken a very long time. She'd been filled with hope, the promise of the land for months. She'd kept an optimistic view–against the odds. But the time spent out here on Jim's claim, though probably healthier, had been so utterly lonesome. The loneliness was compounded by the insecurity, the not-knowing what was going on with this claim business.

It had been a gradual thing. The letter from Tina yesterday, coming right on the heels of having helped Papa and Arnold haul hay for two weeks, brought it like a ripening, boil to the surface. It had left her with a wounded feeling. She'd suddenly felt a loathing for this place that ground at the pit of her stomach.

She hadn't wanted to admit it but suddenly she was tired--sick and tired--of working like somebody's barefoot *hausfrau* in that shoddy old makeshift camp outfit, of baking bread by the ton in a Dutch oven over a fire, of the smell of the canvas tent, of her life revolving around the grub box, the dish pan and the water bucket, of wearing the same three faded dresses over and over.

Ordinarily Minnie's tendency to look on the bright side snapped her out of a bout with gloom and despair.

She'd lashed out angrily at Arnold this morning when he said something insignificant about the temperature of the coffee. Poor Arnold, his only mistake was in just being there. He wasn't *who* or *what* she was angry at. She would tell him she was sorry when she went back to camp–if she ever did.

She was homesick, too, for her Mother and sisters and

little John and wished desperately to be with them. In short, Minnie, the *nice* girl from Gordon, Nebraska, was not feeling too terribly "nice" at this particular point in time.

She knew she should admonish herself for not "rejoicing in all things." But, she guessed she'd just have to work on that tomorrow. Right now she was going to indulge in some more tears.

***

<u>October 2</u>
Papa went to town with Mr. G. G. Fellows, and this evening, brought back Mr. Fellows camp outfit, wagon and team of young horses, which he bought of him. Mr. Fellows took the train out of Lawton for Winona, Minn. 1 load. of hay; cloudy, windy. Carter worked in the cave.

Another would-be settler, Mr. G. G. Fellows, had been culled by the adverse conditions: heat, dust, and lack of a reliable water supply–someone else could have it.

"Wonder what Papa had to pay for that camp outfit, the wagon, and the other team?" She asked Arnold.

He shrugged his shoulders in answer. Arnold didn't want to think about it.

"Do we really need seven horses?"

"Seven?"

"The blacks, the big bay team, the young team bought today," she enumerated.

"...and Red." Arnold added grudgingly. Maybe he took out a loan at one of the banks?"

"I've thought the same thing myself. I wish he'd spend it on finishing out the cave."

Arnold got up to get more firewood.

<u>October 3</u>
Four loads. of hay. Mr. Hyde filed a mile S. of us, which news he communicated to us in a letter.

Mr. Eugene W. Hyde, the man they'd gotten to know

pretty well, a few days ago–the one who'd attended the social at the Deyos' with them–had finally gotten to file. His lottery number being 6053, he was pretty near the end of the list of 6,500 names. His date to file hadn't been until October first. All he'd been able to find was eighty acres. Having filed Mr. Hyde, would return to Kansas to get some tools and other items before settling in. He'd first been nice enough to send his new friends, the Johnsons, a quick note to let them know that he would be returning and to ask them to keep an eye on the "eighty" for him.

<u>October 4</u>
Fri.--two loads of hay before dinner. After dinner Papa & Carter went over to Blue Beaver to squat on an eighty. Took camp outfit along and intended to return on the following day, but seventeen outfits followed their example and our men gave up trying and came home about 10 p.m. I don't know how the rest fared or who was lucky.

"Squat on an eighty?" Minnie shook her head and repeated the phrase as the men pulled away. It sounded funny.

There was a good explanation for what Oliver and Carter, the hired hand, were intending to do, or *had* intended to do before they arrived and saw that seventeen other wagons of squatters had the same idea. At midnight tonight the time period for filing claims would officially end. According to the President's proclamation:

"After the expiration of the said sixty days, but not before, any of the lands not filed upon nor claimed by such time, will be open and available for settlement under the general provisions of the homestead law.(ie. by a "land rush")

This one sentence had caused a lot of confusion. When interpreted by the U. S. Land Office; it didn't have quite the same meaning it seemed to have with the squatters around here.

***

TWO MEN ON horseback came over the crest of the rise and stopped. They sat on their horses for a few minutes looking around. It was late afternoon of Friday, October 4th.

The first to speak was the shorter of the two. He had a beard and an awfully bad mouthful of yellowed teeth. Some of the teeth were short, some long, some missing, some leaning in and some of them sort of twisted around. It was an ugly mouth.

"Ain't tat a purty view?" Fess–the one with the ugly teeth–said looking toward the mountains and wallowing a plug of chewing tobacco around in his mouth.

"Sure is. Now who was it you said was supposed to be proving up on this place?" Zeke asked stepping down from his horse.

"Wudn 'ees name Allen. Otto Allen. Wudn nat it? Yeah, I believe that wuz it." It was Fess speaking now.

"I thought you had all the facts." Zeke, who had a slight cerebral edge on Fess, said accusingly.

"Reckon I do--most of 'em, anyhow. The man's from up in Kansas somewhur." They walked over to a lone elm tree and tied their horses.

"And...?" Zeke prompted.

"...what? And what, dammit?" Fess's feathers ruffled easily.

"Is he coming back? Do you know for sure he's not coming back? How do you know he's not comin' back."

"Now, did I say exactly that?" Fess puffed up like a toad. "Dontcha go twistin' my words!" After an anger-filled pause, he went on, "Whut I said was–if he idn back here by midnight tonight, we got us a homestead!"

They seated themselves in an especially healthy clump of buffalo grass.

"Fess, you idiot! What makes you think this Mr. Allen–if that *is* his name–isn't going to be back or for that matter that we could convince a judge he defaulted? Maybe he's gettin' one of those extensions?"

"Wull do you see him anywhur around?" Fess didn't wait for an answer, just nodded his head once like that was all the proof needed.

"I rest my case," he said definitively, leaning back and

locking his hands behind his head, crossing one leg over the other.

***

OTTO ELLING STEPPED down from the train.

Sure was going to be more convenient, having train access to Lawton. They may not have made it by opening day, but they made it, and now that's all that counted.

Checking his watch he saw that it was 6:35 p.m. It was Friday, October 4th. Since it was so late he'd just get a cot in town for the night and go out to his claim tomorrow.

To be sure he pulled a much folded paper out of his vest pocket and reread the part about the sixty days from August 6th. Yep, it still read the same and he was not anxious to go out trying to find his claim this late in the day.

Picking up his brown valise and bed roll from the loading dock Otto began walking toward the main part of town. Lawton looked absolutely nothing like it had the day he left--August 17th. There had been two month's work accomplished. It showed, too!

Fully five dozen businesses now had wood frame buildings completely changing the look of the whole area. Many of the buildings were of the kind that had the false front, making a small, one-story building appear two stories high. There were still many tents and wagons mingled in along with the new buildings. Some houses were going up in the residential area, too. Though Goo Goo Avenue was still in existence it looked quite deserted. Most of the businesses had relocated on the townsite.

Eventually he found, by asking a couple of questions, that there was still a lodging tent with cots to rent by the night. He reserved a cot for the night before finding a place to eat his supper.

***

"ARNOLD, BRING the wagon and team over here."

"Be sure you get everything out of there, Minnie."

"Pull the tent stakes. Lower the posts." Oliver was giving commands--rallying his troops--both of whom wondered what in the heck had gotten into him.

They'd barely finished breakfast and here was Papa so

full of cheer he was almost giddy. He was bent on moving–taking action–happy as a cow in clover. For a moment or two Minnie wondered if he'd been into the bottle of "spirits" they kept for medicinal purposes. Nah, not Papa.

Papa had been saying that, when it got cooler, they would move their camp up on the hill away from the shade and dampness near the creek. It was getting close to the time of year when they wanted to absorb the heat from the sun not be sheltered from it.

"Looks like today's moving day," Arnold muttered as he passed by Minnie.

"Minnie-girl, you go on up the hill and pick out a place for the tent. Somewhere south of the haystacks but not too far south. Carry a chair or two along with you on your way."

The truth of the matter was this morning Papa was breathing a sigh of relief. No one had approached him to inquire if he had a claim filed on this land. It was safe now to move camp up on higher ground. They could afford to be more visible.

> <u>October 5</u>
> This morning we moved our camp up on the hill near the hay stacks owing to the dampness near the creek. We aren't 1/8 of a mile E. of our old camp. We have no shade here, but the weather is cooler and the sun isn't uncomfortably hot at any time. Two jags of wood fence posts and two l. of hay. This evening papa & I took Carter home, three mi. west of here on Blue Beaver and made the acquaintance of his folks. Coming home we missed our way and were nearly lost when we found ourselves.

The Great Land Lottery had ceased. As of midnight last night, the sixty day filing period was officially at an end. At that moment every unclaimed piece of land in the district became open for settlement. For a few hours this would seem to put everything back into a lawless "land grab" situation.

There had been a lot of confusion around the area over exactly what a person needed to do to claim a piece of unclaimed or relinquished land. This led to some scuffles, stare-downs, standoffs and a few incidents involving firearms.

Most had gotten the word that only the land not yet filed upon at the land office was available to squatters. If a homestead just appeared to be vacant–nobody on it, no improvements begun–didn't mean it hadn't been duly filed on at the land office in Lawton. Many thought they had to be the first one occupying the land as had been the case in the land runs.

The land office personnel had been telling anyone who asked that it would be the person who walked into their office first, the morning of October 5 and filed for the land who would prevail in any contested situation.

There had been over 750 persons in the southern district whose name had been drawn and had been assigned a number, but who failed to appear on their appointed date to file on a claim. This left quite a few empty squares on the map at the land office to be filled on a "first come, first served" basis the morning of October 5. In addition if someone knew a reason why a claimant did not qualify they could win that person's land by contest if they were the first to file a contest on it. Contest cases had been filed in situations where; for instance, one neighbor learned that a young man wasn't 21 years of age; in another case a lady wasn't the "head of household" as she'd claimed–because she had a husband who'd also gotten a number and had a claim six miles from her's. Then there were cases in which a person had previously homesteaded in another state or territory and even though they'd abandoned it, they hadn't cleared up the account through the General Land Office.

Contests of claims could now begin to be heard--as soon as the commissioners had everything in order, had done their research--made some contacts, and were ready to hear the cases.

Oliver Johnson had filed a contest on Jim Reid's claim back in August. He wanted to be very sure no one else had a contest on the books before he did.

When the U.S. Land Office opened it's door at 9:00 a.m.

Saturday morning there was a long line waiting. Interestingly, Register McGuire had received a wire from Washington, to the effect that all papers of those who stood in line at the time the land office opened would be stamped "REC'D 9:00 AM, Oct. 5, 1901". This probably prevented a few brawls. The land office personnel would sort out who had rights to the land later.

> October 6, Sunday
> Papa and I went to church before dinner. This afternoon
> Arnold is hunting Cole, who got away last Tuesday night
> & Papa has walked over west to see some neighbors. Mr.
> Herndon was here this afternoon and got a shave.

***

PAPA HAD indeed been keeping Minnie and Arnold in the dark about "Jim's Claim," though Arnold having spent more time with the men of the Nebraska group during the summer, had more opportunity to pick up pieces of the truth here and there.

Most people around the area assumed that Oliver Johnson had drawn a number and made his own homestead entry on it. At the land office the quarter had an "X" on it, meaning it was taken. And, it was taken–*by Jim Reid, who'd never returned from Nebraska.* Oliver hadn't seen the need to make announcements about it. If someone had suspected that the land on which the Johnsons were camped was not officially on the books as his they could have filed a contest just as well and *might* have won it–seeing that the Johnsons had "settled" there–illegally.

Of course, no one even thought to question whether this land where Papa, Arnold and Minnie were living, busting sod, sinking a well and bringing in load after load of hay wasn't their very own claim. After all, who would put so much effort and money into a place that wasn't their own?

***

ABOUT A WEEK after the end of filing time Papa made an announcement that lifted Minnie's spirits enormously. He lit the kerosene lamp on the table–mosquitoes and June bugs had ceased to be a problem–and said, "Minnie-girl, you can go ahead and write your mother now and tell her to get packed up and ready to leave Gordon. They can leave as soon as school lets out."

"Really?" Minnie squealed in delight drawing a hand to each side of her face.

"Well I think we'd be safe in assuming we'll win the contest on the land. Don't you think?" Papa asked the question as if Minnie had been in on all the discussions–as if she knew everything he did.

Minnie gulped. "Well, I suppose–sure..." How should she know? Why was he asking her opinion? Kinda late to be bringing up the subject for her thoughts now.

Arnold, who'd been lying on his cot–eyes closed–opened one and peered at Minnie wondering if she'd take the opportunity Papa had just given to get some answers to questions she'd had for a long time.

After a bit of contemplation, she decided to ask one question. It took a few starts for her to get the words right.

"Isn't Jim coming ba–?"

"On what grounds–"

"What do you have as evid–"

She cleared her throat. "What are you planning to use as the basis for a contest?"

"Oh, didn't I tell you? Gall durn the thunder! I've been so wound up lately."

Tell us what--Minnie wanted to scream.

"We've got a letter signed by Jim Reid."

"You do? Saying what?" Minnie was shocked. How could he have forgotten to mention something as important as that?

"It's all legal–I think. Got one of those notary clamp-things on it. Would you like to look at it?"

The cold stare in Minnie's eyes, answered his question.

Oliver walked to the tent, went inside and opened the trunk with the carving on it. He slid aside a small mirror on the underside of the lid. From behind it he pulled an envelope.

Chapter 24

Just Beginning

"I meant to have you read this to me awhile back, Minnie-girl, but we've been so tied up with things around here..." Talking nervously, Papa walked back to where she sat. He handed her the envelope.

The return address was Gordon, Nebraska. Minnie withdrew the letter from its envelope and unfolded it.

"What's it say?" Oliver asked, sounding like maybe he already knew.

"It says–" Minnie said testily, taking her sweet time:

"Gordon, Nebraska. October 5, 1901. I, James Reid, hereby relinquish back to the United States all right, title and interest to the land entered by me and described in this Receiver's Receipt #593 of the Lawton Land district. This Relinquishment is made on account of a previous H.D. entry made by me which has never been canceled. James Reid. Subscribed in my presence and sworn to *acknowledged before me this 5th day of October 1901. Fred Hoyt, Notary Public."*

"Relinquish?" Arnold jumped and shouted for joy. "Yee-hah, Jim relinquished! That means we got it. We got it! It's ours." Papa and Arnold jumped and bear-hugged, danced a jig and shook hands, practically all at the same time. Then they both looked over at Minnie who was still seated and staring at the letter.

"Papa, how long have you had this?" Minnie asked, her eyes narrowing in suspicion.

Taken aback by her question and her seriousness–why wasn't she jumping for joy–Papa answered,

"Oh, well let's see...a couple...three weeks I guess, why."

"Well, Papa," she said in an icy voice, "You sure could have saved me a whole lot of worry. If I'd had any idea about this. If I'd only had a hint that Jim was thinking about relinquishing."

A painful silence followed while Minnie decided whether or not to go on. When she did, Papa winced. She was taking him totally by surprise.

She stood up.

"You think I'm still a little child, incapable of any thought or feeling except the ones you give me. You expect unflinching loyalty from me--" Her voice became angrier the more she thought about it. "–as if I were a son but you 'protect' me from life's realities like I'm not quite smart enough or too fragile to handle them. Working beside you in the hayfield should have showed you I was more than that. I am not your baby girl anymore. I'll be twenty-one next April."

"Minnie, I had no idea you were this--"

"Worried? Concerned? Upset? What Papa?" She couldn't stop the intake of a sob. "I've been half-crazy trying to figure out what kind of scheme you had going. Wondering if I–if Arnold and I–were unwittingly breaking the law–being squatters out here, just because YOU decided it was okay."

"Minnie-girl, I thought this letter would be a nice little surprise." He attempted to change the mood with a placating tone.

"Surprise?" No, she would not let him do that. Her head of steam built one notch higher.

"No, Papa." She said angrily with a shake of her head,

willing the hot tears now forming in her eyes, not to run down her cheeks. Her hands clinched into fists.

"Oh, sure, it's a big surprise! And a relief NOW, to know Jim had an idea about relinquishing. Yes, this letter does solve that issue."

Another sob.

"But what about the fact that you witheld this from us. Oh, how I would've loved to have known that something like this was in the works back in September–August–the day we set up camp here. By law, we've been squatters for the last two months, haven't we?"

She went on, "Just how long did you have this little plan going with Jim?"

Papa didn't answer the question.

He stood silent for a long time then he turned and walked to the edge of the lantern light. Without turning around he said. "I'm going to check on the horses."

Minnie sat back down in her chair crying–still furious –she gathered up her apron to cover her face.

After her sobbing subsided, she wiped the last of her tears from her reddened face, she got up to clean up around the grub box and get ready for bed.

Arnold lay silently on his cot–speechless. He'd never in all his life seen *anything* like this.

Papa finally emerged from the darkness into the lantern light of their camp. He stood for awhile looking at the ground.

"Night, Minnie, Arnold. I'm gonna turn in." His voice sounded very tired.

Minnie thought for a long while. Finally, she picked up the letter, walked over to her father arranging his nap sack, and handed him his paper.

***

Clarence approached the creek. It was late in October, a nice day. His legs rustled in the tall prairie grass as he walked toward the west bank of Pecan creek.

He cleared his throat several times, loudly. Trying to make as much noise as possible. He was pretty sure someone might be bathing down there. He was also pretty sure she'd be embarrassed and not the least bit pleased if she didn't have some warning of his approach.

"Minnie." he called too softly.

"Min--nie." a little louder.

Emerging from the water where she was rinsing the shampoo from her hair Minnie thought she heard someone call her name. Her ears were full of water. She couldn't be sure. Her eyes darted along the banks of the creek. She didn't see anyone. Relaxing, she closed her eyes and went under again.

Catching a glimpse of Minnie in the water Clarence's eyes remained on the spot where she'd gone under. He had to look again and then...just one more time. *How beautiful!* Her hair floated out around her like angel wings. The lily whiteness of her skin appeared to shine in the sun. He wanted to sit right down there amid the grass and just watch her. Reluctantly, he turned and retraced his steps, back up the short slope. When just on the edge of the trees lining the creek bank he called again.

"Min-nie?"

There. She'd heard it again. She sat up now alert to any sound or movement. Though she was covered by her camisole and bloomers, the wet, loosely-woven material didn't leave much to the imagination. She crossed her arms over her chest. "Yes?" she called out.

"It's Clarence, Minnie. Didn't want to startle you. Are you decent?"

"Am I what?"

"Are you covered up?"

"Oh, sure, Clarence." She breathed a sigh of relief. "It's okay. Come on down." She scurried over to the old tree trunk that had long ago fallen across the creek bed where she'd left a cotton blanket that she used for a towel. Grabbing it she wrapped it around her shoulders and sat down on the old tree trunk.

She watched her friend approach carrying a bucket in each hand. "What's on your mind, today?" she said cheerfully. He raised the two water buckets in answer.

Clarence Pool's farm had prospects for a good spring. But he'd not yet dug out around it to obtain clean drinking water. Every couple of days it was necessary for him to go either to Pecan Creek to the east or Blue Beaver on the west to get water. Either way it was about a mile walk. If he went west he didn't have a chance of seeing Minnie.

"Needed water again." he said as he came down the path between the trees. "Sure wish I could've found a claim with a stream running through it." he said.

"But...then..." he was approaching her on the dry sandy bank, "I wouldn't have had the opportunity to bother you." He winked at her, teasingly.

"Clarence Pool, how long have you been up there?"

He gave no answer but took an apple from one of the buckets. "Want half?"

"Hey. Don't change the subject." She wasn't angry, just being playful.

"I'll have to take 'the fifth' on that question, Your Honor." he said as he used his thumbnail to cut through the skin all the way around the apple.

"Pardon me? ...*the fifth*? What fifth?" she looked at him puzzled.

"The fifth amendment to the United States Constitution. Ever hear of the bill of rights, Miss Minnie? Y'can't force me to give testimony against myself." he said and with a twist and a snap broke the apple apart along the line he'd made. He handed her half.

"Oh, is that so, Mister law scholar!" she smiled--not the least impressed with his apple trick, she'd seen it before-- and put emphasis on the "Mister." She turned and faced him squarely feeling a new appreciation for her friend. Her eyes fixed on his.

"The truth, the whole truth, and..." he said, but was suddenly treading in the deep blue pools of her eyes.

"...nothing but the truth." she finished his sentence and bit into her half of the apple breaking their gaze.

"My parents are going to be joining me down here." Clarence commented.

"Wonderful. What about your sister, Hellen?"

"Hellen's not sure what she'll do yet. She's committed to teach the winter session of school. She'll come down for awhile when that session is over. Dad purchased the relinquishment on the quarter just west of mine. I filed homestead papers for him on October fifth." Clarence said, finishing his news.

"Papa gave me the go-ahead to write home and tell the

rest of the family to pack up and come on down, soon as school's out. So, our whole family will be living here come springtime." Minnie said, announcing her own good news.

"I'll be so glad to have them here." she went on, "I have missed my sisters and Mom so much. Did I tell you, I have a sister named Helen, as well?"

"No, I don't' believe you did."

"Looks like our community is going to be filling up soon, doesn't it?"

She nodded agreement.

They munched their apple halves in silence for awhile.

Clarence wanted to tell her about his plans; to tell her he was going to Hot Springs to try the mineral baths there- -see if they could help his condition. He wanted to tell her that *she* was the reason. She had given him a reason to take his health and his life more seriously. He wanted to put his arms around her and draw her to him.

***

"THINK IT'D BE BEST if you boys just saddle up and get on outta here. This is my claim and I'm here." Otto pumped his six-shot 12-gauge.

Fess had dozed off–it was his watch. The sound of the gun being pumped startled him. He opened his eyes to find Mr. "Allen" standing, staring down at him.

"Huh? wull hullo Mr. Allen."

"The name is Elling, Otto Elling. This is my claim. You and your friend are going to have to leave."

Luckily, Otto had taken supper in an establishment where a conversation was going on about "the deadline." Listening for half an hour or so, while he ate, he realized that there were lots of folks out sitting on land they thought was vacant tonight. He saw nothing else to do, but rent a horse and ride on out to his claim. His claim was duly filed upon in his name, all the paperwork in order. It might save a lawyer's fee though, if he went out tonight and checked on it.

The moon was bright enough he could see the outline of the mountains to the north and keep his bearings. By watching where he was in relation to Mount Scott, the biggest one with a flattened top, he found his way. Mount Scott was due north of his claim. He'd identified it the day he was out with the locators and made a point of remembering it.

Fess began squirming away from Otto, in the direction of the red coals left from the campfire they'd made earlier. Reaching it, he placed a hand in the middle of the coals burning his hand. He yelled and jumped up to run.

Zeke roused a bit when he heard Fess squalling but it didn't occur to him that someone else was in camp.

Otto hadn't pointed his Remington at anyone yet, but he'd already made up his mind, he'd use it if someone was here and forced the issue.

Seeing that the other fellow wasn't moving yet, Otto walked over to him and gave his rear end a good shove with his boot. He raised his gun and shot once into the air.

"I said, Get up! Get out! Go on!"

He pulled the trigger a second time. Shooting into the air, again.

Now it was Zeke's turn to scramble. And he did—backwards–rapidly. He grabbed his hat and scooted till he could get his feet under him. Then he scampered out in the direction they'd left their horses.

Otto had never seen horses saddled so fast. The man with the scorched hand lifted himself gingerly into his saddle. They rode off into the night with one hollering after the other.

"Zeke..."

"Zeke...wait up."

"Hey, Zeke."

Otto had a good laugh.

After while he settled down by the fire for the rest of the night.

At dawn, he studied his homestead appreciatively from atop the hill. He was pleased. He thanked his lucky stars that running the claim jumpers off had been as easy as it was. By the light of day he shook his head several times when he thought about the risk he'd taken.

He took another long sip of coffee and surveyed his 160 acre "kingdom".

In late October an election was held in Lawton. The job of mayor went to Mr. Leslie K. Ross, while the popular U.S. Deputy Marshal, Heck Thomas, easily won the position of City Marshal. With most of Indian Territory now becoming Oklahoma Territory there wasn't the need for as many federal marshals and deputies. He saw this as an opportunity to "retire" from the dangerous life he'd been accustomed to living. He would take the opportunity to move his wife and two young daughters down from Guthrie, O. T. The next year he bought a lot from Al Jennings (the lawyer, turned bank robber, turned prisoner, turned back to citizen, to gubernatorial candidate to author and film maker) and built a house for his family.

Mattie Beal and her brother were working away on her claim. They'd built a little shack like most other folks--to get started in. Mr. James Woods, the man with the number one draw, was sadly becoming known as "Hog" Woods.

Reuben and Lydia Pool arrived from Iowa in mid-November. They'd shipped enough furniture to set up the bare necessities–a kitchen, living area and a bed. Clarence with the help of his neighbors had put up a one room box house, 12' X 24', with a stove and a chimney pipe so they wouldn't all freeze before spring. Mr. and Mrs. Pool were prepared to watch over their claim as well as their son's while he went to Hot Springs. He felt he must try the hot mineral baths there to see if the treatments would improve his health.

Their daughter Hellen and son Garfield were making plans for a visit in February.

***

MINNIE'S POSITIVE OUTLOOK on life was back. Confront-ing Papa had done wonders for her frame of mind. Yes, she had to deal with those clammy feelings of guilt that occasionally crept into her thoughts. The confrontation was a radical departure from the way she'd been taught. In the long run, though after a lot of soul–searching, she believed she'd done the right thing; done what she had to do. She'd taken a stand for what she believed in. Drawn her own line in the sand; a huge and difficult step, to be sure. But, to her it was an important one. One that differentiated folks with some strength of character from those who could be pushed and pulled around.

And, what had Oliver thought of Minnie's outburst? Well, he'd walked out into the darkness that night and thought for a very long time. The more he walked and thought, the more he realized that what he was feeling–mostly–was pride.

"That's MY girl!" Yep, when all was said and done he found that he was proud of the way she'd stood up to him. And, she had a point. He probably should have let them in on the deal–some of it–maybe.

He wouldn't like it happening again, but just this once... "Hot damn, that's my girl."

THE NEW BLUE dress was finished and it looked nice on Minnie. She wore it to the next gathering of settlers at the Deyos' in late November. They held it out under a large brush arbor close to the churchhouse on a warm Saturday afternoon. There were many new neighbors in attendance including: Reuben and Lydia Pool, the Ringenbergers, Mr. Hyde, Mr. Herndon, Otto Elling and his brother, Carl, who'd joined him from Kansas. Nice gentlemen, Minnie thought.

Otto entertained the group telling about his altercation with the claim jumpers. He'd brought along his fiddle and together with others who brought fiddles, mandolins, harmonicas, one accordion and a dulcimer, they played and sang all the old songs–Westphalia Waltz, Blue-tail Fly, Buffalo Gals–while others chatted and enjoyed getting to know their new neighbors.

Clarence didn't play an instrument and had a voice like a foghorn but he and Minnie enjoyed chatting while the music played. He would be leaving for Arkansas, December second.

Rev. Deyo announced that the application for opening a U. S. Post Office, to be named Taupa, had been filed and approved. Serving the people of this community west and south of Lawton it would be in operation soon after the first of the year. Until a building was built the Deyo Mission would serve as a temporary location.

CLARENCE RETURNED FROM the baths of Hot Springs, on the eleventh of February. He'd been gone ten weeks. He looked and felt much stronger and had put on eighteen pounds.

On a sunny, Sunday afternoon in March, Clarence called on Minnie in a horse and buggy.

"Would you care to go riding with me, Miss Johnson?" He asked in a tone of mock formality barely hiding a smile.

"Well–let me see–I really do have so many things I ought to be doing." Minnie paused and played at seriously consideration.

"But it is a wonderful day..." She said hiding her own smile and making a pretense at being coy. She finally looked up into his face for the first time since he'd returned and said, "I'd love to."

"Whoa-ho," Clarence reined in the dark sorrel mare. They were stopping to enjoy the view of the mountains, from atop a hill north of the mission. He climbed out of the buggy and walked around to Minnie's side to help her out.

"May I help you down, Miss Minnie?" Clarence still feigned formality.

"Oh, my, and such a gentleman you've become, too. What else did you do while you were in Hot Springs." she chided.

Clarence put out the brick to assure that their transportation wouldn't be walking away. Minnie moved toward the splendid view.

"Moody old mountains," he barely heard her say, as if she were speaking to some dear old friends. The usually lavender blue mountains, were a grayish blue today. Breathing in deeply she folded her arms in front of her and clasped the shawl she'd worn for a wrap.

"Beautiful," Clarence said, looking at the mountains–thinking of her. He walked up behind her and put his arms around hers. Silently they looked northward. His body, now so close to her's, warmed at the touch. He'd thought of nothing but her while he was away. Something within him had long since told him this woman was the one. He wanted *her*.

His arms had ached for months to hold her–to only

touch her. His eyes, his throat filled with desire, giving his voice a raspy sound.

"Miss Mina Randina Johnson," he turned her slowly toward him and she allowed herself to be pulled into his embrace. As he spoke the words that were her name, his eyes caressed her hair, her face and then her eyes. Minnie felt warm and soft inside as she released the tight control she'd always kept on her heart.

"Yes," she said as he brought her close. She closed her eyes. She was sure he was going to kiss her and she was very sure she wanted him to.

Oliver soon built a splendid house with running water, five bedrooms and a parlor. Mary and the family loved that house; always referred to it as the best house they ever had. They hosted many community get-togethers on the front lawn. They had seven wonderful years living there.

Minnie and Clarence took their time about marrying. They finally wed in the Johnson home in Lawton on December 18, 1907. "Papa" Oliver wasn't in attendance. He'd left the country the previous summer for Canada, to homestead--one more time.

The Oliver Johnson Home, 1904

HOMESTEAD PROOF—TESTIMONY OF CLAIMANT.

Oliver H. Johnson, being called as a witness in his own behalf in support of homestead entry, No. _6703_, for _NE ¼ Sec 17 T.17 N.R. 13 N.M.,_ testifies as follows:

Ques. 1.—What is your name, age and post-office address?
Ans. _Oliver H. Johnson Age 47. P.O. Tampa. Okla._

Ques. 2.—Are you a _native-born_ citizen of the United States, and if so, in what State or Territory were you born?*
Ans. _Yes. Illinois_

Ques. 3.—Are you the identical person who made homestead entry, No. _6703_ at the _Perry, OKLA._ land office on the _2_ day of _November_, 180 _, and what is the true description of the land now claimed by you?
Ans. _Yes. NE ¼ Sec 17 T.17 N.R. 13 N.M._

Ques. 4.—When was your house built on the land and when did you establish actual residence therein?
(Describe said house and other improvements which you have placed on the land, giving total value thereof.)
Ans. _Mch. 3. 1901. Jan. 3. 1902. House 36 x 36 ft. 2 stories high Granary 16 x 16 ft. Hen House 12 x 16 ft. Barn 16 x 32 ft. Wagon Shed 16 x 32 ft. Worth $1616 ft. Well $100 10 acres Orchard Barn 16 x 20 ft. 20 acres broke, all fenced 2 wires 500 ft. Set 1000 forest trees. Total Value $3000.00_

Ques. 5.—Of whom does your family consist; and have you and your family resided continuously on the land since first establishing residence thereon? (If unmarried, state the fact.)
Ans. _Wife and 9 Children Yes_

Lawton, Oklahoma, Aug. 14, 1901.

INQUIRY

Register and Receiver,

U. S. Land Office,

Valentine, Neb.

Sirs:-

Will you please furnish this office for our official

information the statis of the S. 1/2 of the SW. 1/4, Sec. 4, NE.

1/4 of NW. 1/4, and NW. 1/4 of NE. 1/4 of Sec. 9, T. 33 N., R. 38W.

Very respectfully,

H. D. McHugh
Register.

U.S. Land Office, Valentine Neb

Aug. 17" 1901

Dear Sir:

James K. Reid made H.E. #10579 for the above described tract May 17" 1897. Entry still of record. No contest against it.

Very Respectfully

J.C. Pettijohn of Reynolds

REPLY

Notations in enlarged portion probably read:
C.W. Starling Nov. 9/01
Canc. by rel. Nov. 2/01 -
(illegible)   Nov. 18/01
Sep. 19, 1902 Contest
dismissed. Case closed

NOTICE OF RESULT OF DRAWING FOR LAWTON LAND DISTRICT

July 30 1901

The number assigned to you by the drawing for the Lawton land district is _1011_, and this fixes the order in which your application to make homestead entry of the lands to be opened in that district can be presented to the Lawton land office. Applications will be received, commencing August 6, 1901, at the rate of 125 per day. The lands opened in that district will not make more than, approximately, 6,500 claims. Your entry must be made _Aug. 20_, 1901, or your right under the drawing will be deemed abandoned. Very respectfully,

W. A. RICHARDS,
Assistant Commissioner

Clarence Pool's notification card (above)
Jim Reid's notification card (below)

NOTICE OF RESULT OF DRAWING FOR LAWTON LAND DISTRICT

July 30 1901

The number assigned to you by the drawing for the Lawton land district is _632_, and this fixes the order in which your application to make homestead entry of the lands to be opened in that district can be presented at the Lawton land office. Applications will be received, commencing August 6, 1901, at the rate of 125 per day. The lands opened in that district will not make more than, approximately, 6,500 claims. Your entry must be made _July 12_, 1901, or your right under the drawing will be deemed abandoned. Very respectfully,

W. A. RICHARDS,
Assistant Commissioner

Post Scripts

- By February, 1902 the one room schoolhouses for Pecan, Deyo and Blue Beaver were well on the way to being finished. Schoolboards had been formed. Otto Elling was one of three board members at Pecan School. Reuben Pool was on the schoolboard at Deyo. Among the teachers of these three schools, in those early days were: Minnie Johnson, Helen Johnson, and Clarence Pool. and Hellen Pool.

- Hellen Pool, Clarence's sister, arrived in the territory, in March of 1902. She moved in with her family, and was soon teaching here. She'd left a boy friend and a teaching job in Iowa--both to which she expected to return. She met Otto Elling and it is believed that had something to do with her decision. They say she and Otto met at a prairie fire. She was serving refreshments --he was fighting it. Brother Garfield (Gart) came down at least once in the early days, but married a young lady from Iowa and raised their family there.

- For a couple of years, the congregation of the Deyo Baptist Mission gave their consent for Rev. Deyo to hold separate services for the new white settlers on Sunday afternoons. Arnold Johnson was one of the white people baptized by Rev. Deyo, as was Arnold's future wife Maud Reynolds and her family. Arnold's baptism according to Deyo's meticulous records took place on May 13, 1907. The Deyo Mission parsonage burned, in March 1902. It was soon replaced by one built of native rock that still stands.

- One evening before Otto married he was preparing to go to a pie supper at Deyo School on horseback. He brought his fiddle in it's case out of his small homestead house and started to mount his horse. This particular horse didn't like the idea of having that fiddle on his back wasn't about to stand still for it.. After some pitching and bucking, Otto gave the fiddle and case a toss onto a haystack and proceeded to ride the horse as fast as it could run a mile down and a mile back. As horse and rider came back by the haystack, Otto retrieved his fiddle and they went peaceably on to the pie supper.

- Hellen Pool and Otto Elling, Sr. were married in 1904. They went to the St. Louis World's Fair on their honeymoon. Having by that time "proved up" on his homestead, Otto and Hellen moved to Hays City, Kansas where Otto became the acting Superintendent of the agricultural experiment station. They returned in 1907. In 1908 they began work on a nice home (with a basement--a rarity in this area) just in time for their third child, Carl, to be born January 12, 1909.

Mr. and Mrs. O. H. Elling, Sr. -- 1904

- The home in which Carl Elling was born is still standing and in this century has never left the family. Kermit, the youngest son of Hellen and Otto, lived there with his family, from the 1950s through the mid-1980s. Today, Otto's great-grandson, Carl's grandson, and the author's son (*one and the same person*) lives there with his family.

- Sunday Schools began to be formed and were held in various schoolhouses around the community, until finally in 1908 construction began on a church, to be named Wesley Chapel Methodist Episcopal Church. Reverend George Q. Fenn of Faxon was the first pastor. The church was built on an acre of ground on the southwest corner of Otto Elling's homestead. The Ladies' Aid Society of Wesley Chapel formed on November 13, 1907. They organized and began money making projects such as box socials, ice cream socials, and quilting bees to pay Pastor Fenn's salary, before building on the church began. The minutes of the first few meetings were written by Miss Minnie Johnson. The first meeting was held in Mrs. Otto

Elling's home. Her mother Mrs. R.E. (Lydia) Pool was one of the attendees.

- Over the years there has been some confusion about the location of Taupa. The answer lies in knowing to which Taupa one is referring. According to postal records the Taupa Post Office originated with Rev. E. C. Deyo's application being approved on January 28, 1902. Articles in early Lawton newspapers, announced it's beginning of operation on April 1, 1902. Until that time someone from the neighborhood "usually got all our mail at the Lawton Post Office and brought it to the (Deyo) Mission where we picked it up." The first Taupa Store was a small frame building, about 14 X 16 feet with the post office in the back. It was located eight miles west of Lawton on the Frisco Railroad. The store and Post Office were in the southwest corner of Section 26, 2 north, and 13 west.(one mile north of the Deyo Mission Corner). It lay just north of the railroad tracks but the trains didn't stop there. There was a tall pole with a hook, on which the Postmaster hung the sack of outgoing mail, and the incoming mail was thrown off the train as it passed.

  The Frisco railroad had a switch and siding a couple miles east of this point which was at first called "Hammel." In later years the name of this switch was changed to "Taupa." There was a section house at this point where the section foreman for the railroad lived. *

  Maps of today showing Taupa two miles east of the original Taupa Store and Post Office location are probably using that old Frisco Railroad Switch for reference.

*Prairie Lore, Vol. II, No.2, October 1965; Taupa Store & Post Office, by Roy Peters, pg. 84

January 9, 1902

We Pay Cash for Relinquishments
MASON & HALL
222 D Street

******

Plenty of Pure Water
Water sellers and all others wanting
good pure water
may be supplied at the
steam pump on Miss Beal's land.
Price 5 cents per barrel

******

For a first class
Carriage
to convey you to any part of the city
at anytime day or night--Call me
over
Phone 137 or Phone 129
T. J. Childs

******

Miss M. Duffy
DRESSMAKING
at home or by the day
Corner 6th & A , Lot 7, Block 17

******

R.E. Poole [sic] living ten miles west of town, is in Lawton on business. He informs us that the country is settling up fast and that the white people have organized a good Sunday School out at the Deyo Baptist Indian Mission.

******

Craterville will be another Cripple Creek, dead sure. There is no doubt that Wiggins has discovered a crater rich in mineral. Buy a lot now.

******

W.H. Hornaday has nearly completed a substantial residence on his homestead at the NW corner of town, and hopes to be ready to receive Mrs. Hornaday into their new home. He is the purchaser of the somewhat famous No.3 claim (lost by the original entryman in a card game) and is serene over the possession of the land as though there were no contests pending.

******

Events of 1901

March 4--Inauguration of President Mc Kinley

May 1--Pan-American Exposition opened in Buffalo, New York

July 4--Presidential Proclamations released on this date. One, the opening of theKCA lands. The other setting aside the Wichita Mountains as a Forest Reserve.

August 6--Opening of Lands

September 6--McKinley shot at Buffalo

September 14--Theodore Roosevelt took oath of office

******

THE LAWTON DAILY REPUBLICAN

January 13, 1902

The City National Bank starts new building to move out of the one they wheeled onto the lot on August 6. The new building will be made from red-pressed brick,with white brick and marble ornamentation; two-stories, 86 ft. deep.

******

Indians in Conference

The Kiowa, Comanche, Apache & Wichita Indians are in conference near Anadarko with Lone Wolf presiding. They have met to urge against the distribution of the first payment of the money apportioned on the sale of their lands in the new country. They claim the sale is illegal and do not want to accept the first payment of one-quarter million dollars, but they do want the $70,000 due them for rental on their grass lands. The Indian Commissioner has informed them that they cannot have the latter until they accept the former.

******

January 14, 1902
Fire Buckets

Lawton Cornice Co. 417 Avenue D
Only a few more left. Every business house should have two buckets on their barrels to be used in case of fire to comply with the city ordinance.

******

Mrs. E. P. McMahon
Teacher of Piano & Harmony
Studio 714 C. Ave.

******

January 21, 1902
Time About Up

It has been announced from the best of authority that it will be best for all homesteaders to be ON their claims by February 6. By this the costs of a contest can be avoided. It is not held that this would be sufficient grounds for a contest but the homesteaders should be on the safe side. The lawyer looking for a contest fee has his eye on all such claims and will jump in for himself or some client at the earliest possible moment.

******

January 24, 1902
Teacher Examinations

School Superintendent, Leo A. McBrian and Assistant Examiner J. T. Brnss are holding a school teachers examination today at 8th & D streets. There are 15 applicants.

******

School Across the Track

The people living east of the railroad have a first class school with Mrs. Ridley as teacher. She has 25 pupils ranging from first to sixth grade. The school was badly needed and on account of the tuition in the Lawton school besides the distance and the danger to the little ones in crossing the track the opening of the school was a blessing.

******

Contest on claim # 3 postponed.

Contests were held in the land office. This is the claim originally filed on by Winfield S. Laws of Langston, O. T. It is said he lost it in a poker game.

******

February 1, 1902
The first decision on a contest was rendered at the Land Office.

******

March 3, 1902
News from Taupa
Painter Township
• We are still growing and a better class of people never settled in any country than we have in this township.

• Miss Helen Pool, having finished her school in Iowa, has come to join her family.

• The contract has been let for the school building in Pecan School District, No. 60, for a number one school house, 24 X 36.

• Clarence Pool returned about two weeks ago from Hot Springs much improved in health. It seems good to have him with us again.

• We had 105 in Sunday School on March 2nd.

• At Pecan School Meeting it was voted unanimously that since Uncle Sam gave the bachelors 6 months to get on their land, the school board would give them 6 months more to get married. The Rankin Bros., H. F. Gilbert, Sherman Randall and the Elling Bros. took oath they would fulfill the contract.

• O.H. Johnson is putting up the first windmill in this neck of the woods.

• Rev. E. C. Deyo our Post Master to be, is looking for the mail wagon to drive up to Taupa Post Office soon.

• The man who has Section 3 is a lawyer, doctor, undertaker, minister and a farmer.

Uncle Hiram

******

March 14, 1902
News from Taupa
Painter Township
• A fire got out last Sunday. The wind being brisk, it jumped the fire guard of John Fairchild's and burned several boxes of furniture, etc. The neighbors came just in time to save his house. Mr. Fairchild was not at home at the time, but arrived just as the fire was put out.

• Our School House is being built and when done will be a credit to the community

• Benbow & Horton have just finished O. H. Johnson's irrigating plant. Henry Thompson, their pump man is sure a hummer.

Uncle Hiram

******

March 26, 1902
News from Taupa
Painter Township

• Rev. Deyo will build another house to replace the parsonage that burned.

• Pecan Schoolhouse is almost finished.

• Frank Baker of Atchison, Kansas is visiting his cousin, the Elling Bros.

• Mr. Pool has received a 200 egg incubator brooder. We will know where to go for fried chicken.

• Taupa Post Office starts the first of April with E. C. Deyo in charge.

Uncle Hiram

*****

For the number of lawyers in the city it seems that the legal fraternity suppose the people to be badly in need of advice or that a great amount of litigation will arise. (There are 148 lawyers in 98 law firms)

******

******

******

******

April 12, 1902
Postmaster Schofield of Painter Township came to Lawton yesterday and went home this a.m. She reports that since the recent rains, the streams out that way have been impossible to cross.

Endnotes
Specific Bibliographical References

Chapter 1:
¹"No Horse Race," *The El Reno Democrat*, March 14, 1901, pg 4.

Chapter 2:
² W.S. Nye, Carbine and Lance: The Story of Old Fort Sill(Norman,   OK: University of Oklahoma Press, 1937, 1942, 1969, 1979),299,302,303. paraphrased.

Chapter 4:
³Charles Latham, the son of Tina and Warren Latham is on the left

⁴John O. Johnson, *The "Rutabaga" Johnson Story*, 2nd ed.,pages2,3.

⁵*Ibid.*, #2a.

Chapter 7:
⁶On July 4, 1901, *The El Reno News,* had to go to press without the procla-mation. It quoted a dispatch from the Whitehouse, " The proclamation is due out this week. The proclamation will contain 10,000 words. It will prescribe the plan of drawing outlined in these dispatches."

Chapter 8:
⁷Compiled by Lawton Business and Professional Women's Club, *'Neath August Sun,*1933, 1955, 1985, s.v. "Memories and Reminescences of 1901ers,".

⁸Stan Hoig, *The Battle of the Washita*: *The Sheridan-Custer Indian Campaign of 1867-69* (Lincoln, Nebraska: University of Nebraska Press, 1976).

⁹William T. Hagan, *Quanah Parker, Comanche Chief* (Norman: University of Oklahoma Press, 1993) 78-113.

¹⁰*Ibid.,* #6. A question that David Jerome finally answered--albeit incorrectly, according to Hagan. Mr. Jerome said the offer was for "a trifle over one dollar an acre, while in his report to the Indian Commissioner later , he stated that it figured out to be eighty cents an acre.

Chapter 11:
¹¹*The El Reno That Was*, edited by H. Merle Woods, 1917, 1978, 1985. Copyright H. Merle Woods 1978--transferred to the Canadian County Historical Society.

¹²*Ibid.,#8*

Chapter 12:
¹³Compiled by Lawton Business and Professional Women's Club, *'Neath August Sun*, Edition 4, Dr. LT. Gooch: "Memories and Reminescences of 1901ers,"

¹⁴Many different calculations on the numbers of saloons and gambling joints existed. "There were eighty-six saloons south of the town site and double that number of and locator offices to lend assistance to the newcomer in getting his location, and relieving him of any extra cash he might have." *Neath August Sun"*.

Chapter 13:
¹⁵The Reverend A.B. Carpenter was a highly visible person during the early days of Lawton. A minister of the Christian Church, he came to Lawton with a group of men of the same denomination from Kansas. They intended to start a new church in the new town. They brought with them a huge tent, set it up and placed many cots into it. It was a "safe haven" for gentlemen to rent a cot for fifty cents a night. They posted a guard to stand by discouraging trouble. Before long Lawton's First Christian Church had enough money to purchase a town lot and begin construc-tion of a building.

Chapter 14:
 [16]At least three different reports on the "Lemonade Story" are recorded. This one is a composite. *'Neath August Sun*, pages 186, 188, 190.
Chapter 15:
 [17]Glenn Shirley, *West of Hell's Fringe* (Norman; University of Oklahoma Press,1978, 1990) *pg. 194.*
 [18]Edited by H. Merle Woods, *The El Reno That Was: The Dramatic Start and Early Years of a Historical City of the Prairies* (El Reno, Oklahoma: Canadian County Historical Society, 1917, 1978, 1985) pgs. 40-48.
Chapter 16:
 [19]In 1901, the place was called, Richards. It was named for Governor Richards, former Governor of Wyoming, in charge of the Land Lottery. Today we know it as Richards Spur.
Chapter 18:
 [20]Bert Howard, Editor, "MAY BE A RUN: It Will Be For Mineral Claims In The Wichita Mountains," *The Lawton Daily Republican*, 27 July 1901, First edition, 3.
Chapter 19:
 [21]Harry Wahhahdooah, *DEYO MISSION: 1893 to 1980* (Lawton, Oklahoma:1951).
 [22]Chronicles of Comanche County,Vol V, No.1, Spring 1959, Rev. E.C. Deyo & Deyo Mission by Mrs. Fred R. Harris, assisted by Robert Coffey.pg, 6-8.
 [23]William T. Hagan, *Quanah Parker, Comanche Chief* (Norman : University of Oklahoma Press, 1993, 108
Chapter 24:
 [24]Lawton Land District 1901, *National Archives and Records Administration, Washington D.C;* S11, T1n, R13w "James Reid: HOMESTEAD APPLICATION FILE," #593.

***

Additional Reference Books

• Prepared by Joseph K. Anderson and Susan E. Bearden, *Kiowa-Comanche Apache Land Opening 1901: Homestead Entry Listing: Lawton District, Volume I*: Museum of the Great Plains, Lawton, Oklahoma,1997.
• Ronald S. Barlow, *The Vanishing American Outhouse: A History of Country Plumbing*, Windmill Publishing Company, El Cajon,California, 1992.
• Cambridge Museum, *Centennial Booklet*, 612 Penn Street, Cambridge, NE.
• Laddie J. Elling, phD. *An Oklahoma Landmark:The Otto H. Elling Homestead*, family historical record, 1991.
• Glenn Shirley, *West of Hell's Fringe*, University of Oklahoma Press, Norman, 1978.
• Glenn Shirley, *Law West of Fort Smith*, University of Nebraska Press, Lincoln 1957.
• Bonnie Stahlman Speer, *Portrait of a Lawman: U.S. Deputy Marshal Heck Thomas*, Reliance Press, Norman, Oklahoma, 1996.
• Esther Powell and Ruth Roberson, *Lawton A Child of the Prairie*, C & J Printing, Lawton, Oklahoma, 1965, 1985.
• John O. Johnson, *The "Rutabaga" Johnson Story*, family historical record: 1980 1993.
• Stan Hoig, *The Battle of the Washita: The Sheridan-Custer Indian Campaign of 1867-69*, University of Nebraska Press, 1976

- Colonel W. S. Nye, *Carbine and Lance: The Story of Old Fort Sill*, University of Oklahoma Press, 1937.
- Randolph B. Marcy, *The Prairie Traveler: A Handbook for Overland Expedition*, Applewood Books, Bedford, Massachusetts, 1859;1993.
- Robert S. Sprague, *Grass Money*, (Revised) Robert S. Sprague, Publisher, 1970.

Periodicals

Chronicles of Comanche County, Vol.VII, No.1, Spring 1961, *Henry Andrews "Heck" Thomas*, by Morris Swett, pg. 32-49.

The Lawton Daily Democrat, July and Aug. 1901, Oklahoma Historical Society, OKC. and Lawton Public Library, Lawton, OK.

El Reno American News, October 1901, Oklahoma Historical Society, OKC.

The El Reno News; July 4, 1901, Oklahoma Historical Society, OKC.

The El Reno Democrat; March 14, 1901, Page 4.

Lawton News Republican, August 1901, Oklahoma Historical Society, OKC.

The Plain Dealer Newspaper, March 1901, Altus, Old Greer County, Oklahoma Territory, Oklahoma Historical Society.

Prairie Lore, Vol. II, No.2, Oct. 1965; *Taupa Store & Post Office*, by Roy Peters, pg. 84

Public Records

Comanche County Courthouse Records; Lawton, Oklahoma.

National Archives & Records Administration; Land Entry Files, Washington, DC

Photograph Credits

Pool and Elling Family Albums.

Oklahoma Historical Society; Oklahoma City, OK

The Fort Sill Museum; Fort Sill, OK

Cambridge, Nebraska, A pictoral record; Cambridge Museum, Cambridge, NB.

Esther Powell and Ruth Roberson (deceased) through C& J Printing, Lawton Museum of the Great Plains, Lawton, Oklahoma

Human Resources

Mina Pool, daughter of Minnie Johnson & Clarence Pool; Edmonton,AB. CA.

Brad Pool, grandson of Minnie Johnson & Clarence Pool, Edmonton,AB. CA.

Laddie J. Elling, phd., son of Hellen Pool & Otto H. Elling.

Christine Schallenmueller, daughter of Hellen Pool & Otto H. Elling.

Otto H. Elling, Jr. (Rev.), son of Hellen Pool & Otto H. Elling.

Henry (Hank) Carl Elling, grandson of Hellen Pool and Otto H. Elling.

Towana Spivey, Curator of Fort Sill Museum; Fort Sill, Oklahoma.

The author and Mina Pool, daughter of Minnie and Clarence Pool, in Edmonton, Alberta, Canada.
September, 1997

Ardeth Elling Denney lives with her husband, Jerry, in rural southwest Oklahoma. Born in Lawton, she was raised in the same community south of Deyo Mission in which her grandfather Otto and grandmother Hellen lived and raised their family.

A retired teacher and elementary school principal, Ardeth now enjoys the freedom to pursue other interests.

History has become her avocation.

ORDER FORM
for

LAND LOTTERY: 1901
The Diary of Miss Minnie Johnson

If you are interested in purchasing additional copies of this book, you may fill out this form and send it to the address listed below. You may also order by phone.

Name_____

Street Address_____

City_____State_____Zip_____

No. of copies_____ *$16.95* @   Total Enclosed_____

Blue Beaver Publishing
P.O. Box 6188
Lawton, OK 73506

Toll Free Phone # 1-888-292-5726

e-mail address: blubeavpub@aol.com
Ask about our discounts on quantity orders

HTTP://BLUEBEAVER
PUBLISHING.COM